Kobe University Monograph Series in Social Science Research

The Kobe University Monograph Series in Social Science Research is an exciting interdisciplinary collection of monographs, both authored and edited, that encompass scholarly research not only in the economics but also in law, political science, business and management, accounting, international relations, and other sub-disciplines within the social sciences. As a national university with a special strength in the social sciences, Kobe University actively promotes interdisciplinary research. This series is not limited only to research emerging from Kobe University's faculties of social sciences but also welcomes cross-disciplinary research that integrates studies in the arts and sciences.

Kobe University, founded in 1902, is the second oldest national higher education institution for commerce in Japan and is now a preeminent institution for social science research and education in the country. Currently, the social sciences section includes four faculties—Law, Economics, Business Administration, and International Cooperation Studies—and the Research Institute for Economics and Business Administration (RIEB). There are some 230-plus researchers who belong to these faculties and conduct joint research through the Center for Social Systems Innovation and the Organization for Advanced and Integrated Research, Kobe University. This book series comprises academic works by researchers in the social sciences at Kobe University as well as their collaborators at affiliated institutions, Kobe University alumni and their colleagues, and renowned scholars from around the world who have worked with academic staff at Kobe University. Although traditionally the research of Japanese scholars has been publicized mainly in the Japanese language, Kobe University strives to promote publication and dissemination of works in English in order to further contribute to the global academic community.

More information about this series at https://link.springer.com/bookseries/16115

Akira Negishi · Masako Wakui · Naoko Mariyama
Editors

Competition Law and Policy in the Japanese Pharmaceutical Sector

Editors
Akira Negishi
Graduate School of Law
Kobe University
Kobe, Japan

Masako Wakui ⓘ
Faculty of Law
Kyoto University
Kyoto, Japan

Naoko Mariyama ⓘ
Undergraduate School of Law
Tokai University
Hiratsuka, Kanagawa, Japan

ISSN 2524-504X   ISSN 2524-5058 (electronic)
Kobe University Monograph Series in Social Science Research
ISBN 978-981-16-7816-5   ISBN 978-981-16-7814-1 (eBook)
https://doi.org/10.1007/978-981-16-7814-1

This Springer imprint is published by the registered company Springer Nature Singapore Pte Ltd.
The registered company address is: 152 Beach Road, #21-01/04 Gateway East, Singapore 189721, Singapore

Preface

In the pharmaceutical sector, competition takes place on a global scale. Japan is the world's third-largest pharmaceutical market, selling many drugs developed abroad, while leading Japanese pharmaceutical companies are global players. Although the industry is extensively regulated in Japan, vigorous competition exists, which is vital to a well-functioning pharmaceutical sector. Competition authorities around the world actively enforce competition laws. Therefore, it is essential to understand how competition laws and sector-specific regulations operate in order to run pharmaceutical businesses, conduct research or design policy measures in the country of operation. This book is the first-ever written to explain how Japanese competition law is enforced in the pharmaceutical sector in Japan.

The Japanese competition law, the Antimonopoly Act (AMA), came into force in 1947. It is primarily enforced by an independent administrative body, the Japan Fair Trade Commission (JFTC). The AMA is unique both in substance and procedure, and knowledge of it is becoming important for globalised economic activities. Despite its long history, the linguistic barrier prevents most of the world from knowing about the act. This lack of English literature on the AMA is a serious gap this book intends to fill. Focusing on the pharmaceutical sector, the book demonstrates how the AMA works through the chapters written and edited by expert researchers based in Japan.

The pharmaceutical industry is a challenging one, as a variety of factors, including sector-specific safety and ethical rules, unique trading practices and industrial structure, affect how the market functions. Innovation is at the core of the industry, and intellectual property law and other systems to encourage research and activities help determine the way the market is structured. Such laws and regulations must be considered before one engages in research or policymaking related to competition law. The editors and authors of the book understand this need, which is why competition law in the Japanese pharmaceutical sector is presented so comprehensively. The authors also share their thoughts on the policies and directions the government should take to guide the industry.

The structure of the book is as follows. Part I provides the basic information and highlights contemporary challenges in the Japanese pharmaceutical and healthcare industries. Given the rapid ageing of Japanese society and the growing need to reduce medical costs, various policy measures have been adopted in both the healthcare and pharmaceutical sectors. Ethics, the interests of patients and the effect on competition must be considered when establishing and implementing such measures. At the same time, the promotion of innovation is essential for the provision of high-quality medical care on a sustainable basis. Negishi begins the section by describing the relationship between sector-specific regulation and the AMA in the pharmaceutical sector in Japan and explains the current policy issues that the Japanese pharmaceutical industry faces. This is followed by Sato, who provides an in-depth explanation and analysis of the current situation of the Japanese healthcare system, in which the pharmaceutical industry is embedded. Meanwhile, Tejima outlines the laws and regulations applicable to research and development (R&D), clinical trials, and the manufacturing of and dispensing of drugs, Maeda analyses patent law, data protection and other systems that spur innovation in the sector, and Wakui examines the codes and regulations that guide the relationship between doctors and pharmaceutical companies.

Part II examines various issues of competition law, addressing cutting-edge issues such as whether exploitatively high prices could be regulated by the AMA, how to evaluate co-marketing and other cooperative practices whose importance is increasing, and the way mergers affect innovation in Japan. Negishi provides an overall picture of the AMA regulations by discussing all recent JFTC pharmaceutical cases. Seryo and Takeda, respectably, explain how the AMA applies to horizontal cooperation and mergers amongst pharmaceutical companies. The AMA has a complicated structure and lacks clear case law in relation to many issues, which often makes it difficult to understand. These chapters provide the best explanation for readers, particularly those who are unfamiliar with the AMA.

The second half of Part II focuses on practices characteristic to the pharmaceutical industry. Mariyama examines whether the anti-competitive practice *pay for delay*, or *reverse payment*, by which the original drug company makes payment to generic companies to delay their entry into the market, exists in Japan and how the AMA applies to such conduct. Cheng explores how the *non-challenging clause*, which is often incorporated into patent licensing agreements, should be evaluated under the AMA. He also discusses how Japanese pharmaceutical companies engage in licensing activities. Finally, Abe reviews the competitive landscape for biopharmaceuticals between biosimilars and authorised biologics and suggests policies related to drug pricing, focusing on the need to maintain R&D in the sector, then discusses what role the JFTC should play.

Part III consists of two scholarly articles that delve into economic analyses that help the reader understand industrial structures and trading practices in the pharmaceutical sector in order to create related policies. Nakamura provides a concise overview of the history of the Japanese pharmaceutical industry before exploring the drug discovery process in Japan. Noto provides a clear explanation of the drug pricing and distribution system, and the policy issues the JFTC and Japanese government both wish to address, before presenting an econometric analysis of trading practices that exist in distributing drugs.

The editors would like to express our sincere gratitude to Ms. Keiko Hayasaka for excellent project assistance. Our thanks also go to Kirsten Schlewitz, an editor and researcher in law (http://www.kdsediting.com/), who helped us finish up the English manuscript. This work is supported by JSPS KAKENHI 17 H00959.

Kobe, Japan   Akira Negishi
Kyoto, Japan   Masako Wakui
Hiratsuka, Japan   Naoko Mariyama

Contents

Editors and Contributors

About the Editors

Akira Negishi is Professor Emeritus of Kobe University, where he was the dean of the faculty of law, and Konan University where he was a vice president. At these institutions, he taught competition, consumer and other economic laws. He has published numerous scholarly books, articles and commentaries and led a number of research projects and academic groups in these fields. Professor Negishi was also the president of the Japan Association of Economic Law and the Japan Association of International Economic Law, the chair of the Telecommunication Business Subcommittee, the Information Communication Council, the Ministry of Internal Affairs and Communications (MIC) and the Antimonopoly Forum. He served as a counsellor for the Japan Fair Trade Commission (JFTC), a member of the Advisory Panel on Basic Issues Regarding the Antimonopoly Act, and as the bar examiner for the Ministry of Justice. He has chaired countless expert and advisory groups at the JFTC, MIC and the Ministry of Economy, Trade and Industry. He became a member of the Japan Academy, an honorary organisation that accords special recognition to researchers with eminent academic and scientific achievements in 2018.

Masako Wakui is Professor at the Graduate School of Law, Kyoto University, and Visiting Scholar at Newcastle University, UK. She has previously taught at Osaka City University and Rikkyo University. Her fields are competition law and policy. She has published books and articles on these subjects. She has served as a chief researcher for the Japan Fair Trade Commission (JFTC) Competition Policy Research Centre, as a commissioner at the Osaka Prefecture Labour Relations Commission and as a member of the Interconnection Policy Committee, the Information and Communications Council, the Ministry of Internal Affairs and Communication and various other advisory and study groups at the JFTC and other administrative bodies. Currently, Dr. Wakui is a board member of the Japan Association of Economic Law and the co-head of the Asian Chapter of the Academic Society for Competition Law.

Naoko Mariyama has taught at Tokai University since 2014 and has served as Associate Professor at its Undergraduate School of Law since 2017, where she teaches the Antimonopoly Act. She received her master's from Doshisha University, where she majored in competition law. She was a visiting researcher at King's College London in 2019–2020. She lectured at group training courses held by Japan Fair Trade Committee and Japan International Cooperation Agency on the Antimonopoly Act and on competition policy for developing countries during 2011–2016. Her main research interest is competition law and policy in pharmaceutical industry, and she has published articles on this theme both in English and Japanese. Professor Mariyama has been a member of bid audit committees in two Japanese cities. She is also a regular speaker at the Antimonopoly Study Group and leads the pharmaceutical study group for the Kobe University Innovation and Platform research project.

Contributors

Takanori Abe ABE & PARTNERS, Osaka, Japan; Graduate School of Medicine, Osaka University, Osaka, Japan

Thomas K. Cheng The Department of Law, University of Hong Kong, Pok Fu Lam, Hong Kong

Takeshi Maeda Graduate School of Law, Kobe University, Kobe, Japan

Naoko Mariyama Undergraduate School of Law, Tokai University, Hiratsuka, Kanagawa, Japan

Kenta Nakamura Graduate School of Economics, Kobe University, Kobe, Japan

Akira Negishi Graduate School of Law, Kobe University, Kobe, Japan

Konosuke Noto Keio Research Institute at SFC and Dentsu Inc, Fujisawa, Kanagawa, Japan

Goro Sato School of Law, Okayama University, Okayama, Japan

Shingo Seryo Faculty of Law and Graduate School of Law, Doshisha University, Kyoto, Japan

Kuninobu Takeda Graduate School of Law and Politics, Osaka University, Toyonaka, Osaka, Japan

Yutaka Tejima Graduate School of Law, Kobe University, Kobe, Japan

Masako Wakui Faculty of Law, Kyoto University, Kyoto, Japan

List of Figures

List of Tables

Part I
Healthcare and Pharmaceuticals: Innovation and Regulation in Japan

Chapter 1
Regulation and Competition in the Pharmaceutical Industry in Japan

Akira Negishi

Abstract The Japanese pharmaceutical industry is extensively regulated under two laws: the Act on Securing Quality, Efficacy and Safety of Pharmaceuticals and Medical Devices (PMD Act) and the Health Insurance Act. These laws are administrated by the Ministry of Health, Labour and Welfare (MHLW), which regulates the entire process from entry into the market to the pricing and distribution of products. The necessity and reasonableness of such regulations have been consistently questioned in light of Article 21(1) of the Japanese Constitution, which guarantees freedom to choose an occupation and operate businesses, as well as the Antimonopoly Act (AMA), which establishes the fundamental competition rules that form the basis of the market economy system in Japan. Despite such regulations, vigorous competition concerning development, marketing and pricing exists, with numerous manufacturers and distributors in the Japanese pharmaceutical sector. This chapter outlines the laws and regulations that shape how pharmaceutical markets operate in Japan and describes how these relevant rules interact. It also explores the major challenges the Japanese pharmaceutical industry faces.

Keywords Pharmaceutical industry · Regulation · Antitrust · Competition · Constitutional law

1.1 Introduction

The Japanese pharmaceutical industry is a regulated industry subject to entry restrictions, price restrictions and distribution restrictions imposed by the Ministry of Health, Labour and Welfare (MHLW). The MHLW regulates the sector, primarily based on two laws. The Act on Securing Quality, Efficacy and Safety of Pharmaceuticals and Medical Devices (PMD Act) places entry restrictions on the manufacturing and sales of pharmaceutical products.[1] The purpose of this law is to ensure the quality,

---

[1] Act No. 145 of 1960, as last amended by Act No. 37 of 2019.

A. Negishi (✉)
Graduate School of Law, Kobe University, Kobe, Japan
e-mail: negishi@wine.ocn.ne.jp

effectiveness, and safety of pharmaceuticals, medical devices, and related products, and to carry out the necessary regulations to prevent the occurrence and spread of health hazards due to their use (Article 1). The Health Insurance Act regulates the price and distribution of medical drugs.[2] This law aims to 'provide insurance benefits for illnesses, injuries or deaths or childbirths other than work-related accidents of workers or their dependents, thereby contributing to the stability of people's lives and the improvement of welfare' (Article 1).

Meanwhile, the Constitution of Japan guarantees freedom to choose an occupation and operate a business as long as it does not interfere with public welfare (Article 21, Paragraph 1). Furthermore, the Antimonopoly Act (AMA)[3] outlines the country's competition rules, which constitute the foundation of the market economy. The legitimacy of regulations in the pharmaceutical sector raises issues in light of the Constitution and the AMA.

The regulation of the pharmaceutical sector limits the scope of competition. Within such limits, drug manufacturers, pharmacies and distributors compete with each other. Competition is active in areas such as sales, pricing, patent acquisitions, research and development (R&D), and the launch of new products. Pharmaceutical companies and distributors also engage in mergers and acquisitions to enhance their competitiveness. The AMA prohibits pharmaceutical companies and distributors from avoiding or eliminating competition as an unreasonable restraint of trade and private monopolisation (Article 3) and from employing unfair trade practices (Article 19). The Act also prohibits certain mergers and acquisitions, which may substantially restrict competition in the relevant market (Articles 10 and 15). The AMA prohibitions apply to businesses in the drug industry. The Japan Fair Trade Commission (JFTC), an independent administrative body, enforces the AMA.

1.2 Entry Restrictions for Manufacturing and Sales in the Pharmaceutical Sector

1.2.1 Licences for the Manufacturing and Sales of Pharmaceutical Products

The PMD Act stipulates that obtaining a licence from the MHLW is required before manufacturing and selling pharmaceutical products (Article 12(1)). The MHLW may reject a licencing application if: (i) the quality control method for the manufacture of pharmaceutical products relating to the licence application does not meet the standards stipulated by the Ordinance issued by the MHLW or (ii) the post-marketing safety management method does not meet the standards specified (Article 12-2). The safety management method applies to quality, effectiveness and safety as well as other

---

[2] Act No. 70 of 1922, as last amended by Act No.40 of 2020.
[3] Act No. 54 of 1947, as last amended by Act No. 45 of 2019.

measures relating to collecting and examining information essential for the proper use of medical drugs and the actions to be taken based on the results.

The PMD Act also provides that a person who manufactures and sells pharmaceutical products without a licence from the MHLW may be punished by imprisonment with work for not more than three years or fined not more than three million yen, or both (Article 84 (ii) and (ix)).

1.2.2 Licence for Opening a Pharmacy

A pharmacy is a place where a pharmacist dispenses medical drugs according to a doctor's prescription (PMD Act, Article 2(12)). A pharmacy cannot be opened without a licence issued by the prefectural governor of its location (PMD Act, Article 4(1)). The prefectural governor may reject licence applications if (i) the structural equipment of the pharmacy does not meet the standards set by the MHLW or (ii) the system for dispensing of medicine at the pharmacy, or for selling or providing such medicines dispensed, or, in cases of the business of selling pharmaceuticals, the system for selling and providing pharmaceuticals at the pharmacy does not meet the standard stated in the MHLW Ordinance (Article 5(i) and (ii)). A person who opens a pharmacy without a licence may be punished by imprisonment with work for not more than three years or fined not more than three million yen, or both (Article 84 (i) of the PMD Act).

1.2.3 Licence for Drug Sales Business

A drug sales licence is necessary to sell, store, display or provide medications (PMD Act, Article 24(1)). The three types of licences are *store-based distribution*, *household distribution* and *wholesale distribution* (PMD Act, Article 25). Under the PMD Act, 'drugs' refers to those listed in the Japanese Pharmacopoeia (Article 2(1)(i)). The drugs are further categorised into *medical drugs*, *guidance-requiring drugs* and *over-the-counter drugs*. Although this book focuses on the first category, the regulations relating to guidance-requiring and over-the-counter drugs are summarised below.

Guidance-requiring drugs are medicines that do not significantly affect the human body in terms of their efficacy and effect and are intended to be used by the consumer based on information provided by pharmacists and other pharmaceutical personnel. For the proper use of guidance-requiring drugs, the pharmacist must provide face-to-face information based on pharmaceutical knowledge (PMD Act, Article 4(5)(iii)). In contrast, over-the-counter drugs do not significantly affect the human body in terms of their efficacy and effect. This type of drug can be chosen and used by the consumer based on information provided by pharmacists and other pharmaceutical personnel (PMD Act, Article 4(5)(iv)).

A person who engages in the *store-based distribution* of guidance-requiring or over-the-counter drugs must obtain a licence issued by the prefectural governor of the place where the store is located (PMD Act, Articles 24(1), 25(i), and 26(1)). A licence must be obtained for each store from which the person will distribute. The prefectural governor may reject a licence if the structural equipment of the store does not meet the standards specified in the MHLW Ordinance, if the store lacks a pharmacist or a *registered seller*, or if the system for selling or providing medicines at the store does not conform to the standards specified by the MHLW Ordinance (Article 24(4)). A *registered seller* is a person who has passed the examination established by the MHLW Ordinance to confirm they possess the necessary qualities to engage in the sale or provision of over-the-counter drugs, and is registered by the prefectural governor (PMD Act, Article 36-8 (2)).

A person who engages in *household distribution* to sell or provide guidance-requiring or over-the-counter drugs must also obtain a licence from the prefectural governor of their location (PMD Act, Article 30(1)). The prefectural governor may not issue a licence if a person does not meet the standards stated under the MHLW Ordinance (PMD Act, Article 30(2)). The standard stipulates that a pharmacist or registered seller must be at the store to provide other services necessary for proper household distributorship in the relevant prefecture area.

Wholesale distributors who sell or provide medical drugs to pharmacies, hospitals and clinics must also obtain a licence from the prefectural governor of their location for each business office (PMD Act, Article 34(1)). The prefectural governor may reject a licence application if the structural equipment of the business office does not meet the standards specified by the MHLW Ordinance (PMD Act, Article 34(2)).

A person who sells pharmaceutical products without a licence issued by the prefectural governor may be punished by imprisonment with work for not more than three years or imposed a fine of not more than three million yen, or both (PMD Act, Article 84 (ix)).

1.3 Elimination of Distance Restrictions on Establishing Pharmacies and Lifting of Bans on Online Sales of Over-The-Counter Drugs

1.3.1 Freedom to Choose an Occupation and Distance Restrictions on the Opening of Pharmacies

The Pharmaceutical Affairs Law,[4] the predecessor to the PMD Act, specified the criteria to grant a licence to establish pharmacies, including distance restrictions (Pharmaceutical Affairs Law, Article 6 (2)–(4)).

---

[4] Act No. 145 of 1960.

In 1964, Hiroshima Prefecture decided not to grant a licence to open a pharmacy in Fukuyama City, on the grounds that establishing such a business would violate the distance restrictions stated in the Hiroshima Prefecture Ordinance. The applicant filed a lawsuit against the prefecture to revoke the decision.

On 30 April 1975, the Supreme Court ruled that the distance restriction included in the licence granting criteria violated Article 21, Paragraph 1 of the constitution. The Paragraph stipulates that 'every person has the freedom to choose a profession as long as it does not interfere with public welfare'. The legislator of the pharmacy licence standards explained the primary goal of setting distance restrictions was to ensure safety. Excessive competition due to the overcrowding of pharmacies in some areas may cause management instability, resulting in the risk of supplying defective medicines due to shortcomings in those facilities. The Supreme Court doubted the reasonability of this explanation. The Supreme Court also found it less necessary to enforce such distance restrictions through licence standards, as the Pharmaceutical Affairs Law imposed various regulations on the business activities of pharmaceutical companies to prevent the risk of supplying defective drugs. Ultimately the Court found such distance restrictions limit the location where a person could establish a pharmacy and effectively restrict the freedom of choosing an occupation to a substantial extent. The Supreme Court ruled the distance regulation at issue violated Article 21, Paragraph 1 of the Japanese Constitution.

As a result, the distance restrictions disappeared from pharmacy-opening licence criteria. This change facilitated competition among pharmacies.

1.3.2 Constitution and Prohibition of Online Sales of Over-The-Counter Drugs

As noted earlier, drugs are classified into medical, guidance-requiring and over-the-counter categories. While medical drugs and guidance-requiring drugs demand face-to-face supply and discussion in light of their significant impact on the human body and the resultant possible side effects, over-the-counter medications do not affect users in the same way. Consumers can freely choose and use them based on the information provided by their pharmacists or other pharmaceutical personnel.

The then-Pharmaceutical Affairs Law allowed for the online sale of over-the-counter drugs. However, the MHLW banned it, believing that drug sales should take place in a face-to-face manner according to the MHLW Ordinance promulgated on 6 February 2009. A drugstore that had been selling over-the-counter medicines online filed a lawsuit against the MHLW. The plaintiffs alleged the MHLW rules were illegal, setting regulations beyond the mandate of the Pharmaceutical Affairs Law. They sought confirmation that they could lawfully sell over-the-counter drugs online. On 11 January 2013, the Supreme Court ruled that the uniform ban on online sales of over-the-counter drugs was beyond the mandate of the Pharmaceutical Affairs Law and was unlawful. The Court emphasised the following. First, at the time the law was enacted, there was considerable demand for over-the-counter drug sales online. Second, few experts or general consumers opposed such sales. Moreover, opponents to the ban were present within the government. Third, new regulations on the online sales of over-the-counter drugs severely restricted the freedom of professional activities of those who have made online sales their core business.

Following this Supreme Court judgement, the MHLW changed the rules to allow online sales of over-the-counter drugs. Pharmacists or registered sellers at pharmacies or drugstores could legally sell over-the-counter medicines online. The lifting of the ban increased price competition for over-the-counter medicines.

1.4   Approval for Manufacturing and Marketing of Pharmaceutical Products

A person who intends to manufacture and sell a drug with a drug manufacturing and sales licence must obtain approval for each drug from the MHLW (PMD Act, Article 14). The approval process entails thorough examinations in terms of quality, efficacy and safety. The MHLW tasks the Pharmaceuticals and Medical Devices Agency with performing the necessary assessments. The MHLW then decides whether to approve a drug based on the assessment outcome (PMD Act, Article 14-2). A special system enables the speedy approval of a drug (PMD Act, Article 14-3). The system may be invoked if a drug is urgently necessary to prevent a disease that has a serious impact on lives in the absence of an alternative, and a competent agency abroad has approved the drug.

At the time of writing, Japan needs early approval of new COVID-19 vaccines. Critics say the vaccine approval process in Japan moves exceedingly slowly [10]. Although the expedited special approval system exists, the MHLW is usually extremely careful when approving new drugs because of several severe phytotoxicity cases in the past.[5] Critics expressed their outrage that the COVID-19 vaccine approval was seriously delayed in Japan compared to other countries. Although the drug is in use elsewhere, the MHLW requires clinical trials to be conducted on the Japanese population because it may have different effects depending on race or ethnicity [10]. The MHLW considered adopting measures to shorten the clinical trial stage by utilising the medical information of patients who had not participated in the trial [11].

---

[5] Major phytotoxicity cases include the following: limb defects caused by thalidomide in 1962; retinopathy cases caused in 1969; subacute spinal neuropathy caused by quinoform (known as the *Summon Case*) in 1970; thigh quadrilateral muscle contraction in 1973; human immunodeficiency virus (HIV) infection through blood transfusions, which then led to acquired immune deficiency syndrome (AIDS) in 1983; hepatitis C infections through blood preparations in 1987; uterine rupture/foetal asphyxia caused by labour-promoting agents in 1988; aseptic meningitis brought on by the measles, mumps and rubella (MMR) vaccine in 1992; bone marrow suppression caused by anticancer drug thalidomide in 1993; human infectious prion disease (known as Creutzfeldt-Jakob disease) in 1997.

It is not yet clear if a COVID-19 vaccine has been approved and rolled out in Japan at the time of writing.

1.5 Price Regulation and Competition for Medical Drugs

1.5.1 Price Regulation of Medical Drugs

The prices of medical drugs covered by health insurance under the Japan's universal health insurance system are set by the MHLW (Health Insurance Act, Article 7(1) and (2)). The MHLW lists the medical drugs covered by national insurance that can be used for medical treatment, along with their prices. The prices set in this way are called the *price standards* for medical drugs. Medical insurance providers pay the set price to medical institutions or pharmacies [15].

The MHLW must consult with their advisory body, the Central Social Insurance Medical Council (CSIMC), when setting drug price standards (Health Insurance Act, Article 82(1)). The CSIMC is composed of seven insurance representatives, who pay medical expenses; seven medical practice representatives, such as doctors; six public interest members, including university researchers; and ten expert members.

According to the latest *Criteria for Calculating Drug Prices* published by the CSIMC on 7 February 2020, the prices of new drugs—also called original drugs—are determined based on the *similar drug efficacy comparison method* if similar drugs are on the NHI price list. Otherwise, the drug price is determined by the *cost accounting method*, which is the sum of the cost needed for manufacturing and sales, general and administrative expenses, operating profit, distribution expenses, and the amount equivalent to consumption and the local consumption tax. Prices are adjusted based on the average cost in several foreign countries: France, Germany, the United Kingdom, the United States (CSIMC [1]: Chapter 2 Part 1). In contrast, the price of generic drugs is determined primarily by multiplying the price of the original drug by 0.5 (CSIMC [1]: Chapter 2 2 Part 2 Ib). However, if a similar generic drug is already on the NHI price list, the *similar drug efficacy comparison method* is applied.

1.5.2 Price Competition for Pharmaceutical Products

The drug price standards for medical drugs are revised every fixed period, which is generally every two years.[6] Under Article 77 of the Health Insurance Act, the MHLW conducts a price survey, which constitutes the basis of price revision. The MHLW investigates the actual selling price paid by insurance medical institutions

---

[6] In 2021, the interim drug price revision was implemented for the first time. Prior to this, the revision took place every two years, and if there was no interim revision, it would not have occurred until 2022.

and pharmacies to wholesalers. Such prices are usually below the NHI price, and the standard drug prices decrease each time the drug price is revised. Meanwhile, patients pay the price indicated on the NHI list to medical institutions and pharmacies, so there is no place for price competition. In contrast, price competition exists amongst drug manufacturers selling to wholesalers. Price competition also occurs when wholesalers sell to pharmacies and medical institutions. If price competition in those markets drives the prices down, the NHI list price will be reduced during the next revision. Under such circumstances, the manufacturers and distributors might find it profitable to form price cartels to prevent the NHI prices from decreasing further.

Recently, the JFTC uncovered two cartels, issuing cease and desist and surcharge payment orders. One cartel involved two manufacturers' price-fixing of generic lanthanum carbonate Orally-Disintegrating (OD) tablets used to improve hyperphosphatemia, and the other two manufacturers' price-fixing of generic Calvin tablets used to improve hypertension. The price-fixing hurt the wholesalers they partnered with. On 9 December 2020, the JFTC filed a criminal accusation involving seven people and companies in three wholesalers' bid-rigging and price negotiations cases under AMA Articles 74 and 96. In this case, the Japan Community Healthcare Organisation (JCHO), an independent administrative agency, procured the drugs for its 57 hospitals operated nationwide. One of the four companies that participated in the bid-rigging was the first to file a leniency application with the JFTC before the commencement of JFTC's investigation, so the JFTC did not file an accusation against the company and the prosecutors did not prosecute it. On 30 June 2021, the Tokyo District Court ruled that pharmaceutical wholesalers had engaged in unreasonable restraint of trade. The three companies were each fined 250 million JPY and each of the seven former executives were handed a suspended sentence of 18 months in prison.

The MHLW does not regulate the price for guidance-requiring and over-the-counter drugs. For these medications, competition concerning sales by manufacturers and wholesalers, sales by wholesalers to pharmacies and drugstores, and sales by pharmacies and drugstores to consumers exist.

1.5.3   Price Regulation of Medical Drugs and Promotion of Innovation to Develop New Drugs

The focus on setting the NHI price list is to ensure patients prompt access to medications and to safeguard the sustainability of health insurers' finances. In the past, the prices of new drugs were reduced every two years, similar to other drugs, based on a survey of actual market prices. Substantially innovative medicines were treated in the same way. The issue of drug lag became apparent in the latter half of the 2000s. *Drug lag* occurs when companies do not actively conduct R&D in Japan due to the pricing system, which delays access to innovative drugs [9].

Such a realisation prompted the introduction of a system to add a premium to the cost of new drugs, termed the *new drug premium system*. The drug must fall under the category of *orphan drugs*: drugs publicly solicited for development by the MHLW, drugs with breakthrough additional effects or usefulness at the time of the new listing, or drugs with a new mechanism of action. This system aims to accelerate the development of innovative new drugs and add a premium to the deferment of drug prices during price revision. This allows the drug price to be effectively maintained.[7] The premium system is applicable when no generic drugs have been launched and the original drug has not been listed for more than 15 years, after which the price is deduced from the total amount of the premiums applied at the time of revision of the NHI price list (CSIMC [1]: Chapter 3 Sec 9). The purpose of the new drug premium system is to accelerate sales revenue to incentivise and promote R&D.

This new drug premium system was trialled in 2010, and has been subjected to continuous reviews and revisions (CSIMC [1]: Chapter 3 Sec 9). Although the effect of the premium system has yet to be determined, a serious flaw is that it focuses only on the domestic market. The pharmaceutical industry in Japan is characterised by side-by-side advancements under the escort fleet system, and the new drug premium system also has such characteristics. Unfortunately, the effect of the system is likely to be limited. It is essential for Japan to focus on establishing a competitive advantage in the global market.

1.6 Distribution Regulations for Medical Drugs: AMA and MHLW Distribution Improvement Guidelines

The MHLW published their *Guidelines for Distribution Personnel to Improve Distribution of Medical Drugs* (hereafter *MHLW Distribution Guidelines*) on 23 January 2018, in hopes of increasing the reliability of the drug price surveys. The guidelines are not based on the law and are only used for administrative guidance.

Opaque trade practices have long been a problem in drug distribution. The MHLW is focused on three types of trading practices. First, the drug prices manufacturers charge wholesalers are higher than the prices that wholesalers charge pharmacies, leaving the wholesalers with a loss. Drug manufacturers ordinarily compensate for such losses by paying rebates to wholesalers. Such a practice makes prices meaningless and trading conditions opaque. Second, manufacturers and distributors often deliver medicines before they agree on the prices with their customers. Such a trading custom is called 'unsettled provisional delivery'. Third, the parties engage in 'lump-sum bulk purchases', involving various medications, without setting the price of each drug individually.[8]

---

[7] For more information on the premium system, see Hiroshi Nakamura [9: 27, 30]. For an evaluation of the system, see Kondo [4: 149], Wakustu [16: 171].

[8] Noto [12] conducted a quantitative economic analysis of the trade practices and distribution prices of pharmaceutical products.

The *MHLW Distribution Guidelines* instruct the manufacturer and wholesaler to set the sales price at the appropriate level, taking into account the prices that pharmacies and institutes pay to wholesalers. They further suggest the price for each medicine be set separately—'itemised pricing'—and that the parties should refrain from requesting bargains and low prices without considering the value of the medicine and the distribution cost. After the publication of the guidelines, the percentage of itemised pricing increased significantly. As a result, new problems have arisen; the pharmacies have to bear the difference between the procuring price and sales price [3: 294].

Meanwhile, the *MHLW Distribution Guidelines* impose restrictions on the pricing and trade activities carried out by manufacturers and distributors, thus affecting price competition, competition for customers and other types of competition. Competition issues arise when the MHLW seeks to implement their guidelines through the joint action of manufacturers and wholesalers of pharmaceuticals or their trade associations. Regarding these issues, the JFTC provides the guidance. In its *Guidelines Concerning Administrative Guidance under the AMA*,[9] in which they clarified the following:

> In order to help maintain and promote fair and free competition, it is necessary to leave the pricing of goods or services up to each firm, and administrative organs should take special care to see that any administrative guidance regarding prices, which is not based on any specific provision in law or regulation not restrict or inhibit fair and free competition. The following kinds of administrative guidance, for example, would be apt to pose a problem under the Antimonopoly Act (Article 3, Article 8(i), (iv), and (v), Article 19).
>
> 1. Guidance regarding raising or reducing prices, stating specific figures relating to amount, percentage (range), or the like, which would serve as standards. Such administrative guidance may tempt firms acting together or their trade association to decide to raise or lower prices to the level of the stated standards. 'To decide' in this context may mean not only an explicit decision or agreement but also tacitly agreeing or deciding on a common purpose (the same applies hereinafter).
>
> 2. In a situation in which prices have come down, or the like, guidance which urges self-restraint from selling at discount prices, accepting orders at discount prices, or lowering prices. Such administrative guidance may tempt firms acting together or their trade association to decide to maintain or raise prices.
>
> 3. Requiring reports, through the trade association, on matters which are usually considered the trade secrets of individual firms, such as prices in the particular transactions of member firms. Such administrative guidance may tempt the trade association to take charge of the coordination of such activities, which would result in price fixing.
>
> 4. Giving guidance to manufacturers, distributors, or their respective associations to stabilise the prices offered to their trading partners, including retail prices. Such administrative guidance may invite conduct, which would lead to the maintenance of resale prices. (JFTC 1994: 6–7)

---

[9] JFTC, *Guidelines Concerning Administrative Guidance under the Antimonopoly Act* (1994) <https://www.jftc.go.jp/en/legislation_gls/imonopoly_guidelines_files/administrative.pdf> accessed 1 February 2021.

Thus, actions to implement the *MHLW Distribution Guidelines* potentially cause issues with the AMA. In particular, if the pharmaceutical manufacturers and wholesalers engage in what the guidelines suggest through joint activities or trade associations, they bear the risk of violating the AMA.

1.7 The Relationship Between the Approval of Generic Drugs and Patents on Original Drugs

1.7.1 Approval of Generic Drugs

A generic drug contains the same active ingredient as that of the original drug, and its use, dose, effect and efficacy are basically the same. The approval criteria for medicines under the PMD Act are the same for original and generic drugs, except the latter involves only small clinical trials. These clinical trials are considered bioequivalence studies of the generic drug. Clinical trials of this scale involve only a simple test because the safety of the generic drug has already been confirmed during the trials of the original drug. Therefore, the time needed to approve a generic drug is approximately half the time required to approve an original drug.

Article 69(1) of the Patent Act[10] stipulates 'the effect of a patent right does not extend to the practice of a patented invention for testing or research'. In *Therapeutic Agents for Pancreatic Diseases*, the Supreme Court considered whether the production and use of a drug or chemical substance within the patented invention's technical scope constitutes 'the practice of a patented invention for testing or research' necessary for generic drug approval under Article 69(1).[11] Both production and use are part of the necessary testing to produce the required documents during the drug approval process. The goal is to manufacture and sell a generic drug with the same active ingredients as the drug protected by the patent after the expiration of the patent term. The Supreme Court ruled that such a test constitutes 'execution of a patented invention for testing or research' under Article 69(1) of the Patent Act and does not infringe on the patent right. This ruling helped to expedite the generic drug approval process.

1.7.2 Japanese-Style Patent Linkage System

Although the MHLW promotes the use of generic drugs, it does not approve generic drugs when a patent covers the original drug. There are neither laws nor approval criteria that require the MHLW to impose this restriction. The MHLW also requires

---

[10] Tokkyo ho [Patent Act], Act No. 121 of 1959, as last amended by Act No. 3 of 2019.

[11] Supreme Court, 16 April 1998, 53(4) Minshu 627.

consultation and consensus before adding a generic drug to the NHI price list, where there are concerns that the generic might infringe on the original patent.[12] Again, this practice lacks a legal basis. The MHLW maintains these regulations to ensure a stable supply of generic drugs after their approval. Such MHLW practices are called the 'Japanese-style patent linkage system'.

There is also the practice called *data exclusivity*. As a general rule, a patent term for an original drug is 20 years from the filing date of the patent application (Patent Act, Article 67(1)), which is extendable for the period required for clinical trials and approval process up to examination (maximum 5 years) (Patent Act, Article 67(4)). The manufacturer of the original drug must collect data regarding efficacy and safety while in actual use at medical institutions after approval of the drug, and then undergo re-examination. The re-examination process established under PMD Act Article 14-4 usually takes eight years (a maximum of ten years). During this period, the MHLW does not accept applications for approval for a generic drug, even when the patent relating to the original drug has expired.[13] This MHLW practice creates *data exclusivity*, which prolongs the period when only the original drug is on the market.

Critics of MHLW operations point out it is unclear how the MHLW approves drugs and generates the listing system in practice. Another issue is their processes deter the entry of generic drugs into the market. In addition, manufacturers and distributors of the original drug cannot tell if the manufacturer of a generic drug has applied for approval until it occurs [2, 13]. The MHLW should not delay the generic drug approval process. It should suffice to refrain from approving its sale until after the expiration of the original drug's patent and re-examination period. Ensuring a stable supply of generic drugs is achievable in this way. Given the significant effects of allowing generics into the market, thorough examinations of whether such a system is appropriate should be conducted and discussed, and explicit provisions should be added to the PMD Act.

As stated earlier, the MHLW requires coordination between the original and generic manufacturers before adding a generic drug to the NHI price list. It is exceedingly doubtful whether such a practice is compatible with the AMA. It is not clear what type of coordination occurs following MHLW guidance. However, such coordination risks violating the AMA. Such a practice may be deemed private monopolisation given an original drug manufacturer's exclusion. Alternatively, an agreement between the original and generic manufacturers may constitute an unreasonable restraint of trade.

---

[12] Notification from the Director of the Economic Affairs Division, Medical Affairs Bureau, MHLW, Iryoyo kohatsu iyakuhin no yakuji ho jo no shonin shinsa oyobi yakka shusai ni

kakaru iyakuhin tokkyo no toriatsukai [Pharmaceutical patents in relation to the approval review and NHI price listing of generic drugs for medical use under the PMD Act], 5 June 2009 <https://www.mhlw.go.jp/web/t_doc?dataId=00tb5511&dataType=1&pageNo=1>.

[13] Notification of the Director-General of the Pharmaceutical and Food Safety Bureau, MHLW (2014) Iykauhin no shonin shinsei ni tsuite [Application for approval of pharmaceuticals] <https://www.mhlw.go.jp/file/06-Seisakujouhou-11120000-Iyakushokuhinkyoku/0000092759.pdf>.

1.7.3 Competition Between Original and Generic Drugs

When generic drugs were first introduced, doctors and patients worried about their effects. Currently, the use of generic drugs is steadily increasing in Japan. The Japanese government is trying to promote generic drugs to prevent an increase in medical insurance in its ageing society. The price of generic drugs is half that of the original drugs. The government aims to raise the utilisation rate of generic drugs to 80% by September 2020 [14: 76, 82]. To achieve this, the government has adopted several measures, including the introduction of a medical fee evaluation system under which medical institutions earn more when they use generic drugs. The government also changed the prescription format to promote generics as the default option and created a system to increase the basic dispensing fee paid to pharmacies based on the dispensing ratio of generic drugs [14: 83–86].

Under the current MHLW practice, the agency approves generics after the expiration of the maximum 25-year patent period and the maximum 10-year re-examination period for the original drug. After receiving approval, manufacturers of generics begin to compete with those of the original drugs. The original drug manufacturers produce the *authorised generic* (AG), which can overwhelm generic markets. The AG is a generic drug manufactured under the original drug manufacturer's patent licence to its affiliated company or the generic drug manufacturer. The original drug manufacturer acknowledges the AG is the same as the original drug, ensuring most doctors and patients readily trust the AG. The AG also has an advantage in the approval process because it contains exactly the same ingredients as those of the original drug. The data of the original drug can be used in the bioequivalence test described above. This means the AG can skip the tests needed before its eventual approval, and more easily enter—and often flood—the market. As such, competition in generic drug markets has intensified with the presence of AGs [3: 40, 52].

1.8 Conclusions

At the time of writing, Japan is in the midst of the COVID-19 outbreak. Although vaccine development in Japan was not significantly delayed, PMD Act regulations postponed the marketing approval of vaccines developed overseas, which caused the rolling out of the vaccination programme to begin later than hoped.

In light of such experiences, the MHLW established the 'Accelerated Parallel Plan' to speed up the entire process, from basic research, the development of a vaccine, pharmaceutical approval, production and commercialisation [7, 8]. The intention of the plan is to accelerate the R&D of domestic seeds by conducting clinical and non-clinical research at an early stage in parallel with basic research, management of the fast-track processes, and outsourcing testing and documentation to specialist companies. The plan also sets out an accelerated regulatory approval process, which involves vaccines developed both in Japan and abroad. Regarding the former, efficient implementation of clinical trials and shortening of review periods for vaccines are planned, while for the latter, domestic clinical trials will be enhanced and the time necessary for review and approval will be shortened. The plan also refers to the development of a production system in parallel with R&D, which supports the early growth of a large-scale production system. To achieve this, the Japanese government issued a supplementary budget to support R&D and established a fund to create a parallel production system [5, 6].

This chapter reveals the MHLW extensively regulates the pharmaceutical industry in Japan. The extent to which the rules established by the MHLW will be effectively implemented remains to be seen.

References

1. Central Social Insurance Medical Council. (2020). Yakka santei no kijun ni tsuite [Criteria for calculating drug prices] <https://www.mhlw.go.jp/content/12400000/000593956.pdf>.
2. Ichihashi, T. (2018). Nihon ni okeru patent linkage no unnyou jitsumu [Patent linkage practice in Japan]. *Hōritsu Jiho, 89*(8), 35–40.
3. Jiho. (2019). *Yakuji handbook 2019 [2019 handbook on pharmaceutical affairs]*. Tokyo.
4. Kondo, S. (2018). Iyakuhin sangyo shinko to yakka sei-do [Promotion of pharmaceutical industry and pricing system]. In K. Oguro, & T. Sugahara (Eds.), *Yakka no keizaigaku [The economics of NHI prices]*. Nikkei.
5. Ministry of Health, Labour and Welfare. (2020a). Dainiji hosei yosan an sanko shiiro [Second supplementary budget plan for 2020: Reference material].
6. Ministry of Health, Labour and Welfare. (2020b). Dai-sanji hosei yosan an sanko shiryo [Third supplementary budget plan for 2020: Reference material].
7. Ministry of Health, Labour and Welfare. (2021a). Shingata coronavirus wakuchin no soki jitsuyoka ni muketa kosei rodo sho no torikumi [MHLW measures to facilitate early commercialisation of the COVID-19 vaccine]. <https://www.mhlw.go.jp/content/10900000/000635 865.pdf>.
8. Ministry of Health, Labour and Welfare. (2021b). Kaihatsu jokyo ni tsuite [On developments] <https://www.mhlw.go.jp/stf/seisakunitsuite/bunya/0000121431_00223.html>.
9. Nakamura, H. (2018). Yakuzai seidono kangaekata, tokucho okucho to yakka wo torimaku kadai [The principle characteristics of the NHI price system and related issues]. In K. Oguro, & T. Sugahara (Eds.), *Yakka no keizaigaku [The economics of NHI prices]*. Nikkei.
10. Nikkei. (2021a). Isuraeru korona vaccine sessyoku saisoku, zinko niwari cho ni: Nihon no okure kiwadatsu (Israel, the fastest corona vaccination roll-out, with a population of over 20% vaccined: Japan's delay stands out)(15 January 2021) p.3 mMorning edition, : 3. Article ID NIRKDB20210115NKM0036.
11. Nikkei. (2021b). Shinnyaku soki shonin he shishin (Guidelines for early approval of new drugs) Nikkei Sokuho (18 January 2021). Article ID NIKNWS-DGXZQODF0703B007012021000000.
12. Noto. (2018). Iyakuhin ryutsu ni okeru ryutsu kakaku to torihiki kanko [Distribution prices and trade practices in distribution of medicine]. In K. Oguro, & T. Sugahara (Eds.), *Yakka no keizaigaku [The economics of NHI prices]*. Nikkei.
13. Shinohara, K. (2018). Nihongata patent linkage seido no shomondai [Japanese-style patent linkage system] I, Law and Technology 80, 29; Nihongata patent link-age seido no shomondai [Japanese-style patent linkage system] II, Law and Technology 81, 9–15.
14. Sugahara, T. (2018). Kohatsu iyakuhin ni kakaru seisaku kadai: fukyu sokushin saku to kohatsu iyakuhin riyo ritsu no kettei youin [Policy issues related to generic drugs: Promotional measures

and determinants of generic drug use]. In K. Oguro, & T. Sugahara (Eds.), *Yakka no keiz-aigaku [The economics of NHI prices]*. Nikkei.

15. Takahashi, M. (2016). Nihon no yakka seido ni tsuite [About the Japanese drug price system]. <https://www.mhlw.go.jp/file/04-Houdouhappyou-11123000-Iyakushokuhinkyoku-Shinsakanrika/0000135596.pdf>.

16. Wakustu. N. (2018). Kenkyu kaihatsu incentive to iyakuhin kaihatsu [R&D incentives and development of drugs]. In K. Oguro, & T. Sugahara (Eds.), *Yakka no keizaigaku [The economics of NHI prices]*. Nikkei

Chapter 2
Competition and Cooperation: Building a Sustainable Healthcare Delivery System in a Society with a Declining Population

Goro Sato

Abstract In response to social changes such as the declining birth rate, ageing population and rapid workforce decline, the Japanese government has implemented regulatory reforms in the healthcare delivery system, including the introduction of collaboration promotion policies. The urgent demand for medical care that arose in 2020 to cope with the COVID-19 pandemic further demonstrates the necessity of a sustainable healthcare delivery system. This requires a major legal shift from competition to cooperation, which necessitates revisiting competition policy in the healthcare sector. It is vital to clarify the challenges facing the healthcare system and to consider how competition policy relates to the establishment of a sustainable healthcare delivery system. This chapter first analyses the legal framework of, and recent reforms to, the healthcare delivery system in Japan from the perspective of competition policy. It then reviews the challenges the system faces. The chapter concludes by discussing the issues to be considered further when creating a sustainable healthcare delivery system and enacting competition policies.

Keywords Healthcare delivery system · Declining population · Competition policy · Sustainability · Regional infrastructure

2.1 Introduction

In Japan, baby boomers will reach the age of 75 or over by 2025. The country will be comprised of a markedly ageing society, with one in three citizens aged 65 or over and one in five aged 75 or over. At the same time, the Ministry of Health, Labour and Welfare (MHLW) forecasts that Japan's working-age population will decline from 65.3 million in 2017 to 60.82 million in 2025, and to just 52.45 million in 2040. In response to these social changes the government has introduced regulatory reforms to the healthcare delivery system, including policies to promote collaboration. The urgent demand for medical care that arose in 2020 to cope with the COVID-19

G. Sato (✉)
School of Law, Okayama University, Okayama, Japan
e-mail: gorosat@cc.okayama-u.ac.jp

pandemic further demonstrates the necessity of a sustainable healthcare delivery system.

This requires a major legal shift from competition to cooperation, which necessitates revisiting competition policy in the healthcare sector. If the regulations are meant to promote cooperation, the government should consider whether the application of competition law and policy be limited and restructured. If so, current policies must be examined to determine which type of competition policy should be developed and which perspective from which it should emerge. Furthermore, as the COVID-19 disaster demonstrated, Japan must urgently establish a way to prevent the collapse of the healthcare system that is flexible enough to meet the demand that may arise during a crisis. Therefore, it is necessary to clarify the challenges facing the healthcare delivery system and to consider how competition policy relates to the creation of a sustainable healthcare model.

In the following chapter, I first analyse the legal framework and recent reforms of the healthcare delivery system in Japan through the lens of competition policy (Sect. 2.2), then review the challenges the system faces (Sect. 2.3). Finally, I present the issues to be considered in the future when building a sustainable healthcare delivery system and competition policy (Sect. 2.4).

2.2 Laws Relating to the Healthcare Delivery System: From the Perspective of Competition Policy

2.2.1 The Basic Legal Structure of the Healthcare Delivery System

Japan's healthcare system is characterised by universal coverage under a dual system of regional and occupational health insurance, and emphasises the 'private' nature of clinics and hospitals in which insured patients have free access to medical institutions and their staff [1, 2].

Japanese healthcare services are primarily provided by private medical institutions; as of 2019, approximately 80% of all hospitals (8300) and 95.5% of all general clinics (101,471) were privately owned and operated [3]. Meanwhile, small- and medium-sized hospitals with less than 200 beds accounted for about 80% of all private hospitals. The Medical Care Act (MCA)[1] stipulates that hospitals and other healthcare facilities should be permitted to open if they meet the prescribed requirements and procedures (Article 7(4)), and few restrictions are placed on the use of names of departments in hospitals and clinics (Article 6-6). In addition, Japan uses the *free access system*, which allows patients to choose medical institutions based on their own judgment, without any restrictions such as prior screening by insurers. The free access system encourages the expansion of the supply of services by private medical

---

[1] *Iryo ho*, Act No. 205 of 1948, as last amended by Act No. 79 of 2018.

institutions and improves opportunities for the public to receive medical treatment. Free competition—in terms of freedom of entry and exit—between medical institutions also plays a role in ensuring the quality of healthcare.

The price of medical services is set by the medical fee system where the universal health insurance system is in place. The health insurance system in Japan is comprised of government-managed health insurance, union-managed and other employee health insurance, and national health insurance, which covers self-employed and small business employees. This system was established in 1961, with the basic principle that all citizens should be able to receive medical care at any time and in any location, without worrying about money or institution choice. Since its inception, the system was designed to ensure and maintain the health of the Japanese people through some form of public medical insurance coverage, and to provide all citizens with medical care of uniform price and quality, assuming that there are no qualitative differences in medical care between institutions.

Neither the MCA nor the Medical Practitioners Act[2] contain any provisions regulating prices charged by medical institutions, which are essentially free to set their prices for medical treatment. While fees are set by the government under the Health Insurance Act,[3] they only apply to the price of insured medical acts covered by public medical insurance. It is possible for medical institutions to provide these free medical services to patients who prefer not to use public medical insurance, and in this way set different prices from the medical fee. However, under the universal health insurance system, most patients opt for services covered by insurance in order to pay less out of pocket. For this reason, the medical fees set under the Health Insurance Act and other laws effectively constitute a government-determined price for medical treatment.

When medical treatment is carried out under public health insurance, the institution submits a medical fee statement, called a *receipt*, to the National Health Insurance Federation or the Social Insurance Agency Fee Payment Fund. The medical fees are itemised and calculated on the receipt, and the insurer, such as the national government or a health insurance association, pays the medical institution. At present, medical fees are generally paid on a piece-rate basis. The fees for medical treatment are determined by a public notice issued by the MHLW following a decision of the Central Social Insurance Medical Council (CSIMC). The same fee is paid to clinics and hospitals. As such, the fees are considered official prices.

Another feature of the healthcare sector is that, apart from prices and regulations on the number of hospital beds in certain areas, the government takes a liberal approach, refraining from imposing any direct regulations, aiming to cement property rights and guarantee medical institutions' freedom of operation. Medical institutions are permitted to make capital investments such as the purchase of expensive medical equipment, and to promote and advocate for their specialty practices.

This system leads to the uneven distribution of medical institutions. To address this problem, in 1985, the MCA was amended to ensure the more efficient use of medical resources and the systematisation of medical supplies by introducing

---

[2] *Ishi ho*, Act No. 201 of 1948 as last amended by Act No. 79 of 2018.

[3] *Kenko hoken ho*, Act No. 70 of 1922 as last amended by Act No. 8 of 2020.

a medical planning system that includes private medical institutions.[4] Under this system, each prefecture formulated a plan that stated the number of beds it would need, how it would create an emergency medical system, and introduce a system that would secure and train medical personnel.

Under the MCA, prefectures must submit medical care plans in order to ensure the medical care delivery system works smoothly, in line with the basic policy established by the MHLW as well as the conditions of reported by the region (Articles 30-3 and 30-4). Local and national governments must take necessary measures to improve the healthcare delivery system in areas with a shortage of hospitals and clinics (Article 30-5). Owners and managers of hospitals should also make efforts to maintain their facilities, instruments and equipment and keep the institution open and running (Article 30-6). To achieve the goals stated in the medical plan, or when particularly necessary, a prefectural governor may make recommendations to a hospital or other establishment regarding its business operations or increasing the number of hospital beds (Article 30-11).

Unfortunately, serious problems arose, such as the collapse of regional healthcare system due to a shortage of doctors, nurses and other staff, and the closure of key hospitals. As such the MCA was further amended in 2006 to formulate a basic policy for Japan's healthcare delivery system.[5] This amendment expanded the necessary details included in the medical plan and implemented measures to secure medical personnel. The institutional changes resulting from this amendment were substantial.

2.2.2 Medical Services and the Antimonopoly Act

The Antimonopoly Act (AMA) applies to all business sectors. In contrast, medical laws are sector-specific regulations applicable only to the healthcare sector. The relationship between the AMA and medical law is generally understood as follows, assuming the provision of medical services is subject to the AMA [4].

The AMA is Japan's fundamental economic law that, in principle, requires the application of fair and free competition regulations to all business sectors. On the other hand, the healthcare sector is subject to entry and price controls under medical laws and the health insurance system. It is a regulated industry in which free competition is restricted. However, this restriction does not imply a lack of competition—there is room for service and price competition within the regulatory framework. Therefore, application of the AMA to competition in the health sector is mandatory.

Such a position is supported by case law. In *Kannonji Medical Association*, the Tokyo High Court ruled that a business association's restriction of the establishment of new medical institutions and the promotion of specialised medical units to protect

---

[4] Iryo ho no ichibu wo kaisei suru horitsu, Act No. 109 of 1985.

[5] Ryoshitsuna iryo wo teikyo suru taisei no kakuritsu wo hakaru tameno iryoho to no ichibu wo kaisei suru horitsu, Act No. 84 of 2006.

their members' vested interests violated Articles 8(3) and (4) of the AMA.[6] The court stated:

> Although there is little room for price competition in the provision of medical care, there are many aspects in which the principle of competition operates in terms of the content and quality of the medical care provided, and it is necessary to secure the interests of consumers and promote the sound development of medical services through fair and free competition.

The ruling continued:

> The medical planning system established by prefectures is intended to correct the uneven regional distribution of medical resources by regulating the uncontrolled increase in hospital beds and to ensure functional coordination between medical facilities, thus restricting free competition to that extent. However, as an exception to the free competition required by the AMA, the restrictions on the provision of medical care are only in line with the purpose of the Medical Care Law, which is 'to ensure the system for providing medical care and thereby contribute to the maintenance of the health of the people', and the means are limited to those within the scope permitted by the Medical Care Law. Medical institutions are also required to improve the quality of their provision of medical services through the principle of free competition, within the framework of public regulation under the Medical Services Act.

2.2.3   Recent Healthcare Reform: From Competition to Cooperation

The healthcare delivery system, established as a network promoted private hospitals and institutions, needs to cope with the recent decline in Japan's population. As such, healthcare policy reform is occurring under the motto, 'from competition to cooperation'.

2.2.3.1   Introduction of a System to Promote Cooperation

Regional Medical Care Plan and Regional Medical Plan Coordination Board

In 2014, hospitals and clinics competed with each other to provide outpatient care, which hindered the differentiation of medical institutions and the development of a system of cooperation—particularly involving the allotted number of hospital beds. Under such circumstances, they developed a plan to resolve these issues, called a 'regional medical care plan'. The purpose was to achieve functional differentiation amongst institutions and cooperation on the number of hospital beds in each region.

Under the regional medical care plan, 341 medical care areas were created based on estimates of future populations across Japan that would need access to secondary medical care. Each medical care area estimated the number of hospital beds they would require by 2025 for each level of patient care: high acuity, acute, chronic and recovery. A Regional Medical Care Plan Coordination Board was established for

---

[6] Tokyo High Court, 16 February 2001, 1740 Hanrei Jiho 13 (*Kannonji Medical Association*)

each area. The measures were implemented in June 2014 by the Act for Securing Comprehensive Medical and Long-term Care in the Community.[7] The goals are to promote differentiation amongst institutions and cooperation regarding the number of hospital beds that would be required, created through consultations with medical professionals to ensure an efficient and effective medical care delivery system in each region. In March 2015, the MHLW set out its *Guidelines for the Formulation of Regional Medical Care Plansv*, and in line with these guidelines, all prefectures formulated regional medical care plans by the end of fiscal year 2016 to be implemented in April 2018.

The number of current hospital beds is reported to the Regional Medical Care Plan Coordination Board. The board then estimates the number of hospital beds that will be required in 2025 under each regional medical care plan, and evaluates the number of hospital beds stated in the plan. They then determine whether there is an uneven regional distribution of beds, and whether either a surplus or shortage of beds is expected. Issues are resolved through consultation among the parties concerned, with the aim of establishing a sustainable healthcare delivery system by 2025. Under this system, a consultation is initially held to assess the functions of local hospitals and clinics. This is followed by information sharing through the reporting system of hospital bed functions (high acuity, acute, chronic and recovery). Then, consultations are held on projects to be included in prefectural medical care plans, as well as on other matters related to achieving the goals of the regional medical care plan. The aim is to establish the necessary number of beds in each region and to ensure adjustments are made in accordance with regional conditions.

Doctor Recruitment Plan

In March 2019, the MHLW published its *Guidelines for the Development of a Plan to Secure Doctors*. During fiscal year 2019, each prefecture formulated its own 'Plan to Secure Doctors' based on the MHLW *Guidelines* as part of its regional medical care plan. Prefectures began to implement their plans in 2020, with the final target year 2036. To comply with the guidelines, each region creates a 'physician maldistribution index', applying a formula considering medical demand, population and demographic composition and changes, patient flow in and out of the country, geographical conditions such as remote areas, gender and age distribution of doctors, and the type of maldistribution of doctors (area, department, inpatient/outpatient) to predict the number of doctors needed. Areas with a large number of doctors (high-density areas) and with a small number of doctors (low-density areas) are identified based on these indices. When an uneven distribution of doctors is found, adjustments are made through consultation, and doctors are dispatched from the high-density to the low-density areas to correct maldistribution.

---

[7] *Chiiki ni okeru iryo oyobi kaigo no sogoteki na kakuho wo suishin suru tameno kakei horitsu no seibi to ni kansuru horitsu (Iryo kaigo sogo kakuho suishin ho)*, Act No. 64 of 1989 as last amended by Act No. 52 of 2020.

Outpatient Medical Care Plan

The MHLW published its *Guidelines for Securing Healthcare Provision Systems for Outpatient Medical Care* in March 2019. During fiscal year 2019, each prefecture formulated a 'Plan to Secure Outpatient Doctors' as part of its medical care plan, in accordance with said guidelines. This plan was implemented in fiscal year 2020.

Under this plan, each area creates a 'outpatient doctor maldistribution index', taking into consideration medical demand, population and demographic composition, patient in- and outflow, geographical conditions such as remote areas, gender and age distribution of doctors, and the type of maldistribution of doctors (area, inpatient/outpatient). Based on this index, prefectures determine the current doctor maldistribution in secondary medical care areas, which contain 200,000–300,000 people. The secondary medical care areas that fall into the top 33.3% are designated as 'areas with a larger number of outpatient doctors (large-number areas)'. The system encourages new doctors in short-supply areas who do not provide ambulatory care functions (vaccinations, home care, school visits, public health initiatives, and initial emergency care in the community at night and on holidays) to learn new care techniques, changing or adding to their specialties. To inspire such change, prior to opening new clinics information about the region is provided to the practitioners. The notification form for new practitioners contains a space for them to give their consent to take on ambulatory care functions that are in short supply in the area. This consent is also confirmed through a pre-opening consultation. Should a new practitioner refuse to take on an outpatient function in short supply in the area, an ad-hoc meeting is held, and the new practitioner is requested to attend the meeting. If they do not, the ad-hoc meeting is attended by the senior incumbent staff members who requested the new practitioner, and the results of that discussion are published.

Plans for the Efficient Use of Medical Equipment

According to the MHLW, 'As the population is expected to decline in the future and an efficient healthcare delivery system is being established, it is necessary to take action to ensure that medical equipment can also be used efficiently' and so the agency created the *Guidelines for Ensuring the Healthcare Provision System for Ambulatory Care* in March 2019. Each prefecture formulated a plan for the efficient use of medical equipment during fiscal year 2019 as part of its medical care plan. These plans were implemented in 2020. The five types of medical equipment covered are mammography, radiotherapy, computed tomography (CT), magnetic resonance imaging (MRI) and positron emission tomography (PET).

To enhance the efficient use of medical equipment, each region developed an index to visualise the deployment of medical equipment in each region, mapping institutions with such equipment. This information is provided to prospective purchasers, and discussions are held on the joint use of medical equipment, often through consultations on outpatient care. If the purchase is rejected, the reasons are stated at a meeting on outpatient care.

The recent regulatory reforms have promoted cooperation on hospital beds since 2017, and on doctors, outpatient care and medical equipment since 2020. The common approach consists of providing data-based visualisations of the current situation to the concerned medical institutions, and encouraging them to reach a consensus through consultation or voluntary action.

2.2.3.2   Establishment of an Organisation to Promote Regional Cooperation: The Regional Medical Alliance

In 2016, the regional medical alliance system was established. It promotes the sharing of functions and operations amongst medical institutions and provides opportunities to achieve the goals of the regional medical care plan. The purpose is to foster cooperation rather than competition in order to best ensure a high quality and efficient healthcare delivery system in the region. The prefectural governor certifies a general incorporated association that meets the necessary criteria as a regional medical alliance corporation. At the time of approval, consideration is given to consistency with the regional medical care plan, and the opinions of prefectural medical councils are heard. Medical corporations that operate two or more hospitals or other medical institutions are eligible to participate in the regional medical alliance. Non-profits that engage in projects that contribute to the establishment of a comprehensive community care system, such as nursing care services, are also eligible to participate.

These alliances work to enhance and promote regional cooperation. They provide comprehensive regional care by taking advantage of the characteristics of group hospitals and improve management efficiency through their integrated management. Activities carried out by the alliance include reorganisation of departments, joint training of doctors, joint purchase of medicines, lending of funds, investment in related businesses, reassignment of doctors, formulation of rules for accepting emergency patients, and home life support through home nursing and other services. Since the creation of the system, 21 alliances have been accredited as of 12 February 2021.

2.3   Challenges Facing the Healthcare Delivery System

Despite being able to lean on the basic legal structure outlined in Sect. 2.2 and the recent institutional reforms, the healthcare delivery system continues to face certain challenges.

2.3.1   Recent Healthcare Reform: From Competition to Cooperation

As indicated, private medical institutions account for about 80% of the medical institutions in Japan. Furthermore, 80% of private medical institutions are small-

or medium-sized hospitals with fewer than 200 beds. Many small- and medium-sized hospitals are geographically distanced from each other and so the promotion of cooperation and differentiation continues to be a policy issue. However, adopting a common approach concerning the number of hospital beds allocated to each institution (from 2014) and plans regarding physicians, outpatient care and medical equipment (from 2020) has helped address existing problems. In addition, from a legal perspective, a high degree of freedom—apart from drug pricing—exists.

However, during the latter half of 2020, combating COVID-19 became an urgent need, yet the current level of cooperation and existing division of roles amongst healthcare service providers has proved insufficient. At the time of writing in February 2021, the proportion of hospital beds accepting patients with COVID-19 in Japan is less than one-tenth of that in Europe and the United States. No progress has been made in the division of roles amongst institutions, which would have allowed large hospitals to concentrate on the treatment of COVID-19 patients whilst small hospitals provided other medical services. One factor may be insufficient cooperation between hospitals. In Japan, the number of hospital beds per 1000 is about 13, much higher than the fewer than 3 per 1000 in the United Kingdom and the United States (Organisation for Economic Cooperation and Development [OECD] [5]). The cumulative number of infected persons is relatively low: about 0.3% of the population. On 27 January 2021, the proportion of beds accepting COVID-19 patients was 0.87%, or about 14,000 beds, whilst the proportion of beds for urgent and serious illnesses was 2%. In the United Kingdom, the number of infected people relative to the population was about 6%, which was higher than Japan's rate, yet more than 20% of all hospital beds were being used for COVID-19 care. It may be argued that the United Kingdom is responding to the pandemic by utilising its healthcare resources more flexibly. Although the number of hospitals and hospital beds in Japan is one of the highest in the world, it can be argued the country falls short in the efficient use of its healthcare resources.

Six hospital-related organisations, including the Japan Medical Association and the All-Japan Hospital Association, announced they will establish public–private councils in each prefecture to promote cooperation and the division of roles between public and private hospitals.[8] Despite systematic efforts, these issues remain, as efforts have been limited. Deliberations amongst regional healthcare coordination boards often end in unsuccessful discussions due to the difficulty reaching agreement amongst competitors and the fact that council member composition is skewed, involving only members of the healthcare profession. In addition, the regional medical alliance system is not functioning efficiently. As these entities are incorporated associations that require extensive collaboration to establish, and are committed to strengthening cooperation while maintaining independent management, the number of certified organisations currently stands at just 21. Recent policy changes should make it possible to better coordinate the acceptance of patients and to change the assignment of healthcare personnel amongst hospitals, regardless of whether they are in the public or private sector. Although these changes could be

---

[8] Nihon Keizai Shimbun, 4 February 2021, 3.

applied to the COVID-19 pandemic, they have yet to be used to further cooperation in this area.

Overall, progress on cooperation is weak. The degree of cooperation varies greatly from region to region. Considering the situation caused by the pandemic, future legal regulations will likely require a shift to a system based on economic incentives that promote cooperation. Initiatives such as rewarding cooperation through remuneration for care provided and clarifying the division of roles—including financial support for public hospitals—are likely to be introduced.

2.3.2 Methods of Delivering Healthcare Services

In April 2020, the MHLW announced a temporary and exceptional measure based on the spread of COVID-19. Due to patients' increased difficulty in receiving care in medical institutions, those wanting diagnoses and prescriptions via telephone or telecommunication devices could do so through consultation with a physician—including initial examinations—to the extent deemed medically feasible. Prior to this measure, face-to face consultations were required for initial examinations. Diseases approved for online examination were limited to lifestyle-related diseases.

On 29 October 2020, the MHLW further announced a policy change, lifting the ban on online initial examinations when the patient's 'family physician' examines the patient. On 21 December, Prime Minister Yoshihisa Suga instructed the ministry to report whether to make the measures for online examinations permanent by June 2021. MHLW Minister Tamura explained he reached an agreement with the relevant government officials on a permanent policy to be implemented once the pandemic settles, limiting online initial medical examinations to family physicians. The Study Group on Review of Guidelines for Appropriate Implementation of Online Medical Care established within the MHLW is currently deliberating the rules for online health examinations.

Those supporting the point of view of the Japan Medical Association argue the ban on online health exams should be lifted only for family physicians who possess the patient's basic data that make a diagnosis possible. They consider it risky to see a patient for the first time via online examination as information about the patient is limited. Others contend the younger generation's access would be restricted because few have a family physician.

The introduction of online healthcare services is commendable in terms of ensuring access, as it improves healthcare delivery for those who do not have medical facilities near their homes. The effectiveness of online healthcare is especially high for patients who have seen a particular physician for an extended period. The question for the future is how to divide the roles between face-to-face and online healthcare. Along with the expansion of online healthcare, it is necessary to promote evidence-based healthcare by accumulating various data using digital health applications.

2.3.3 Securing Physicians and Efficient Use of Medical Equipment

In the future, the expected rapid decline of those in the working population suggests it will become difficult to secure human resources such as physicians and nurses who are essential contributors to healthcare delivery services. The primary purpose of establishing a plan to bring in more physicians is to correct their uneven distribution and reform the way they work as well as implement restrictions on overtime work. Such reforms should enable healthcare professionals to continue working in a sustainable manner and expand application of the competition principle in the labour market in part by creating regulations on freelancers, which contributes to maintaining sustainable provision of services.

No public regulation of any kind governed the purchase of high-priced medical equipment until the plan for its efficient use was incorporated into the healthcare delivery system in 2020. Across the country, no effort had been made to avoid excessive and duplicative investment in localities to promote the efficient allocation of healthcare resources. Japan is known for having an exceedingly large number of CTs and MRIs. Based on a 2019 survey by the Organisation for Economic Cooperation and Development (OECD), the number of CTs and MRIs owned in Japan per 100,000 population is 111.49 and 55.21, respectively, the highest in the world. For comparison, the percentage of CTs is 67.2 in Australia and of MRIs is 39.1 in the United States. Japan's delivery system is problematic as it leads to excessive costs. The Ministry of Finance points out in its fiscal year 2018 budget execution survey that the number of CTs in all prefectures and of MRIs in almost all prefectures are far higher than the OECD average of 2.6 CTs and 1.6 MRIs. The survey states, 'It is necessary to consider allocations in a way that propels the efficient use of existing healthcare resources and from the perspective of avoiding excessive investment in medical institutions'. From 2020, the efficient use of medical equipment has been incorporated into the plan for outpatient healthcare. Still, as these are voluntary measures, ensuring their efficiency will be an issue. Furthermore, the introduction of medical equipment functions as a means for medical institutions to attract young physicians, so it is difficult for these institutions to reduce their investment costs.

2.3.4 Planning Administration Implementation Methods and Ensuring Effectiveness

Recent regulatory reforms have created coordination councils to promote cooperation. The common approach of these councils is to visualise data and encourage voluntary measures through consensus-building in deliberation meetings. Councils exist because it is difficult for the public sector to set and implement uniform numerical standards. Moreover, they are a response to regional diversity. This approach is

considered a *public–private collaboration*. In principle, the role of public government agencies is limited to setting up a forum for deliberation and distributing the
necessary data-driven numbers. Consequently, coordination takes place according
to local conditions through a deliberative system. However, the system's limitations
mean it may function as a forum to protect the vested interests of medical institutions.
As councils cannot implement binding measures, agreements are reached only to the
extent that the interests of each medical institution are not damaged.

2.4 Building a Sustainable Healthcare Delivery System and Competition Policy

One of the characteristics of the Japanese healthcare service market structure is the
large proportion of private hospitals, most of which are small- and medium-sized
institutions. The 'private' sector plays a central role in the provision of healthcare
as public hospitals have been reduced in size and numbers due to budget deficits.
Because the legal framework is based on the market economy, few compulsory
measures have been implemented. Freedom of business and the protection of property rights are honoured but despite the formulation of a plan for healthcare the degree
of implementation remains insufficient. Recent policy issues have been addressed by
through systems under which deliberative councils encourage voluntary efforts. Such
policy issues include differentiation amongst medical institutions, securing physicians, development of outpatient care and the efficient use of medical equipment.
Countermeasures against COVID-19, which began in 2020, have exposed the challenges of the current healthcare delivery system. This section presents issues from a
medium- to long-term perspective.

2.4.1 Re-examination of the Nature of the Competition Policy

Due to changes in healthcare-related legislation and policies ('from competition to
cooperation') that address Japan's declining population, it is necessary to reconsider
the way to implement competition policy. Factors responsible for population decline
include the ageing population, accompanied by a rapid decrease in the working
population and a declining birth rate. How should competition policies respond to
the introduction of a system based on cooperation that will also ensure sustainability?
Population decline is a structural factor that impedes the maintenance of the healthcare delivery system. It reduces the number of service demanders and makes the
delivery of multiple options difficult due to fewer service suppliers. Competition
policy should be shaped differently at the national, regional and sectorial level to
respond to policy issues arising from structural population decline.

2.4.2 Competition and Sustainability in Healthcare Delivery Systems

The healthcare policy introduced recently broadly aims at establishing legal support for a sustainable healthcare delivery system in response to social changes. Yet it is still difficult to determine the relationship between competition and sustainability, and whether the former can contribute to the establishment of the latter. It all depends on which values are considered compatible with the objectives of competition law.

The AMA has rarely been applied to the healthcare sector in Japan, and the discussion tends to be limited to advocating for the application of competition laws to the appropriate extent. This is based on the dichotomy of application or exemption from the AMA. Such a view dictates the scope of applications of the AMA becomes narrower when the scope of exemptions expands. Although this perspective is appropriate and remains valid, such a dichotomy is unlikely to be sufficient. Examination from the point of view of competition policy is necessary not only within the AMA's scope, but also within the areas where the AMA is inapplicable.

2.4.3 The Necessity of Securing Service Users' Interests

The consultation approach, discussed earlier, is the system currently in use to promote cooperation in healthcare reform. This approach has its merits, such as reducing regulatory costs and responding flexibly to regional needs. However, as medical institutions participate on a strictly voluntary basis, the opinions of regulatory authorities and supply-side actors are not often heard. As a result, competition authorities risk not prioritising the securing of interests of those who receive medical services.

The expected improvements in price and quality via competition, which presumes the existence of multiple options, is likely to be difficult given the decreasing numbers of service options from which consumers can choose. Decreased service options include reduced demand in Japan due to population decline as well as difficulties in obtaining input factors on the supply side. Examples include a decline in the number of physicians, restrictions on their overtime work and an increase in the number of specialists. As healthcare is essential to daily life, it is necessary to maintain and improve the quality of services while ensuring the possibility of service selection. However, as it is hard to evaluate services based on price (especially for medical services paid for by insurance, which have officially controlled prices), it is necessary to establish a method for assessing quality from the demander's view, using other factors. In the future, when designing a system that emphasises sustainability and allows for regional monopolies, it will be extremely important to evaluate the quality of services from the perspective of users.

2.4.4 Population Decline and Competition Policy as Impediments to Sustainability

Healthcare has the character of a regional infrastructure industry that is indispensable for the lives of local residents. In a regional society with a declining population, education and public transportation also possess the characteristics of regional infrastructure industries. Therefore, the study of a sustainable healthcare delivery system may provide insights to other fields. In general terms, it is necessary to examine the nature of the competition policy that maintains regional infrastructure industries in a society with a declining population. A situation in which it becomes difficult to maintain service delivery systems due to a declining population could occur structurally, nation-, region- or sector-wide. When considering competition policy, institutional reforms to promote cooperation and organisational integration are underway as a response to population decline. To ensure sustainability as part of competition policy, it is necessary to consider whether regional monopolies should be permitted in certain sectors through exemption legislation. Important considerations include how to ensure the interests of users, how to evaluate the quality of services from the viewpoint of users, how to consider the relationship between the public and private sectors, and how to respond to regional and industry characteristics.

2.5 Conclusions

This chapter outlines the basic legal framework, recent regulatory reforms, challenges, and medium- and long-term issues surrounding the Japanese healthcare delivery system from the viewpoint of competition policy. Japan is responding to the social needs arising from its declining population. This response is based on the premise of a decidedly liberal legal system and has introduced a degree of cooperation that encourages voluntary responses. However, COVID-19 countermeasures exposed problems such as the lack of integration and comprehensiveness that continue to plague the healthcare delivery system. At this stage, it is difficult to predict whether the COVID-19 pandemic will result in rapid progress in regional cooperation through systems such as the regional medical alliance system. If the approximately 8000 hospitals, most of which are private institutions, continue to respond without sufficient cooperation, the healthcare delivery system will not be up to the challenge, and the perspectives presented in this chapter will become more necessary.

Broadly, Japan seeks to implement a sustainable healthcare delivery system in response to the social demands of a declining population and the need to meet budgetary restraints. The question is how to think about the relationship between competition and sustainability. There are various ways to consider the latter in relation to competition, including examining the legal systems and enforcement authorities of a country [6]. Approaching the issue from the perspective of regional diversity, rapid changes in population composition, industries that are indispensable to people's lives, and the establishment of a sustainable healthcare delivery system, population decline is a structural factor that hinders sustainability. On the other hand, viewing competition policy from the perspective of protecting the interests of users should prompt policies that encompass sustainability while reflecting the principles of competition law.

This chapter focuses on systems that promote cooperation. It discusses the construction of a sustainable regional healthcare delivery system from the perspective of competition policy. Innovation is significant, as it can play a complementary role in building a sustainable system by utilising technology. Health services users could choose multiple medical services through the use of artificial intelligence (AI) (e.g., supplementing imaging diagnosis through AI), undergo remote surgery by surgical support robots or simply take advantage of online medical care. Furthermore, the quality of medical services (including prevention) is expected to improve through the use of digital health systems. Technology could contribute to overcoming impediments to sustainability resulting from population decline. Specifically, digital health and competition policy are major issues to be considered in the future.

References

1. Ishida. M. (2012). Iryo teikyo seido [Healthcare delivery system]. In Nihon Shakaihoshoho Gakkai [Japan Association of Social Security Law] (ed) *Shin Koza Shakaihoshoho 1: Korekara no iryo to nenkin* [New course on social security law 1: Future medical care and pension], Horitsu bunka, 172–[191]
2. Shimazaki, K. (2020). *Nihon no iryo* [Japan's health care] (p. 372). University of Tokyo Press.
3. Ministry of Health, Labour and Welfare. (2019a). *Reiwa gannendo irho shisetsu (dotai) chosa* [Dynamic survey of medical institutions and hospital reports].
4. Negishi, A. (2001). Ishikai ni yoru iryokikan no kaisetsu to no seigen to dokkin ho [Restrictions on opening medical clinics and the AMA]. *Hanrei Jiho, 1755*, 172–175
5. Organisation for Economic Cooperation and Development. (2020a). Health statistics 2020. https://www.oecd.org/health/health-data.htm.
6. Organisation for Economic Cooperation and Development. (2020b). Sustainability and competition, OECD Competition Committee Discussion Paper, 27. http://www.oecd.org/daf/competition/sustainability-and-competition-2020.pdf.

Chapter 3
Drug Regulation in Japan

Yutaka Tejima

Abstract Medications are borne out of medical research, which plays a vital role in the healthcare sector. Japan's national policies to promote research and development (R&D) and create new businesses are set out in the Health and Medical Care Strategy Promotion Act. The rules regulating medical research are established based on the Declaration of Helsinki. Additionally, the Clinical Research Act and other legal rules exist to ensure citizens' trust in clinical research. Medical products are regulated primarily under the Act on Securing Quality, Efficacy and Safety of Pharmaceuticals and Medical Devices (PMD Act). Approval for the manufacture of medicinal products is subject to careful review, and promotional activities for such products are strictly regulated. In the event of an accident involving a medicinal product, the question of whether the government or the pharmaceutical company should be held liable arises. A remedial system for health damage caused by the proper use of medicinal products also exists. Although remedies are not limited to damage caused by unknown side effects, a certain set of requirements, different from that for civil liability, must be met to for the plaintiff to be allowed recourse to this system.

Keywords PMD Act · Clinical research · Product liabilities · Safety regulation · Healthcare sector

3.1 Introduction

This chapter outlines the current state of pharmaceutical laws and regulations in Japan.[1] I first explain the discipline of the medical research that precedes pharmaceutical manufacturing. I then review the rules relating to drugs and discuss compensation for damages caused. Pharmaceuticals are borne out of scientific research, and play a large role in medical care. The vital role of scientific research is clear from the

Y. Tejima (✉)
Graduate School of Law, Kobe University, Kobe, Japan
e-mail: ytejima@kobe-u.ac.jp

[1] This chapter is an English abridged version of Chap. 7, Yutaka Tejima, Introduction to Medical Law (Yuhikaku, 6th edition, scheduled to be published in 2021).

A. Negishi et al. (eds.), *Competition Law and Policy in the Japanese Pharmaceutical Sector*, Kobe University Monograph Series in Social Science Research,
https://doi.org/10.1007/978-981-16-7814-1_3

fact that where there is inadequate medical research, pharmaceutical development is insufficient. The 2014 Act to Advance Health and Medicine Strategy stipulates basic principles, national responsibilities, necessary measures and other fundamental matters involving cutting-edge research and development (R&D) related to health and medical care and the creation of new industries.[2] The law also requires the preparation of plans to comprehensively and systematically promote government measures on matters necessary for promoting health and medical care strategies. As such, the law aims to promote health and medical strategies and contribute to forming and sustaining a healthy society in which much of the population has a long life span.[3]

3.2 Necessity and Methods of Medical Research Regulation

Human beings have greatly benefited from advances in medicine. However, there are still many unexplained mechanism in the human body, and many diseases cannot be eradicated by current medical treatment. The progress of medicine and medical care lies in continuous research activities carried out under fierce competition. Because pharmaceutical products are ultimately provided to individuals, it is essential to carry out clinical research on humans.

Legal regulations help to ensure the protection of the human rights of subjects in medical research. However, legal rules are rigid and do not always fit into rapidly changing medical research areas. For this reason, in Japan, the general framework of medical research is based on guidelines. Medical research aims to contribute to humankind's well-being, and it is expected that it be carried out with goodwill. In reality, human rights violations have not been rare in the past. Therefore, the Nuremberg Code states no medical research should be conducted without the subjects' consent.[4] The World Medical Association drafted the Declaration of Helsinki, based on the Code, in 1964.[5] This established the principle by which obtaining consent from the subject is essential. The Declaration of Helsinki is regarded as a fundamental rule of medical research in Japan, where clinical research norms are based on its position. The Japanese Ministry of Health, Labour and Welfare (MHLW),

---

[2] Act No. 48 of 2014, as last amended by Act No. 94 of 2018

[3] The law provides that activities must be carried out with the aim of contributing to the growth of the Japanese economy while improving the quality of medical care overseas (Article 2). Fundamental policies include promotion of R&D (Article 10); improvement of the environment for R&D (Article 11); ensuring fair and proper implementation of R&D, which refers to observance of laws, regulations and administrative guidance or guidelines; consideration of bioethics and appropriate management of personal information (Article 12); establishment of an examination system for practical application of outcomes of R&D (Article 13); creation of new industries and promotion of overseas expansion (Article 14); and promotion of education and human resources (Articles 15 and 16). The national government's cabinet must decide and publish its findings on health and medical strategies (Article 17). The medical field R&D promotion plan is prepared by the Japan Agency for Medical Research and Development (Article 19).

[4] Nuremberg Code 1947.

[5] World Medical Association, Declaration of Helsinki 1964.

together with other ministries and agencies,[6] has published ethical guidelines based on the type of research, noting they are based on the principles stipulated in the Declaration of Helsinki.[7] The *Ethical Guidelines for Medical Research Involving Human Subjects* recognise the importance of clinical research and set out the basic policy to promote appropriate compliance, focusing on the dignity of individuals and respect for human rights. The guidelines cover medical studies involving human subjects conducted to prevent and diagnose diseases, improve treatment methods, understand the causes and conditions of diseases, and improve patients' quality of life. They require researchers to secure participants' consent, protect personal information and submit their research to review by an ethics committee. The guidelines further require the heads of research institutes to disseminate ethical considerations, establish ethical review committees and refer issues to them, and disclose clinical research plans.

3.3 Laws and Regulations Related to Medical Research

In the past, the only legal regulation on medical research was the Act on Regulation of Human Cloning Techniques, which prohibits only specific types of research.[8] Research scandals led to the enactment of the Clinical Trials Act,[9] which brought legal regulations on medical research to the fore. Then, as medical care data are useful for drug development, the Act on Anonymized Medical Data That Are Meant to Contribute to Research and Development in the Medical Field,[10] (the Next Generation Medical Infrastructure Act) was implemented, setting out the rules relating to such data. The law is not a legal regulation of medical research itself, but of its underlying information. The usefulness of data obtained through medical care for drug development was made clear when big data provided information regarding effective drugs to combat COVID-19.

---

[6] In addition to the Ministry of Health, Labour and Welfare (MHLW), the other ministries involved are the Ministry of Education, Culture, Sports, Science and Technology (MWXT) and the Ministry of Economy, Trade and Industry (METI).

[7] For example, the Ethical Guidelines for Human Genome/Gene Analysis Research (29 March 2001, last amended 1 December 2008); the MEXT and MHLW Guidelines for Clinical Gene Therapy Research (27 March 2002, last amended 2014); the MEXT and MHLW Ethical Guidelines for Epidemiological Research (17 June 2002, last amended 1 December 2008); and the MHLW Ethical Guidelines for Clinical Studies (30 July 2003, last amended 28 December 2004). The Ethical Guidelines for Medical Research Involving Human Subjects will be replaced by the Ethical Guidelines for Life Science and Medical Research Involving Human Subjects in June 2021. At the same time, the Ethical Guidelines for Human Genome/Gene Analysis Research will be abolished.

[8] Hitoni Kansuru kurohn gijutsu nadono kisei ni kansuru Houritsu, Act No. 146 of 2000, as last amended by Act No. 31 of 2014.

[9] Rinsho Kenkyu Ho, Act of No. 16 of 2017.

[10] Iryo bunyano kcnkyukaihatsu ni shisurutameno tokumei kakou johoni kansuru Horitsu, Act No. 28 of 2017, as last amended by Act No. 44 of 2020.

3.3.1 Outline of the Clinical Trials Act

The Clinical Trials Act aims to ensure the trust of people involved in clinical research, particularly the subjects, and thereby contributes to the improvement of health and hygiene. It outlines procedures for conducting clinical research, measures for the appropriate implementation of activities to examine and issue opinions by the accredited clinical research review committee, and a system for disclosing information regarding the provision of funds for clinical research (Article 1).

'Clinical research' refers to research that clarifies the efficacy or safety of a drug for human use. 'Specific clinical research' is clinical research conducted courtesy of research funds from a pharmaceutical manufacturer or related party, as well as clinical studies using pharmaceuticals that have been approved by the Pharmaceutical Machinery Law and certain studies in which unapproved drugs are used (Article 2).

The MHLW must establish implementation standards for clinical research, including the implementation system, structural equipment of facilities and confirmation of implementation status (Article 3). Researchers in general and specific clinical studies are obliged to comply with the standards (Article 4).

Those wishing to conduct a specific clinical study must prepare and submit a detailed implementation plan that describes legal matters for each particular clinical trial to the MHLW and listen to the accredited clinical research review committee's opinions (Article 5). The implementation plan is legally binding (Article 7). The researcher must notify the MHLW if even minor changes to the plan are made (Article 6).

It is necessary to obtain the consent of specific research subjects in advance (Article 9). The information provided includes the purpose and content of the specific clinical research, a description of the drug and other products to be used, and information regarding the manufacturer or distributor of the drug or the person or entity providing research funding. It is also necessary to implement measures to protect personal data that could identify specific individuals, such as names (Article 10). Those involved in the research must maintain confidentiality (Article 11). They must create and store records for each subject (Article 12). In the event of an outbreak of a disease, disorder or death, or infectious disease suspected to be caused by a component of the specific clinical research, it must be reported to the accredited clinical research review committee and the relevant clinical researcher must take necessary measures (Article 13). Finally, researchers may be required to report to the MHLW (Article 14 and subsequent articles).

The MHLW may order the researcher to suspend the research or take other emergency measures necessary to prevent the occurrence and spread of health hazards arising from the research (emergency order, Article 19). A violation of orders or regulations may prompt the MHLW to instruct the researcher to change the implementation plan or take other necessary measures to correct the violation (Article 20). These rules also apply to those who conduct clinical research (Article 21).

When a manufacturer or distributor of pharmaceutical products or related parties provide research funds or other supplies for a specific clinical research study, the entities or persons must sign a contract agreeing to matters specified by the MHLW Ordinance (Article 32). These entities or persons must also publish information regarding their funding (Articles 33 and 34).

3.3.2 Next Generation Medical Infrastructure Act

The Next Generation Medical Infrastructure Act establishes fundamental policies and national responsibilities, requires certification of persons engaged in processing anonymous medical information, and sets out rules regarding medical information and the handling of anonymous information. The purpose of the law is to promote cutting-edge R&D related to health and medical care and the creation of new industries, thereby contributing to the formation of a healthy society (Article 1). The Act consists of 50 articles. *Medical information* includes information about a specific individual's physical and mental condition and history. Handling such information requires special care to avoid unfair discrimination and prejudice against the individual or their offspring due to physical or mental conditions. To constitute medical information, data must be described or recorded following a format specified by a Cabinet Order; expressed using voice, action or other methods; and be able to identify a specific individual or include a personal identification code. *Person* is a specific individual identified by medical information. *Anonymously processed medical information* refers to information about an individual obtained by processing medical data so that a specific person cannot be identified, and the medical information cannot be restored. The Japanese government is responsible for taking necessary measures regarding anonymously processed medical information to contribute to research and development in the medical field (Article 3). The government establishes basic policies regarding various measures (Article 4). Researchers must carry out public relations activities, planning optimisation and information system maintenance (Articles 5–7). The law stipulates businesses handling such information must comply as well.

3.4 Legal Regulations for Pharmaceutical Products

3.4.1 Introduction

Although medications play a significant role in helping people overcome illness, in many cases, drugs cause other health problems. The fact that collective phytotoxicity cases have occurred indicates not all medicines are not fully safe.

Billions of yen are invested in pharmaceutical development, but only a handful of pharmaceuticals result in practical use. Competition in the field is fierce. While certain drugs generate enormous profits if successful, it is also necessary to promote the development of medicines that cannot be commercialised because of the small number of patients they help. The Act on Securing Quality, Effectiveness, and Safety of Pharmaceuticals and Medical Devices (PMD Act)[11] plays a central role in the regulation of pharmaceuticals, quasi-drugs, cosmetics, medical devices and regenerative medicine products in Japan. The PMD Act consists of 91 articles.

The Pharmaceutical Affairs Law,[12] the predecessor of the PMD Act, was enacted in 1943 under wartime controlled economy, but its content was mainly related to pharmacists' work. The new Pharmaceutical Affairs Law was adopted in 1948[13]; it also concerned the status of pharmacists. The law was amended in1960,[14] forming the basis of the PMD Act. The pharmacist status rules were separated and became the Pharmacists Law, while the Pharmaceutical Affairs Law focused on pharmaceutical products. The latter formed the basis of Japan's pharmaceutical administration. As the importance of medical devices has increased recently, the PMD Act was written to cover a broader scope of medical devices, not limited to pharmaceutical products. The name of the legislation has also changed.

3.4.2 The Act on Securing Quality, Effectiveness, and Safety of Pharmaceuticals and Medical Devices

3.4.2.1 Overview

The PMD Act ensures the quality, effectiveness and safety of pharmaceuticals, quasi-drugs, cosmetics, medical devices, and regenerative medicine and related products. It also sets out rules to prevent the occurrence and spread of health hazards due to their use. Furthermore, the Act stipulates regulations for designated drugs should be established and necessary steps be taken to promote the research and development of products such as pharmaceuticals, medical devices, and regenerative medicine, which have an exceptionally high medical need. Through these regulations, the law aims to improve health and hygiene (Article 1). To achieve this goal, the Act stipulates the responsibilities of the national and local governments, pharmaceutical-related businesses, pharmaceutical-related persons, and the general public (Articles 1–2–1–5).

The *pharmaceutical products* referred to in the PMD Act are (i) those listed in the Japanese Pharmacopoeia[15]; (ii) those intended to be used for the diagnosis, treatment, or prevention of human or animal diseases, except machinery and equipment; and (iii) items designed to affect the structure or function of the human or animal body

---

[11] Iyakuhin, Iryokikitouno hinshitsu, yuukousei oyobi anzenseino kakuho tounikansuru Horitsu, Act No. 145 of 1960, as last amended by Act No. 37 of 2019.

[12] Yakuji Ho, Act No. 145 of 1960.

[13] Yakuji Ho, Act No. 48 of 1943.

[14] Yakuji Ho, Act No. 197 of 1948.

[15] Ministry of Health, Labour and Welfare, Japanese Pharmacopoeia < https://www.mhlw.go.jp/stf/seisakunitsuite/bunya/0000066597.html > accessed 21 January 2021.

and are neither machinery nor equipment (Article 2). *Medical device* refers to a device or machine used for the diagnosis, treatment, or prevention of human or animal diseases, or that is intended to affect the structure or function of the body as specified by a Cabinet Order. *Regenerative medicine products* are designed to be used to reconstruct, repair, or form the structure or function of the human or animal body or for the treatment or prevention of diseases. Among those intended for use in medical treatment or veterinary medicine, those cultured or otherwise processed into human or animal cells, such as those introduced into animal cells and containing genes expressed in the body, constitute regenerative medicine products. *Biological products* are pharmaceuticals, quasi-drugs, cosmetics, or medical devices manufactured using living organisms other than humans or plants as raw materials. They require special attention to maintain health and hygiene, and the MHLW designates them as such after hearing the opinions of the Pharmaceutical Affairs and Food Sanitation Council.

Approval is required to manufacture pharmaceutical products on a commercial scale (Article 12). The factory must meet the standards for doing so (Article 13). The MHLW may ask the Pharmaceuticals and Medical Devices Agency (PMDA) to investigate potential problems at the time of issuance or renewal of manufacturing approval (Article 13–2).

Approval for manufacturing pharmaceutical products is given to each item at the time of application after the examination. The application must be accompanied by materials related to clinical trial results and other necessary data, and the materials must be collected and prepared according to the standards set by the MHLW (Article 14). The method of conducting clinical trials to collect this data is called *good clinical practice*. The MHLW may also have the organisation carry out examinations related to the pharmaceutical products (Article 14–2).

In particular instances, the MHLW may consider the Pharmaceutical Affairs and Food Sanitation Council's opinions and give special approval (Article 14–3). Special approval may be issued where a drug needs to be used urgently to prevent the spread of disease or other health hazards that may have a severe impact on the lives and health of people, and where there is no suitable method available other than the use of the drug. The drug must have been approved by a foreign government for sale, provided or stored or displayed for sale in a foreign country, and the foreign government must have a drug manufacture and sale authorisation system, whose rigidity is comparable to that of Japan.

3.4.2.2   Clinical Trials

To be approved as a medical drug, scientific evidence to support the drug's efficacy and safety is necessary. Studies conducted on humans to collect data for this purpose are called clinical trials. The PMD Act defines *clinical trials* as an examination to collect data on clinical study results (Article 2 (1)).

Clinical trials include several phases. Phase I is a clinical pharmacology study that aims to demonstrate the safety and pharmacokinetics of a drug by administering it to healthy subjects. Phase II trials are exploratory trials, the primary purpose of which is to explore the drug's therapeutic effect on patients. Phase III trials are confirmatory trials; they confirm the safety and efficacy of the drug in hundreds of people to demonstrate therapeutic benefits. After successful Phase III trials, the MHLW grants approval and the drug is then manufactured and marketed. Subsequently, Phase IV trials are conducted as a clinical study after marketing. This study examines long-term safety and associated issues.

Clinical trials are indispensable for the development of pharmaceutical products, and the PMD Act generally requires MHLW standards be followed when requesting clinical trials (Article 80–2). However, the rule does not apply when the drug's use on the subject is urgent and unavoidable, or when the MHLW is notified of the clinical trial within 30 days from the start date.

A clinical trial must be conducted within 30 days after the date of notification. The MHLW conducts the necessary investigations to prevent health hazards that may arise from the planned trial.

The clinical trial sponsor, or the person conducting the clinical trial, must adhere to certain standards. They must report to the MHLW if they become aware of (i) the occurrence of diseases, disorders or deaths suspected to be due to side effects of the drug under study; (ii) the occurrence of infectious diseases that may have arisen due to the use of the drug; or iii) other issues related to the efficacy and safety of other drugs under study, as specified by the MHLW. When the MHLW finds it necessary to prevent the occurrence or spread of health hazards due to the use of drugs in clinical trials, the ministry may order a change, suspension or cancellation of the clinical trial or take other necessary measures. The ministry gives such orders to those who intend to request or have requested a clinical trial, those who intend to conduct or have conducted a clinical trial by themselves, or those who have received a clinical trial request. The person who requests or conducts the clinical trial by themselves has a confidentiality duty.

3.4.2.3   The Display and Advertisement of Pharmaceutical and Related Products

The PMD Act generally prohibits pharmacies from selling certain drugs to anyone without a prescription (Article 49). Handling methods for pharmaceutical products are stipulated, and directions printed on container labels (Article 50), items are in package inserts (Article 52), they are provided with a description method and notification, and warned of the prohibition on sales and awards (Article 55). The package insert must not contain false or misleading information on the drug's effects, or describe effects that have not been approved (Article 54). This rule also applies to medical devices (Articles 63–65–6).

Given the nature of pharmaceutical products, advertising, describing, or disseminating explicit or implicit false or exaggerated claims; inappropriate advertising; and advertising of pharmaceutical products before approval are prohibited (Articles 66–68). It is also forbidden to advertise, describe or disseminate misleading information that may falsely guarantee efficacy.

3.4.2.4   Measures to Ensure the Safety of Pharmaceutical Products

Manufacturers and distributors of pharmaceutical products must collect and examine information related to the efficacy and safety of pharmaceutical products, as well as other information necessary for their proper use, and provide such information to medical personnel to raise awareness (Article 68–2). Records and preservation are also required (Article 68–5, 68–7, and others).

When manufacturers and distributors of pharmaceutical products become aware that their use may cause or increase health hazards, they should collect and dispose of such products, suspend sales, provide information to the public and take other necessary measures to prevent use. Healthcare professionals should cooperate in implementing the actions needed (Article 68–9). In addition, individuals may become aware of diseases or disorders, deaths or other complications suspected to be caused by side effects of drugs. When they become aware of these matters specified by the MHLW, they must report them (Article 68–10).

3.4.2.5   Supervision and Information Gathering

The MHLW or the prefectural governor may request reports, conduct on-site inspections or ask questions when necessary to confirm whether the manufacturers and distributors comply with instructions (Article 69). When the MHLW finds it necessary to prevent the occurrence or spread of health hazards caused by pharmaceuticals, the ministry can take emergency measures to avoid health hazards (Article 69–3). The ministry may also order the disposal of such products (Article 70), carry out an inspection (Article 71), issue an improvement order or take other recourse (Articles 72–72–4). It is also possible to revoke approval, permission, registration or special approval (Articles 74–2, 75, 75–2, 75–3).

3.4.2.6   Designation of Orphan Drugs

After considering the Pharmaceutical Affairs and Food Sanitation Council's opinion, the MHLW may designate the drug or medical device as one to be used for rare diseases (Article 77–2). This occurs when an application for a drug or medical device targets fewer individuals than the number specified by the Ministerial Ordinance. Once manufacturing and import approval is obtained, the use value is particularly excellent. In such a case, the national government must endeavour to secure the funds necessary to promote drug trials and research (Article 77–3).

3.4.2.7 Penalties

The PMD Act stipulates various penalties for violation, including bribery and breach of confidentiality obligations for natural persons and corporations (Articles 83–6–90).

3.4.3 Act on the Safety of Regenerative Medicine

Regenerative medicine refers to medical treatment performed using regenerative medicine technology, which includes using cell-processed products for medical treatment such as repair, reconstruction, or formation of the human body structure or function, and the treatment or prevention of human diseases. The Act on the Safety of Regenerative Medicine[16] clarifies the measures to be taken by those who intend to provide regenerative medicine in order to ensure the safety and bioethics of regenerative medicine technology. A government ordinance specifies the technologies to which the Act is applicable, where measures to ensure safety and other measures to secure compliance with the Act are necessary. The Act also sets out a certification system for manufacturers of specific cell-processed products. The Act aims to improve the quality of medical care, health and hygiene by promoting the prompt and safe provision and dissemination of regenerative medicine (Article 1). Regenerative medicines and their technology are assessed according to the degree of risk to human life and health and sorted into one of three categories. The strictness of the rules varies accordingly. The MHLW Ordinance outlines the requirements relating to personnel and structural equipment that hospitals should have, the measures to take to ensure the safety of the technology, and health hazards compensation methods for each of the three categories.

A person or institution interested in providing regenerative medicine must first prepare a plan and submit it to the MHLW (Article 4). To implement regenerative medicine, a health provider must offer appropriate explanations and obtain consent from patients regarding matters necessary for proper implementation (Article 14). The provider must take necessary measures to prevent personal information leakage, loss or damage, and implement other appropriate measures to manage personal data (Article 15). They must create and store records (Article 16) and report to the Certified Regenerative Medicine Committee, the MHLW and the Health Science Council when they become aware of a disease, disorder or death suspected to be caused by the provision of regenerative medicine (Articles 17–19). When the MHLW deems it necessary to prevent the occurrence or spread of health hazards, the ministry may order the managers of hospitals or clinics that provide regenerative medicine to take emergency preventative measures (Emergency Order, Article 22). If necessary, the

---

[16] Saisei iryo no anzenseinokakuho touni kansuru houritsu, Act No. 85 of 2013, as last amended by Act No. 98 of 2018.

MHLW can also issue improvement orders (Article 23) and carry out on-site inspections (Article 24). A certified regenerative medicine committee has been established for use in regenerative medicine. The committee examines the plans and states their opinions (Articles 26–34).

3.5 Relief for Accidents Caused by Medicines

3.5.1 Introduction

Drugs are foreign substances to the human body, whether natural or manufactured. They are often administered with an eye toward their primary and secondary effects. However, even with this in mind, the administration of medicine may cause unwanted health hazards, which vary from minor to severe reactions.

3.5.2 Responsibility of the National Government

The national government is responsible for regulating medications. In the event of damage caused by drugs, the patient or family may pursue remedies based on Article 1, Paragraph 1 of the State Redress Act.[17] Because the pre-1979 Pharmaceutical Affairs Law did not stipulate the government's obligation to patients regarding drug safety, whether the government could be held responsible for health hazards due to the neglect or non-exercise of authority was debatable. However, a Pharmaceutical Affairs Law amendment clarifies the responsibility of the national government, and PMD Act also outlines the government's responsibility. If the government is found to have violated its obligation to ensure safety, it can be held liable for damages.

3.5.3 Product Liability of Pharmaceutical Manufacturers

If pharmaceuticals, medical devices or related products are deemed unsafe in light of the level of science and technology available at the time of manufacture and distribution, the manufacturer, distributor and related entities may be liable for damages to the victim(s) based on negligence under the Japanese Civil Code or the Product Liability Law.[18]

---

[17] Kokka Baisho Ho, Act No. 125 of 1947.

[18] Seizoubutsu Sekinin Ho, Act No. 85 of 1994, as last amended by Act 45 of 2017.

Previously, it was difficult to pursue the negligence liability of pharmaceutical companies, which was a serious issue.[19] This problem was alleviated to a considerable extent through the Product Liability Law. However, it is still hard to hold pharmaceutical companies responsible due to the *development risk defence*. After taking the anticancer drug Iressa (Gefitinib), a patient died of interstitial pneumonia. The issue went to court to determine if the product was as safe as it could have been. The Supreme Court denied it was flawed.[20] It is not rare that what was understood as medical malpractice by an individual doctor, or an error in the use of medicines, later turns out to be phytotoxicity. This becomes known when drugs of the same type frequently cause damage, signalling they are defective in their own right. When this happens, the doctor's responsibility becomes the pharmaceutical company's responsibility.

3.5.4 The Pharmaceutical and Medical Devices Agency and the Health Hazard Relief System

Even if medicine is used correctly, it still may be a health hazard. In this case, it is difficult to pursue liability against drug manufacturers and medical personnel. Japan's drug side-effect relief system is a system that provides medical costs, pensions and funeral fees without a finding of negligence for damage caused by the drug. Contributions from pharmaceutical manufacturers are the primary source of revenue for this system. This system provides remedies for illnesses, disabilities, and deaths that occur when prescription drugs prescribed by medical institutions, over-the-counter medicines purchased at pharmacies, etc. are correctly used. However, the system does not cover cases where medication is used differently for lifesaving, and thus, damage is expected.

Health hazards covered by the benefits are not limited to those caused by unknown side effects of medicines, but damages must be severe enough to meet a certain threshold. Furthermore, it is necessary to meet the requirements that it is not a side effect of an excluded drug, and the person responsible for the liability must not be able to be identified. In the event of damage, the victim or their bereaved family makes a written request to the PMDA. The agency will then make a decision request to the MHLW and, after referring the issues to the Pharmaceutical Affairs and Food Sanitation Council, determine whether benefits should be granted. The PMDA operates a phytotoxicity damage relief system and a damage relief system for biological product

---

[19] The Supreme Court denied the national government was responsible for retinopathy caused by the antibacterial agent chloroquine. Supreme Court, 23 June 1995, 49–6 Minshu 1600. The courts affirmed the obligation to ensure drug safety and determined the national government was liable for the disorder caused by subacute myelo-optico-neuropathy (SMON) disease brought on by the intestinal regulator quinoform. Niigata District Court, 30 June 1994, 849 Hanrei Times 279. The Tokyo High Court affirmed the manufacturer's responsibility for hearing loss caused by the tuberculosis drug streptomycin. Tokyo High Court, 23 April 1981, 1000 Hanrei Jiho 61.

[20] Supreme Court, 12 April 2013, 67–4 Minshu 899.

infections. The agency also works for subacute myelo-optico neuropathy (SMON) victims, provides health damage benefits for HIV patients infected by blood products and to hepatitis C-infected patients under the Hepatitis C Relief Measure Act.[21]

A victim may bring the case to the court to determine whether a remedy will be granted. The courts denied a causal relationship in the case of a youth's death, caused by abnormal behaviour after Tamiflu was administered to treat influenza.[22] Another example is that of hepatitis C caused by gamma-globulin preparations and plasma fractionation preparations. In this case, the Supreme Court rejected the claim that it should be covered in light of the relief law's purpose.[23]

---

[21] Tokutei Fiburiogen seizai oyobi tokutei ketuekigyokodai-IX inshi seizai niyoru C gata kan-en kansen higaisya wo kyusai surutameno kyuhukinn no sikyu ni kannsuru tokubetsusoti Ho, Act No. 2 of 2008, as last amended by 2017.

[22] Tokyo District Court, 14 October 2016, 2335 Hanrei Jiho 4.

[23] Supreme Court, 17 September 2015, LEX/DB25541742.

Chapter 4
Collaboration Between the Patent System and Pharmaceutical Regulations for Drug-Discovery Innovation in Japan

Takeshi Maeda

Abstract Due to the high risks and costs involved, it is vital to provide incentives for drug development. The patent right and re-examination system (data protection) are crucial to dominating the competition in drug development. Monopolisation of pharmaceuticals is enforceable by Japanese patent and pharmaceutical regulations. Pharmaceutical regulations partly define the scope and duration of patent rights. On the other hand, they themselves are a means of enforcing monopolies. Patent linkages enforce patent rights in pharmaceutical procedures. Monopoly profits based on patent rights depend on the National Health Insurance (NHI) drug price standard, the official price list for medicines in Japan. In this way, the patent system and the pharmaceutical regulations work together to provide incentives to create pharmaceuticals.

Keywords Patent · Drug-discovery · Pharmaceuticals · Patent linkage · Data protection · Clinical trials

4.1 Introduction

It is crucial to secure incentives for drug creation in order to promote the development of pharmaceuticals. The patent system, which allows a certain degree of monopolisation of research and development (R&D) results, thereby ensuring the opportunity to recover invested costs, is essential for this to work. What is unique about this is the patent system works together with pharmaceutical regulations to provide a legal means of monopoly. This chapter will clarify the legal cooperation mechanism between the patent system and pharmaceuticals in Japan, including patent linkage and data protection.

T. Maeda (✉)
Graduate School of Law, Kobe University, Kobe, Japan
e-mail: tmaeda@harbor.kobe-u.ac.jp

4.2 Incentives for Drug Discovery

The way to ensure incentives for drug discovery is through patent rights and data protection. This section will review the state of competition in drug research and development (R&D) and explain how patent and data protection works.

4.2.1 Competition in Pharmaceutical R&D

Pharmaceutical products are developed through basic research, non-clinical studies and clinical studies. After obtaining regulatory approval, they are released into the market. The development of a pharmaceutical product takes, on average, 9–17 years from the start of research until final approval is granted. The probability of success is extremely low: only 1 in 20,000–30,000. The R&D cost for each new active ingredient is close to 100 billion yen, a cost that has increased in recent years.[1] The costs and risks of R&D for drug development are incredibly high. Therefore, the original drug manufacturers must recover these costs using the new active ingredients they develop. For this reason, companies focus their efforts on the development of drugs called 'blockbusters'. They also concentrate on improving drugs with these new ingredients, aiming to maximise the revenue from a single new active ingredient. Developing improved drugs is relatively low-cost and low-risk, and it is more efficient to use a single successful active ingredient in multiple ways.

When developing a new active ingredient, drug manufacturers face competition that can best be understood in three stages: inter-mechanism competition, within-mechanism competition and competition involving an identical active ingredient [4]. Within-mechanism competition is the competition for the development of new active ingredients with the same mechanisms that occur after discovering a new mechanism and is sometimes fierce [4]. For example, statins are used to treat hyperlipidaemia by lowering Low-density lipoprotein (LDL) cholesterol in the blood by using a mechanism to trigger HMG-CoA reductase to suppress cholesterol synthesis in the liver. Under the current patent system, a manufacturer does not necessarily have a monopoly over a new mechanism; thus, when competition to use a new mechanism arises, the pioneer is not necessarily the winner. In the case of statins, Merck launched their new drug first. To incentivise companies develop new drugs with new mechanisms, policies that reward for the development of follow-on drugs are considered necessary [4]. On the other hand, since competition within a mechanism may produce superior innovation, it may not be desirable to restrict it.

Competition within the identical active ingredient occurs between brand name and generic drugs, or between different generics caused by generic drugs' entry into the market. Original drug manufacturers develop improved drugs to increase the

---

[1] Yamanaka [7], Ministry of Health, Labour and Welfare (2013) 'Pharmaceutical Industry Vision 2013: A Dimensional Approach to Winning the National Competition in the Drug Discovery Environment', p. 11 and its reference 15.

value of a new active ingredient as well as strengthen and extend their monopoly by obtaining patent rights for the improvements. In Japan, the government promotes the use of generic drugs to reduce the financial burden on patients and National Health Insurance. It is best if generics become available after the original manufacturer has obtained a sufficient return on investment.

4.2.2 Monopoly Through Patent Rights

The most important measure to secure incentives for drug discovery is obtaining patent rights. Patent rights play a role in establishing monopoly rights in both within-mechanism competition and competition within the identical active ingredient.

4.2.2.1 Protection of Active Ingredients

A product patent on an active ingredient is the basic patent needed to protect pharmaceutical products. It places a monopoly on the active ingredient in question, manufactured by any process and for any use.

Protection is limited if the applicant merely identifies a pharmaceutical use for a known substance or discovers a new manufacturing method. In the former, the invention can be protected as a *use invention*, as described in the following section. In the latter, the applicant can apply for a patent on the invention of a method for producing, and can monopolise the invention only for the active ingredient produced through said method.

Patents on active ingredients may cover other active ingredients using the exact mechanism. For small-molecule drugs, it is possible to obtain protection for an abstracted scope using a Markash-style claim, which may be considered beyond the technical idea disclosed in the patent specification, and may lack the enablement or support requirements (disclosure requirements).[2] In biologics, functional claims may allow other active ingredients using the exact same mechanism to be covered by the patent right.[3] However, functional claims may also violate the technical idea disclosed in the specification.[4]

Patents on active ingredients usually restrict competition to the identical active ingredient and create a monopoly for the original drug manufacturer. Those who discover a new mechanism may obtain patents to control the competition within the mechanism and create a monopoly. Patents on the mechanism of action could

---

[2] IP High Court, 4 September 2018, 2017 (ne) 23,087 [Antiviral drug].

[3] IP High Court, 30 October 2019, 2019 (ne) 10,014 [Antigen Binding Protein for Proprotein Convertase Subtilisin Kexin Type 9 (PCSK9)].

[4] IP High Court, 3 October 2019, 2018 (ne) 10,043 [Antibodies and antibody derivatives of Factor IX/ Factor IXa].

be considered invalid if they lack disclosure requirements. Thus, setting a standard for disclosure requirements would control the nature of competition within the mechanism.

4.2.2.2 Protection of Improved Pharmaceuticals

Patent rights can also protect improved medicines. The discovery of a new efficacy or effect of a known active ingredient or a new dosage and administration of a known drug can lead to patent protection as a *use invention*. In addition, if researchers discover that combining multiple active ingredients is effective, they can obtain a patent for the combination drug as a product patent.

Under Japanese patent law, the invention of methods to treat, operate or diagnose humans lacks industrial applicability requirements and is not eligible for patent protection.[5] Therapeutic methods such as a new use or combining active ingredients are not eligible for patent protection except as an invention of a product with limited use. This is called a use patent. A use patent applies only to the act of producing or transferring a product for the said use.[6] Unfortunately, cases in which a product is considered 'for the said use' are unclear (see the discussion on package inserts described in Sect. 4.3.1.2.

In principle, a patent for an improved drug can only monopolise the improved part of the drug. However, a use patent or a patent for a combination drug may extend to the act of producing and transferring the active ingredient itself. In certain cases, a patent right on an improved drug can monopolise the active ingredient itself.[7]

4.2.3 Monopoly Under Re-Examination ('data Protection')

The pharmaceutical re-examination of a product is used to reconfirm the efficacy and safety of a new drug after a certain period following its approval. Until this period has passed, the clinical trial data of the original drug cannot be used to support the approval of a generic drug. Therefore, the re-examination period plays the same role as the data protection period in other countries.

---

[5] See Part III, Chapter 1, Sect. 4.3.1.1 of the Examination Guidelines for Patents and Utility Models and the Tokyo High Court, 11 April 2002, 1828 Hanrei-Jihoh 99 [Method for optically displaying a surgical operation in reproducible form].

[6] See Patent Act, Article 2(3)(i), and IP High Court, 28 July 2016, 2016 (ne) 10,023 [Meniere's disease therapeutic drug].

[7] Osaka District Court, 27 September 2012, 2011 (wa) 7576/78, [Pioglitazone (1)], and Tokyo District Court, 28 February 2013, 2011 (wa) 19,435/6 [Pioglitazone (2)], whether the manufacture and sale of a single drug constituted indirect infringement of a combination drug patent was the issue (both non-infringement).

4.2.3.1 Outline of the Re-Examination System

To market pharmaceutical products, marketing approval is needed for each product as stipulated in Article 14(1) of the Pharmaceutical Affairs Act.[8] Article 14(13) of the Act must be met for partial change approval. An approved *new drug* (a drug with active components, quantities, directions, dosage, efficacy and effects, which are obviously different from those of already approved pharmaceuticals) must undergo re-examination within three months after the expiration of the period designated by the Minister of Health, Labour and Welfare (MHLW).[9] The re-examination period is ten years for orphan drugs, eight years for new active ingredients, four years for new indications (six to eight years for pioneering drugs), four years for new directions and dosage drugs and approximately six years for drugs for specific uses (e.g., paediatric drugs).[10]

The purpose of the re-examination system is to confirm the efficacy and safety of new drugs by collecting data on actual use at medical institutions, as the information obtained in clinical trials is limited. However, during the re-examination period, the data involved in the approval of the brand-name drug cannot be used to support the application for approval of the generic drug. Therefore, the re-examination period functions as a monopoly period in which the manufacturer of the original drug is protected. As such, the re-examination period is sometimes called the data protection period.

The legal basis for the re-examination period to act as a data protection period is as follows. An application for the approval of a new drug must be accompanied by the test results of clinical trials as well as other materials, as specified by the MHLW Ordinance (Pharmaceutical Affairs Act, Article 14(3)). Article 40(1)(i) of the Enforcement Regulations of the Pharmaceutical Affairs Act outlines the details of the required materials. Article 40(2) stipulates that the materials may be omitted if they are 'deemed to be publicly known in terms of medicine and pharmacology' or if there are other reasonable grounds ' however, in principle, 'during the period of re-examination of a new drug', the materials 'shall not be deemed to be publicly known in terms of medicine and pharmacology'. It is sufficient for generic drugs to

---

[8] *Iyakuhin, Iryokiki-tou no hinshitsu, yuukousei oyobi anzensei no kakuho-tou ni kansuru houritsu,* Act No 145 of 1960, as last amended by Act No 63 of 2020.

[9] Article 14-4(1)(i) of the Pharmaceutical Affairs Act.

[10] See Pharmaceutical Affairs Act, Article 14-4(1)(i); Enforcement Regulations of the Pharmaceutical Affairs Act, Article 57; Notification No. 0831-11 issued by Director-General of Pharmaceutical Safety and Environmental Health Bureau, 31 August 2020, 'Concerning the Re-examination Period of Medical Drugs'; Notification No. 0831-16 issued by the Director of Pharmaceutical Evaluation Division, Pharmaceutical Safety and Environmental Health Bureau, 31 August 2020, 'Concerning the Administration of the Re-examination Period'.

attach materials demonstrating bioequivalence with the branded drug after the re-examination period. Nevertheless, during this period, they cannot apply for approval unless they conduct clinical studies equivalent to those of the branded drug.[11]

Biosimilars (subsequent entry biologics) should be proved equivalent in terms of efficacy and safety through more rigours clinical trials, because their active ingredients are not entirely identical to those of original biologics.[12] However, this does not mean the reliance on the original drug clinical trial data disappears. The re-examination period is still a way for biologics to maintain their monopoly. There is no mechanism for special treatment of biologics in Japan, such as the US Biologics Price Competition and Innovation Act (BPCIA).

4.2.3.2 Purpose and Function of the Re-Examination System

There are two theories on the purpose of the data protection system in the United States: one promotes innovation in drug discovery [1, 5] and the other provides incentives for the generation of useful data [6].

The purpose of the re-examination system in Japan is, in principle, to reconfirm efficacy and safety. However, it may also serve the purpose of securing incentives concerning drug innovation, for the following reasons. First, it is believed equivalent to the data protection portion of the TPP Agreement.[13] Second, it expectedly plays a role of exclusivity for original drugs. Third, the difference in the length of the re-examination period for each drug is explained by the drug creation incentives. Finally, the purpose of the Pharmaceutical Affairs Act includes 'promotion of research and development of drugs' (Article 1 of the Act). In any case, the re-examination system, together with the patent system, functions as a mechanism that encourages drug discovery innovation.

A study from 2005 investigated the 'Effective Patent Term', the period from the date of drug approval to the expiration date of patent rights, including the extension period. It reveals that the effective patent term ranges from 5.33 to 19.31 years (average 11.74 years), and only 6.3% of patents are protected for fewer than eight years [3]. Judicial precedents indicate the patent scope during the extension period is limited to substantially the same scope as the approved drug (see Sect. 4.3.2.2). Thus, for many cases, the period during which exclusive rights over the new active ingredient are available is even shorter. Therefore, the re-examination period ensures a minimum exclusivity period for developing new drugs and reduces drug discovery companies' risk.

---

[11] The details of the documents attached to the application for approval are specified in Notification No. 1121-2 issued by the Director-General of Pharmaceutical and Food Safety Bureau on 21 November 2014, 'Application for Approval of Pharmaceuticals'.

[12] Notification No. 0304007 issued by the Director-General of Pharmaceutical and Food Safety Bureau on 4 March 2009, 'Guidelines for Ensuring the Quality, Safety and Efficacy of Biosimilars'.

[13] The Trans-Pacific Partnership Agreement, Art. 18.50-51. Its application was suspended under Art. 2 of the Comprehensive and Progressive Agreement on Trans-Pacific Partnership (CPTPP).

4.2.4 Summary

As the costs and risks associated with the R&D of drugs are incredibly high, original drug manufacturers focus their efforts on developing new active ingredients that generate high profits and are used in the development of improved drugs, aiming to recover their investment from a single new active ingredient.

Competition over drug development can be classified into an inter-mechanism competition to discover a new mechanism of action, a within-mechanism competition for the newly discovered mechanism and a competition within the identical active ingredient. Ensuring exclusive remuneration for those who discover a new mechanism of action promotes innovation and provides incentives for drug creation. Moreover, while monopolising a new active ingredient for a certain period is essential to secure incentives for creation, promptly promoting generic drugs after providing sufficient opportunities for return on investment is also necessary given the cost difference between the two.

Patent rights over new active ingredients are an important means for controlling competition within the identical active ingredients and enable drug discovery companies to establish a monopoly, which can be strengthened and extended by obtaining patents on improved drugs. Patent rights can also control competition within the same mechanism and build a monopoly; however, such broad patent rights are not always enforceable because they go beyond the patent disclosure. The re-examination period, sometimes referred to as the data protection period, is the period during which, following approval, one can monopolise the approved drugs for a certain period. The re-examination system complements the patent system, controls competition within the same active ingredient and guarantees a minimum period of exclusivity for the drug.

4.3 Monopoly Achieved Through Cooperation Between the Patent System and Pharmaceutical Law

Pharmaceutical monopolies are achieved through cooperation between the patent system and the Pharmaceutical Affairs Law. This section outlines their interaction.

4.3.1 The Relationship Between the Patent System and Pharmaceutical Regulations

This subsection offers an overview of the pharmaceutical approval system and how it affects the patent system and vice versa. It also demonstrates that the pharmaceutical approval process can be a means for imposing monopolies, as well as enforcing patent rights through the courts.

4.3.1.1 Marketing Approval, Price Listing and Japan's National Health Insurance

The marketing of a pharmaceutical product requires marketing approval under Article 14(1) of the Pharmaceutical Affairs Act (or partial change approval under paragraph 13), as mentioned in Sect. 4.2.3.1. Without approval, even the company holding the patent rights concerning the drug cannot practice the invention.

In addition to approval, the marketing process requires the drug to be listed in the National Health Insurance (NHI) Drug Price Standard (see Sect. 4.4.1 below). Only after it is listed can it be covered by health insurance, because inclusion on the NHI price list is a prerequisite for a drug's use by medical institutions.

The package insert (Pharmaceutical Affairs Act, Article 52) description binds the actual way of using the drug [2]. It contains information on the approved and NHI-listed drug usage, dosage, effects and efficacy. The off-label use of a drug, which is a use other than that for which it was approved and placed on the NHI Drug Price List, cannot receive insurance benefits. The Health Insurance Law[14] stipulates that insurance physicians provide health insurance treatment in accordance with the provisions of the MHLW Ordinance, and Article 19(1) of the Regulations for Insurance Medical Institutions and Insurance Medical Treatment instructs insurance physicians to not apply or prescribe drugs to patients other than those specified by the MHLW. Only drugs listed in the National Health Insurance Drug Price Standards are available for treatment covered by insurance.[15] Medical institutions are required to submit a specification of remuneration (receipt) when billing the insurer for medical treatment, so off-label use is curtailed. Such restrictions reduce the probability of a drug being used for purposes other than those stated in the package insert.

4.3.1.2 Interaction Between Pharmaceutical Regulations and the Patent System

As explained in Sect. 4.3.1.3, drug companies cannot market a drug without approval, and the NHI list can, in itself, be a means to enforce monopoly. Besides, pharmaceutical regulations often affect the scope of patent protection. The contents of the drug package insert may determine whether the marketing of the drug constitutes patent infringement. As the act of producing and transferring the product for a designated use alone could constitute an infringement of use patent, the description in the package insert is a decisive factor on whether it is 'for a designated use', which will

---

[14] Article 72(1), *Kenko Hoken Hou*, Act No 70 of 1922, as last amended by Act No 8 of 2020.

[15] MHLW Ministerial Notification No. 106, 'Notices established by the Minister of Health, Labour and Welfare based on Medical Treatment Regulations, Pharmaceutical Treatment Regulations, and Medical Treatment Standards', 6 March 2006.

determine if infringement has occurred (see Sect. 4.2.2.2).[16] Additionally, pharmaceutical regulations may affect the duration and limitation of patent rights, as will be discussed in Sect. 4.3.2.

Conversely, the existence of patent rights may affect the approval and NHI listing procedures. This is the so-called patent linkage, which will be presented in Sect. 4.3.3.

4.3.1.3 Enforcement of Monopoly Through Pharmaceutical Approval Procedures

The first step in enforcing a patent monopoly on original drugs is for the manufacturer to obtain a judicial court order prohibiting competitors from marketing the drug. The Patent Act[17] states the patentee has the exclusive right to work the patented invention as a business. The 'working' of a product invention is the act of producing, using, transferring, lending, exporting, importing and assigning the product (Patent Act, Article 2(3)(i)). The act of working on a patented invention without permission of the patentee constitutes an infringement of the patent right, and the patentee may demand the person who infringes or is likely to infringe on their patent to cease and desist (Patent Act, Article 100). In this way the patentee of an active ingredient can prohibit the production, transfer, or any other act relating to a drug with the same active ingredient.

Alternatively, a brand-name company can legally enforce a monopoly on its drugs by legally preventing others from obtaining approval or inclusion on the NHI price list. As mentioned in Sect. 4.2.3.1, a generic company cannot obtain approval for its drug during the re-examination period of the original drug. Therefore, even if the original company does not take any further steps, the monopoly of the drug will automatically continue through this period, as the generic company would not be approved and they would not be included on the NHI price list. Furthermore, patent linkage can enforce the patent right by prohibiting the generic drug from being approved or listed on the NHI price list.

Currently, new drugs are added to the NHI Drug Price Standards four times a year, while generic drugs, items reported to the Committee on Drugs (biosimilars also fall under this category), and new kit products are listed twice a year.[18] It creates a time lag of several months between approval and the actual start of sales. The existence of this time lag has a non-negligible impact on the de facto monopoly period.

---

[16] The doctrine that the description of a package insert plays a decisive role in deciding whether a competing product constitutes infringement is sometimes called 'label theory'.

[17] Article 68 of *Tokkyo Hou* Act No 121 of 1959, as last amended by Act No 3 of 2019.

[18] Notification No. 0207-2 issued by the Director-General of Health Policy Bureau and the Director-General of Health Insurance Bureau on 7 February 2020, 'Handling of NHI Drug Price Standard Listing of Prescription Drugs'.

4.3.2   Impact of Pharmaceutical Regulations on Patent Rights

This subsection examines the extension of patent duration and trials conducted in order to apply for approval, an example of how pharmaceutical regulations affect patent rights.

4.3.2.1   Registration of Extension of Duration

The first example of the impact of pharmaceutical legislation on the patent system is the registration of patent term extension. In principle, the duration of a patent right is 20 years from the date of filing (Patent Law, Article 67). However, for pharmaceuticals, the term after obtaining marketing approval is much shorter than 20 years because of the long time required for clinical trials. Because the patentee loses the opportunity to enjoy the benefits of market monopoly while waiting for approval, the Patent Act permits an extension of the duration of the patent of up to five years of the period required for the approval.

Duration extension registration requires for marketing approval to be necessary for the working of the patented invention (Patent Act, Article 67-7(1)(i)). When a company develops a new active ingredient, it is often the case that after the initial approval under Article 14(1) of the Pharmaceutical Affairs Act, the company often obtains a partial change approval under Article 14(13), multiple times, by adding new indications or dosages, changing or adding new formulations. Whether or not the extension could be registered again based on multiple approvals was open to interpretation.

Prior to 2011, the practice of the Japan Patent Office (JPO) was that obtaining 'other approvals with the identical active ingredient and efficacy' (e.g., approvals differing only in formulation or manufacturing method) was not necessary to work the patented invention.[19] However, two Supreme Court decisions, *Pasif 30 mg*[20] and *Bevacizumab*[21], revised JPO practices.

Current JPO practice follows the Supreme Court's decision in *Bevacizumab*: re-extension is not granted.

> When, in light of the type and subject matter of the patented invention, as a result of comparing the two approvals with respect to examination factors directly related to the substantial identity as a pharmaceutical product, it is found that the manufacture and sale of the pharmaceutical product, subject to the prior approval, encompasses the manufacture and sale of the pharmaceutical product, subject to the latter approval.[22]

---

[19] Patent/Utility Model Examination Guidelines, Part VI, 3.1.1(3), before the revision in December 2011.

[20] 28 April 2011, Minshuu Vol. 65, No. 3, p. 1654.

[21] 17 November 2015, Minshuu Vol. 69, No. 7, p. 1912.

[22] Patent/Utility Model Examination Guidelines, Part IX, Chapter 2, , 3.1.1(1).

Therefore, if a different ingredient or formulation, or an indication or dosage not included in the prior approval, is approved, the patent duration can be extended multiple times.

The practice of repeatedly allowing such 'fragmented' extensions has its critics, who argue it delays the release of generics to the market, which is considered good public health policy. One cannot deny that multiple extensions with different scopes and durations reduce predictability.

Scopes for extended patent rights.

The scope of the extended patent is limited to the working of the patented invention on the object of approval (the object to be used for the purpose specified in the approval) (Patent Act, Article 68-2). Because pharmaceutical products are approved by specifying the dosage and efficacy, the patent extends on its use specified in the approval.

The IP High Court, Grand Bench decision in *Oxaliplatin*[23] recognises that the patent scope extends beyond the approved drug itself. The decision states the patent right 'extends not only to the approved "product" (pharmaceutical product) specified by "components, quantity, dosage, administration, efficacy and effects", but also to the product that is substantially identical to the pharmaceutical product', and that a product is included in the scope as a substantially identical product if it has only 'slight differences or formal differences in the overall view'.

Certain scholars contend the extended patent scope should cover products likely to compete with the approved drug. The extension system does not allow a brand-name company to build a monopoly by extending the patent unless its scope encompasses highly substitutable drugs. However, judging the degree of substitution on a case-by-case basis would be detrimental to the parties' predictability. It is necessary to draw a clear line somewhere using the commonality of components, efficacy, dosage and administration of drugs as an indicator.

4.3.2.2   Trials Leading to the Application for Approval

There is debate over whether the exception for experiments and research under Article 69(1) of the Patent Act includes experiments performed to apply for approval. While conducting clinical trials is essential to obtain marketing approval, doing so during the term of the patent would technically be considered patent infringement. However, according to the Supreme Court, patent rights do not extend to experiments necessary for the application for approval to market a generic after the expiration of the patent. If follow-on drug makers cannot market their drug promptly after the expiration of the patent, it is practically equivalent to extending the duration of the patent. The Court determined that conducting experiments necessary to obtain data for an application for approval, as mandated by Article 14 of the Pharmaceutical Affairs Act, does not constitute patent infringement because it is 'working the patented

---

[23] 20 January 2017, Hanji No. 2361, p. 73.

invention for experimental or research purposes', as defined in Article 69(1).[24] This decision indicates conducting clinical trials or other experiments before the patent expires in order to market a drug after the expiration of the patent does not constitute a patent infringement.[25]

4.3.3 Patent Linkage: The Impact of Patent Rights on Pharmaceutical Regulations

Patent linkage is a system in which the infringement of new drug-related patent rights is considered in the approval process to market follow-on drugs (i.e., generic drugs and biosimilars). Patent linkage was first adopted in the United States, then introduced in many countries, including Japan. On the other hand, many countries, including those in the European Union, do not use patent linkage.

The purpose of patent linkage is to ensure sufficient protection of the original drug while facilitating the prompt entry of follow-on products when patents expire, by eliminating uncertainty regarding the sale of follow-on drugs. The advantage of patent linkage for the patent holder or original drug manufacturer is reliability and rapid enforcement of patent rights. It also eliminates uncertainty as to whether the product generic drug manufacturers are marketing infringes on a patent before it goes to market.

4.3.3.1 Two-Step Patent Linkage

The patent linkage system in Japan consists of two steps.

Step 1: Withholding of Approval when in Conflict with Patent Rights

The first step is a scheme to deny the approval of drugs that conflict with patent rights. This denial has no explicit basis in the Pharmaceutical Affairs Act, but is based on the discretion of the MHLW, which is explained in the Director's Notifications of 1994 and 2009.[26] This treatment is the so-called administrative discretion. The MHLW can deny approval for reasons other than those described in Article 14(2) of the

---

[24] Supreme Court,16 April 1999, Minshu Vol. 53, No. 4, p. 627.

[25] The Tokyo District Court, 22 July 2020, 2019 (Wa) No. 1409 held that the 1999 Supreme Court decision was also applicable to bridging studies conducted in Japan after receiving marketing approval from a foreign drug regulatory authority.

[26] Notification No. 762 issued by the Director of Evaluation and Registration Division, Pharmaceutical Affairs Bureau, Ministry of Health and Welfare on 4 October 1994, 'Handling of Drug Patent Information for Approval Review', and Notification No. 0605001 issued by the Director of Economic Affairs Division, Health Policy Bureau/Notification No. 0605014 issued by the Director of Evaluation and Licensing Division, Pharmaceutical Food Safety Bureau on 5 June 2009, 'Handling of Drug Patents for Marketing Approval Review and NHI Drug Price Listing of Generic Pharmaceuticals'.

Pharmaceutical Affairs Act, as the decision on whether a product is suitable as a drug should be left to a high level of professional discretion. Drugs that conflict with patent rights are not approved due to concerns regarding a stable supply.

Only substance and use patents concerning the active ingredients of already approved drugs are relevant to patent linkage. Patents on dosage, efficacy and administration are considered; however, the extent to which they can be linked is unclear. Patent information is collected by the holder of the original drug approval or the patent holder submitting a Drug Information Report Form to the Pharmaceuticals and Medical Devices Agency (PMDA),[27] which the MHLW entrusts with the approval review work. Unlike the United States' 'Orange Book',[28] this patent information is not public; thus, generic drug manufacturers cannot know in advance which patents will become relevant. If there is a substance patent on an active ingredient, the generic drug will not be approved at all. In contrast, in the case of a use patent, it is possible to obtain approval excluding the conflicting efficacy, dosage and administration. This is referred to as a 'skinny label'.

Consequently, we can point out the following problems. Whether patent infringement exists is determined by examiners making inquiries to generic drug manufacturers based on the Drug Information Report Form, and the MHLW seems to understand that the difference in views is not a problem since the scope of rights for substance and use patents is relatively clear. However, considering that the technical scope of functional claims and use inventions is not clear, with the scope of extended patents even more unclear, there should be many cases in which a dispute exists. Additionally, the treatment of patent invalidation is unstable, which means that the patent should be considered valid even if it has been judged invalid by the JPO or the court until it is finalised; however, there are some cases in which the PMDA has approved drugs in certain cases without considering patents.

Step 2: Prior Adjustment in NHI Drug Price Listing

The second step in Japanese patent linkage is prior adjustment before the product is placed on the NHI drug price list. This adjustment is based on a notification issued by the MHLW to the Japan Pharmaceutical Manufacturers Association (JPMA).[29] The MHLW asks those who wish to list generic drugs on the NHI drug price list to conduct prior adjustments with the patent holder. They list only those items without a patent dispute for which a future stable supply is possible, since drugs involving a patent dispute cannot be stably supplied. Its legal nature seems administrative guidance by the MHLW (see Procedure Act, Article 32).

Prior adjustments cover all kinds of patent rights. However, it is just a dialogue between the patentee and the generic drug manufacturer. If there is a dispute between

---

[27] Article 14-2 (1) of the Pharmaceutical Affairs Act and Article 15 (v)(a) of the Act on the Pharmaceuticals and Medical Devices Agency.

[28] The Orange Book contains a list of patents considered by the US Food and Drug Administration for generic drug approval.

[29] Notification No. 0115001 issued by the Director of Economic Affairs Division, Health Policy Bureau on 15 January 2009, 'Listing of Generic Drugs in the National Health Insurance Drug Price Standard'.

the two parties, the MHLW seems to list the drug only after the generic manufacturer submits a letter that guarantees stable supply. While this system corresponds to Article 18.53(1) of the TPP Agreement, it does not meet its requirements, in that notification to the patentee is not mandatory, and the only way to resolve a dispute is through ordinary litigation procedures.

On the other hand, the United States' 'Orange Book' lists and publishes relevant patents under the Hatch–Waxman Act, and anyone who files an abbreviated new drug application (ANDA) for a generic drug that relies on the clinical trials of the original drug must notify the patentee. An ANDA is considered patent infringement; thus, the patentee can file an infringement suit, called an ANDA suit, and the approval will be suspended for as long as the suit is in court.

4.3.3.2   Providing Incentives for Generic Drug Applications

The US patent linkage system grants the first generic drug manufacturer to file an ANDA contesting the validity or technical scope of a patent 180 days of market exclusivity, which incentivises generic drug manufacturers to enter the market by rewarding them for taking the risk of being the first to do so. This contributes to the widespread use of generic drugs in the country, despite frequent litigation and reverse payments.

Japan has no such system. Instead, the first generic drug manufacturer to enter the market risks incurring more damages than the second if patent infringement is found later. The first entrant risks liability for damages equivalent to the amount of revenue lost due to the reduction in drug prices following the generic drug launch (see Sect. 4.4.2 below). It is necessary to ensure that generic drugs can enter the market by eliminating the risk of patent infringement beforehand.

4.3.3.3   Patent Linkage for Biologics

The same patent linkage applies to biosimilars such as generic drugs, although this is not made clear in the MHLW's notification.

A unique patent linkage system for biologics (original drugs) is available in the United States under the BPCIA. The abbreviated Biologics License Application (aBLA) for marketing approval of a biosimilar, involves a procedure called the 'patent dance', an interaction between the original company and the follow-on company to identify relevant patents and, if necessary, to file a patent infringement suit, which is much more complicated and sophisticated than an ANDA suit. Such a system is required for biosimilars in the U.S., probably because identifying the relevant patents for biosimilars is not easy, and the follow-on drug makers want to reduce the risk of patent infringement in advance.

4.3.3.4 Problems with Patent Linkage in Japan

Japanese patent linkage consists of the first step—withholding approval when substance or use patents are infringed, and the second step—prior adjustment, a discussion amongst all relevant generic drugs. Although stakeholders praise the system and it contributes to smoothing the negotiation process, it has several problems.

The criteria for selecting patent rights for which approval is withheld at the first step are not clear. In certain cases, it is difficult for the MHLW/PMDA, which are not patent experts, to interpret the patent scope, such as use patents and extended patents. Such uncertainty reduces predictability, and patent linkage will not only fail to protect branded drugs but may even hinder the early entry of generic drugs.

Another issue is that Japanese patent linkage lacks a mechanism to resolve disputes fairly and transparently. The current system avoids unnecessary disputes when the gap between the involved party views is minor, but it is ineffective and unfair when the conflict between the parties is significant.

In addition, the current system, which lacks a clear legal basis, is contrary to the rule of law and may deprive parties of the opportunity to seek judicial review on property rights. The first step of patent linkage is just administrative discretion, and the second step is merely administrative guidance. The rules must be clearly explained in legislative statutes, and it is necessary to secure a place to receive a legitimate judgment in the event of a dispute since this is a matter that significantly affects the rights and duties of citizens.

To avoid these issues, Japan should consider a system corresponding to Article 18.53(1) of the TPP Agreement. Disputes over patents should be clarified at an early stage of the approval and NHI price listing procedures so the judiciary can make a prompt decision while considering the systems in other countries, such as the United States, and taking into consideration that the disclosure of relevant patents in advance is not necessary. Such a system will further protect brand-name drugs and make it easier for follow-on drugs to enter the market.

4.4 NHI Drug Price Standard

The National Health Insurance (NHI) Drug Price Standard determines the revenue obtained from drug monopolies. The Standard refers to the official price of prescription drugs and defines the price of drugs when paid by the medical insurance pays to the insured medical institutions and pharmacies. According to Article 76(2) of the Health Insurance Act, the NHI price is determined by the Minister of the MHLW. The Minister conducts necessary investigations when calculating NHI prices (Health Insurance Act, Article 77(1)) and sets NHI prices after consulting with the Central Social Insurance Medical Council (*Chuikyo*; Health Insurance Act, Article 82(1)). A drug is included on the NHI drug price list if a drug maker submits a request to the MHLW after receiving marketing approval.[30]

The NHI Drug Price Standard is a list that defines the range of drugs available for insurance purposes and a price list for prescription drugs. Such a system has two purposes: one is to control rising drug costs and ensure patient access to medicines paid by insurance, and the other is to secure incentives for R&D of innovative new drugs. The latter purpose has much in common with the intellectual property system.

4.4.1 How to Calculate the NHI Price

The method of calculating NHI prices is set by the *Chuikyo* and is made public.[31] It differs for new drugs and generic drugs.

4.4.1.1 The NHI Price for New Drugs

The method of calculating the NHI price differs according to whether a similar drug exists. If so, the NHI price relies on the Similar Efficacy Comparison Method (I), which matches the daily NHI price of a new drug to that of the most similar existing drug. New drugs that show a higher degree of usefulness than similar drugs include a Supplemental Allowance of 5–120%, which includes a Premium for Usefulness (I) (II), Premium for Marketability (I) (II), Premium for Paediatric Use and Premium for the *Sakigake* Designation Scheme.[32] The Supplemental Allowance aims to raise NHI prices for drugs that require strong incentives for creation.

Even if similar drugs exists, drugs without novelty—three or more drugs with similar pharmacological effects—are not eligible for the supplemental allowance. In these cases, resolution depends on the Similar Efficacy Comparison Method (II), in which the price will be the lowest for similar drugs over the past several years.

If there is no similar drug, the Cost Calculation Method is adopted, in which selling expenses, distribution expenses and operating income are added to the cost of production and sales. The operating profit margin is calculated according to the degree of innovation when compared to existing drugs. The Cost Calculation Method is also subject to the Supplemental Allowance.

---

[30] Notification No. 0207-2 issued by the Director-General of Health Policy Bureau and the Director-General of Health Insurance Bureau on 7 February 2020, supra note18.

[31] Notification No. 0207-1 issued by Director-General of Health Insurance Bureau on 7 February 2020, 'Standards for Drug Prices Calculation'.

[32] A scheme that designates drugs first developed in Japan and are expected to show significant efficacy at an early stage of clinical trials, aiming for early commercialisation (approval in six months, half the usual time for drugs).

Finally, the NHI price is calculated by applying the Foreign Average Price Adjustment[33] and Inter-specification Adjustment[34] in the case of Similar Efficacy Comparison Methods.

4.4.1.2   The NHI Price for Generic Drugs

When generic drugs are first placed on the NHI drug price list, the NHI price will equal that of the brand-name drug multiplied by 0.5. However, if the number of drug brands for internal use exceeds 10, the NHI price will be multiplied by 0.4. The price of generic drugs is sufficiently lower to encourage a rapid shift to generics.

Biosimilars have a special provision, where the price is 0.7 (0.6) times instead of 0.5 (0.4) times that of the original drug. Furthermore, the price may rise to 10% more depending on the difficulty of the clinical trials, which ensures incentives for biosimilar development, as their R&D costs are higher than those of generics. The NHI price of an authorised generic of biologics ('bio-AG') is also the same as a biosimilar. It aims to ensure an appropriate competitive environment with biosimilars, although bio-AGs do not incur the same R&D costs.[35]

4.4.1.3   NHI Price Revision and Price Maintenance Premium

NHI prices are now revised annually.[36] The prices for already-listed drugs are calculated using the Market Price Weighted Average Adjustment Range Method. The NHI price is simply the price at the medical institution or pharmacy, and the price delivered by the wholesaler to these institutions is not fixed. This method adjusts the NHI price based on the prevailing market price of the sales price established by the wholesaler. As a result of competition, NHI prices usually decrease with each revision.

The general rule includes a few exceptions. For example, the NHI price of long-listed drugs is to be reduced in order to promote their replacement by generics. Conversely, the Premium to Promote the Development of New Drugs and Elimination of Off Label Uses (Price Maintenance Premium; [PMP]) is closely related to the promotion of innovation.

The purpose of PMP is to maintain prices by decreasing the price reduction from NHI price revisions. The eligibility requirements for PMP are that it must be less than 15 years since the initial NHI price listing and no generics have been listed,

---

[33] An adjustment made when there is a large discrepancy between the price of a new drug and that of a foreign (American, British, German, French) drug with the identical composition and formulation.

[34] An adjustment made based on the relationship between the NHI price and a similar drug when calculating the NHI price of preparation with the identical active ingredient and formulation, but different content.

[35] Authorised generic makers can manufacture biologics that are completely identical to the original only if the original drug manufacturer provides its relevant technology.

[36] The NHI prices used to be revised every two years but are revised annually as of 2021.

and must be a Covered Item, which includes orphan drugs, products under public solicitation for development, drugs subject to the Supplementary Allowance at the time of the NHI drug price listing, drugs with innovative and useful novel mechanisms of action, items designated under the Sakigake Designation Scheme, and drugs for drug-resistant bacteria.[37]

PMP aims to accelerate the creation of new drugs by appropriately evaluating innovative new medicines during the patent term. It allows patent holders, especially those who have developed new drugs that require incentives for creation, to maintain high prices during the patent term and sell them exclusively, thus earning greater profits.

4.4.2 Interaction Between the NHI Drug Price System and Patent Law

As described above, one of the purposes of the NHI drug price system is to secure incentives for the creation of new drugs. In this respect, the NHI price system shares the same purpose as the patent system. The patent system grants monopoly rights, while the NHI price system determines the profit margin during the monopoly period.

A case in which the patent system and the NHI drug price system directly interacted saw damages awarded based on the NHI price reduction caused by the entry of generic drugs.[38] The issue was whether the reduction of drug prices due to the lack of PMP requirements caused by the listing of generic drugs on the NHI drug price list had a reasonable causal relationship to patent infringement, which the court affirmed. This case suggests that only the first generic drug manufacturer to enter the market is liable for damages resulting from the reduction of drug prices. The patent system and the NHI price system are intertwined in the case, and it negatively affects the incentives for generic drug manufacturers to enter the market (see also Sect. 4.3.3.3).

4.5 Conclusion

This chapter reviews the risks and costs of the R&D of original drugs and the competition in drug development. It outlines how patent rights and the re-examination system (data protection) affect competition. It also clarifies the legal mechanism through which the patent system and the pharmaceutical law collaboratively enforce monopolies on certain drugs, showing the pharmaceutical law partly regulates the scope and duration of patent rights. The law itself is a means to enforce monopolies and patent linkage. The chapter also demonstrates monopoly profits through

---

[37] Supra note31.

[38] Tokyo District Court, 27 July 2017, 2015 (Wa) 22,491.

patents depend on the NHI drug price standard, which considers the incentives for drug creation. In this way, this chapter clearly shows how the patent system and pharmaceutical regulations in Japan work together to provide incentives for creating pharmaceuticals.

Acknowledgements This work was supported by JSPS KAKENHI, through Grant Numbers JP19K01422, JP18H05216.

References

1. Eisenberg, R. S. (2007). The Role of the FDA in Innovation Policy. *Michigan Telecommunication and Technical L Review 13*, 345.
2. Ishino, M. et al. (2017). Iyaku Yoto Hatsumei wo meguru genjo ni tsuite (On the Present Situation Concerning Pharmaceutical Use Inventions), *70*(9) Patent 86 (2017).
3. Masuda, S. (2005). Iyakuhin Chitekizaisan Hogo no Genjo to Kadai—Encho Tokkyo-ken Bunseki kara miru Sinyaku Tokkyo Hogo Kikan (Current Status and Issues of Pharmaceutical Intellectual Property Protection: New Drug Patent Protection Period from the Perspective of Analysis of Extended Patent Rights), *55*(13) Chizai Kanri (Intellectual Property Management) 1909.
4. Nagaoka, S. (2019). *Drug discovery in Japan.* Springer.
5. Roin, B. N. (2009). Unpatentable drugs and the standards of patentability. *Texas L Review 87,* 503.
6. Thomas, J. R. (2014). Toward a theory of regulatory exclusiveness. In R. L. Okediji, & M. A. Bagley, (Eds.), *Patent law in global perspective* (Vol. 345).
7. Yamanaka, T. (2017). Jenerikku vs Burokkubasuta—Kenkyu Kaihatsu, Tokkyo Senryaku kara mita Iyakuhin Sangyo no Shinso (*Generic vs. Blockbuster*: The True Story of the Pharmaceutical Industry from the Perspective of R&D and Patent Strategy). Kodansha, Tokyo.

Chapter 5
Corruption and Conflicts of Interest in the Pharmaceutical Market: Regulation of Pharmaceutical Companies' Gift-Giving Practices

Masako Wakui

Abstract Pharmaceutical companies often give gifts to doctors or pay them to recommend or prescribe their products. Such practices not only pose a risk to patients' recovery, but also cause excessive medication use, increase medical costs and undermine merit-based competition amongst pharmaceutical companies, causing severe inefficiency in society. Japan's regulatory approach towards pharmaceutical companies' gift-giving practices is lenient and ineffective, with the criminal code prohibiting bribery only in relation to public officials. Most doctors who privately provide medical services are not able to be reached by the law. Furthermore, only the individual, not the company, is penalised under the criminal code. Although the Antimonopoly Act and the Act against Unjustifiable Premiums and Misleading Representations regulate attempts to entice customers using unfair means, a violation results only in a cease-and-desist order. The detailed rules set out in the Fair Competition Code are rarely enforced by the industry's self-regulatory body, which issues only a warning and guidance to violators. Disclosure, rather than prohibition, has become the primary way to control pharmaceutical companies' profiteering practices. However, disclosure alone is insufficient to ensure a proper distance remains between doctors and pharmaceutical companies. Given the serious harms and inefficiencies that may be caused by gift-giving practices, such regulatory systems must be overhauled to effectively prevent such unfair and inefficient methods of competition.

Keywords Pharmaceutical industry · Corruption · Conflict of interest · Code of conduct · Physicians

5.1 Introduction

Prescribing doctors decide which and how many medications a patient uses. Ensuring that doctors make the right decision is vital for both patients and the general public, who ultimately bear the cost through public health insurance. Doctors' medication

M. Wakui (✉)
Faculty of Law, Kyoto University, Kyoto, Japan
e-mail: wakui@law.kyoto-u.ac.jp

© The Author(s), under exclusive license to Springer Nature Singapore Pte Ltd. 2022   69
A. Negishi et al. (eds.), *Competition Law and Policy in the Japanese Pharmaceutical Sector*, Kobe University Monograph Series in Social Science Research,
https://doi.org/10.1007/978-981-16-7814-1_5

choices also affect the pharmaceutical industry, as the company that developed the medication will not earn any revenue unless the medicine is prescribed. A doctor's decision, however, may be distorted by gifts and payments provided by the pharmaceutical company, and the patient, not the doctors, could suffer from a resulting improper drug prescription. Patients without medical knowledge are unable to judge whether a doctor's prescription is appropriate. As such, it is critical to implement rules to ensure that doctors' decisions are not distorted by pharmaceutical companies' gift-giving and payments.

The relationship between physicians and pharmaceutical companies is a serious issue in Japan.[1] Recently, the Fair Trade Council of the Pharmaceutical and Medical Devices Industry [4] issued a warning to doctors against a particular medical device manufacturer, having discovered it was paying approximately 200 million yen (about 1.8 million USD) per year to 20 doctors. This raises the question of whether similar practices occur with prescription drugs. In the following chapter, I examine the potential impact of gifts and payments on the pharmaceutical market and assess whether the current regulatory system in Japan is sufficient to deter harmful and inefficient prescription practices. I conclude by discussing the necessary reforms.

5.2 The Impact of Gifts and Payments to Doctors

5.2.1 Medication Choice

More than 80% of the medication used in Japan is prescription drugs [25]. Only doctors can issue a prescription, and pharmacies must provide medication accordingly.[2] The majority of prescribed medications are covered by public insurance, and doctors typically choose drugs based on the National Health Insurance (NHI) Drug Price Standard, issued by the Ministry of Health, Labour and Welfare (MHLW), which lists the prices of drugs covered by insurance. Patients lack medical knowledge, and their influence on doctors' prescribing behaviour is limited. There are

---

[1] In Japan, hospitals and clinics formerly dispensed drugs directly to patients. This practice was considered problematic because doctors tended to prescribe excessive medications in order to earn a higher income (Rodwin [44]: 190). To resolve this issue, the government adopted a policy that prescription drugs should be provided by independent pharmacies established outside these institutions. Japan implemented an insurance-payment system under which hospitals and clinics, as well as pharmacists, earn more if they comply with the government's policy. Currently, only 30% of prescription drugs are dispensed within hospitals and clinics. Critics argue the current insurance-payment system only benefits pharmacies, which provide medication following a doctor's prescription, without creating any material added value. To counter such criticism, the Ministry of Health, Labour and Welfare (MHLW) encourages pharmacies to offer more assistance, such as monitoring and advising on patients' drug use [32].

[2] Iryohin, Iyakukiki to no hinsitsu, yukosei oyobi anzensei no kakuho to ni kansuru horitsu (Act on Securing Quality, Efficacy and Safety of Pharmaceuticals and Medical Devices [PMD Act]), Act No. 145 of 1960, as last amended by Act No. 63 of 1989, Art 49; Yakuzaishi ho (Pharmacists Act), Act No. 146 of 1960, as last amended by Act No. 63 of 2019, Art 23.

often several possible prescription options to manage or cure particular symptoms, and doctors have discretion in choosing which to use. Doctors in Japan often specify the brand name of the drug when writing a prescription; only about half of the prescriptions refer to drugs by their generic names [24]. Thus, doctors also influence the choice of drug manufacturer.

5.2.2 Pharmaceutical Company Gift-Giving and Payments to Doctors

Pharmaceutical companies influence doctors' prescription choices via several avenues. They promote their drugs to doctors through medical representatives,[3] often providing incentives such as calendars and pens, paying for lunches and dinners, sending mid-year and year-end gifts according to Japanese custom, arranging entertainment such as invitations to expensive golf tournaments, and making payments in the form of gratuities for lectures and advice. These gifts may distort doctors' decision making, either consciously or subconsciously.

Another way pharmaceutical companies sway doctors' opinions is to have influencers, such as professors and doctors who work for prestigious hospitals, write and speak about specific drugs. Pharmaceutical companies pay and give gifts to these influencers as incentives. Doctors may also voluntarily promote certain drugs if they are involved in the research on the product. Such collaboration is indispensable for medical research [31], where the opportunities, materials and financial aid provided by pharmaceutical companies are essential for doctors engaged in research.

For a medication to be prescribed and compensated by insurers, the government must first approve and add it to the NHI price list. Doctors are involved in drug approval and the compilation of the NHI Drug Price Standard. The MHLW also relies on groups of doctors, often members of relevant societies of specialised medicine, to establish guidelines of care as reference (Tejima [60]: 149–51). Pharmaceutical companies may give gifts to these doctors to solicit a favourable outcome.

5.2.3 Potential Adverse Effects of Gifts and Payments

The gifts and payments given to doctors may lead to over-prescribing and a distorted preference for a particular brand of drug. The first and foremost negative impact of this is the delay or preclusion of patient recovery. The doctor has a contractual relationship with the patient, under which they are obliged to act in good faith to promote

---

[3] The information provided by the medical representative is an important source of pharmaceutical information for doctors, although today more online tools are used, particularly since the outbreak of the COVID-19 pandemic in 2020 [57].

the patient's interest (Yonemura [63]: 99). Prescriptions that benefit a pharmaceutical company instead might constitute a breach of this requirement. The doctor's behaviour also might constitute corruption, as the doctor abuses their entrusted power for personal gain [42]. Delays in a patient's recovery cause suffering not only to the individual, but also to their family. In addition, over-prescription also burdens the national healthcare system by increasing costs.

Gifts and payments can adversely affect the economy and society by distorting merit-based competition amongst pharmaceutical companies, where better-quality, low-cost medications are not used, resulting in inefficiency. The gifts are often wasteful and allocate economic resources inefficiently. In general, companies' expected monopoly profit tends to be used up to obtain such profit [41], and so there must be a mechanism to ensure that these expenditures are beneficial to society, such as for research and development (R&D). Supplying stationery and luxurious foods does not appear to serve the greater social good.

Furthermore, pharmaceutical companies' promotional efforts may inhibit the entry or expansion of businesses, particularly small- and medium-sized companies that lack financial resources. Economies of scale facilitate brand recognition; for example, the giant drug manufacturer Pfizer can spread the cost of brand recognition more easily across its product portfolio than can small pharmaceutical companies. Therefore, when competition is based on brand-name recognition, large pharmaceutical companies tend to have a competitive advantage.

5.2.4 The Relationship Between Doctors and Pharmaceutical Companies in Japan

Waseda Chronicle, a private think tank established by investigative journalists, collected donation data and created a database to show that pharmaceutical companies pay a substantial amount to doctors [21]. Ozaki [40] explain that the payments unrelated to research are typically made in the name of information provision related expenses and fees for lectures, consulting and writing. Pharmaceutical companies also provide research funding. Meanwhile, the known non-monetary benefits include luxurious boxed lunches and dinners. This gift-giving relationship starts from when students enrol in medical school [48–49].

It is difficult to establish the extent to which such gift-giving and payment practices affect prescriptions, either directly or indirectly. Surveys show doctors tend to believe the gifts do not affect their prescription choices [35, 50]. There may be a mechanism to counter such solicitation efforts, possibly involving specific medical training and ethical values. However, the research conducted worldwide indicates gifts and payments do affect doctors' decision making [8, 28], and doctors tend to incorrectly believe that a gift would not influence their behaviours [18,29,45], which suggests what doctors say about the effect of gifts and payments is not necessarily true.

Several studies [9, 19, 56, 62] on the relationship between pharmaceutical companies and key persons, such as medical professors and well-known doctors, or the influence of standard treatment guidelines, reveal that about 90% of doctors involved in the development of standard treatment guidelines for various diseases received some form of payment from pharmaceutical companies. Saito et al [52] show that pharmaceutical companies also make payments to orthopaedic professors and speciality board members. Ozaki [39] finds this practice also exists when publishing research results in international journals.

The payments may either be remuneration for the doctor's service, which the pharmaceutical companies do need, or to finance doctors' activities, such as clinical trials and post-marketing surveillance. There is nothing wrong with doctors carrying out collaborative or commissioned activities, and pharmaceutical companies should be able to make such payments as long as the amount is fair. The same holds true for the provision of materials, such as testing drugs and supporting services. However, serious problems arise when doctors fabricate data and falsify research outcomes to benefit pharmaceutical companies. In *Novartis (valsartan),* the employees of a pharmaceutical company falsified data produced from what was claimed to be physician-led clinical studies. The company donated scholarships worth hundreds of millions to university courses run by the professors and doctors involved in the study [36, 54]. Such data falsification also occurred in *Takeda (candesartan cilexetil)* where a pharmaceutical company (Takeda) conducting a physician-led clinical trial provided funding to Kyoto University totalling over 3.7 billion JPY [37].

Meanwhile, the Financial System Subcommittee of the Ministry of Finance [5] demonstrated that more money is spent on advertising and sales than on R&D in the Japanese pharmaceutical industry, and that the ratio of sales, general and administrative expenses to R&D expenses tends to be higher than in other countries. Hayashi [12] estimates the total cost of lunches (each 2000–3000 JPY, or approximately 18.00–28.00 USD) distributed at drug briefings is several billion yen at university hospitals alone across Japan.[4] These figures cast serious doubt on the appropriateness of resource allocation in the pharmaceutical sector. The Science Council of Japan [55] warns that the number of young researchers working in basic medicine in Japan is declining. This is considered to be due to financial difficultirs that graduate students and post doctoral researchers encounter [34]., The annual payment toward the Japan Society for the Promotion of Science (JSPS) Fellowship, which supports the livelihood of small number of postdoctoral researchers, is 4,344,000 JPY per person [15]. Given that pharmaceutical companies spend money earned through the public insurance system, there must be a better use for it than buying lunches.

Such expensive promotional activities may also deter the entrance and expansion of small- and medium-sized companies into the market. Ohara [38] was concerned that trading practices and large promotional expenditures in the Japanese pharmaceutical sector would deter foreign pharmaceutical companies' entry into the Japanese

---

[4] Hayashi [12] estimates that a weekly pharmaceutical briefing at a relatively small university hospital with 340 medical staff would result in an annual expenditure of over 25 million JPY.

market. Later, Takeuchi [59] showed that large foreign companies overcome such barriers by forming even closer ties with doctors in Japan.[5]

In summary, although it is not entirely clear to what extent gifts and payments affect doctors' prescribing behaviours, either directly or indirectly, such practices are prevalent and likely to induce pharmaceutical companies to spend more on promoting drugs. Financial ties also distort competition among pharmaceutical companies.

5.3 Japanese Laws and Regulations Regarding the Relationship Between Doctors and Pharmaceutical Companies

The situation above indicates pharmaceutical companies and doctors are not governed by strict regulations regarding gift-giving and payments. In the following section, I examine the current state of legal rules and their enforcement.

5.3.1 Current State

5.3.1.1 The Criminal Code and Bribery Offenses

The Penal Code of Japan[6] makes a public official liable if he or she accepts or demands a bribe in connection with his or her duties, punishable by imprisonment for a term not exceeding five years (Article 197). Bribing a public official is also punishable by up to three years' imprisonment or a fine of up to 2.5 million JPY (Article 198). Doctors working for public hospitals and national and municipal universities are either public officials or deemed as such.[7] However, there are no such anti-bribery laws that apply to doctors practising privately, who constitute the majority of doctors

---

[5] Another harm the gift-giving practice might cause is patients' distrust of physicians, which could discourage them from visiting doctors or complying with instructions. The Japan Pharmaceutical Manufacturers Association (JPMA) [16] found that 85% of respondents trust prescribed drugs, while about half consider drugs to be overused. The same study also reveals those who do not trust prescribed drugs tend to comply with instructions on how to take less medication (70%) compared to those who trust them (90%). Such a correlation was observed in the past by Yomiur. 'Kokumin ha "kusuri zuki" ja nai' ('Japanese people are not "medicine lovers"') (Yomiuri Shimbun, 4 April 1977). In the 1970s, medical institutes provided medication, and the doctors' overmedication practices, called *kusuri-zuke* (pouring drugs)—which was motivated by greed—was a social issue. In the survey, about 45% of the respondents said they 'more or less' trust their doctors, while 13.4% of the respondents said they did not trust their doctors very much or at all. The most common reasons for such mistrust were because they were 'money-making' (54.4%) and 'they give me too much medicine' (39.2%).

[6] Keiho, Act No. 45 of 1907, as last amended by Act No. 72 of 2008.

[7] See e.g. Kokusitsu daigaku hojin ho (National University Corporation Act), Act No. 112 of 2003, last amended by Act No. 11 of 2019, Art 19; Dokusitsu gyosei hojin kokuritsu byoin kiko ho (Act

in Japan [26]. Although bribes include a vast variety of benefits and are not limited to financial gains, the gifts customarily provided in Japan, such as mid-year and end-of-year gifts, are not considered bribes unless the value of the gift is substantial. The offence can only be committed by an individual and not by companies; therefore, no criminal penalty can be imposed on pharmaceutical companies. Several criminal cases have been reported in which doctors and individuals acting at the behest of pharmaceutical companies have been guilty of this offense.[8] Furthermore, public prosecutors do not prosecute every public doctor who demands or receives a bribe from pharmaceutical companies.[9]

5.3.1.2 The Pharmaceutical Affairs Law and the Clinical Trials Act

The Pharmaceutical Affairs Law[10]prohibits misleading advertising of medicinal products (Article 66), a violation of which is punishable by imprisonment for a term not exceeding two years or a fine not exceeding two million JPY (Article 85). The MHLW issued detailed guidelines on the provision of information by pharmaceutical companies stating that when they refer to external research and studies, the company must clearly specify the details of any goods, money or services they provide in return.[11] However, the latter is only a guideline, and its violation is not necessarily considered illegal misrepresentation (Ito et al. [13]: 66).

Meanwhile, the Clinical Trials Act[12] requires pharmaceutical companies to disclose any research funds, donations or remuneration provided to doctors conducting clinical trials (Article 33). By doing so, the law tries to ensure that informed consent is obtained from research subjects. However, the law does not

---

on the National Hospital Organisation, Independent Administrative Agency), Act No. 191 of 2002, as last amended by Act No. 67 of 2004, Art 14.

[8] Over the last two decades, the court decisions in which bribery by individuals working for pharmaceutical companies to doctors was found illegal include Sendai High Court decision of 31 August 2009, No. 68 of 2009 (U) (bribery of a municipal hospital doctor); Tokyo High Court decision of 21 April 2004, No. 2446 of 2002 (U) (bribery of a university doctor); Nagoya District Court decision of 31 March 31 1999, 1679 Hanrei Jihou 155 (payment of 256 million JPY as compensation for favourable treatment in joint R&D). Other high-profile cases made known to the public through the media include Hirakata Municipal Hospital, in which the director was arrested and convicted (Asahi, 12 May 2001, 33); Nara Prefectural Medical University (Yomiuri, Osaka edn) 17 December 2000, 3); Kyoto University Hospital (Yomiuri, 27 November 1996, 25) (payment to a university lecturer for clinical trials).

[9] Asahi, 4 April 1997 (Toyama edn) (Toyama City Hospital's head of surgery collected money to finance a year-end party); Yomiuri, 12 March 1999, 19 (University staff requested money to celebrate the retirement of a professor); Yomiuri, 17 August 1999, 26 (Osaka edn) (A professor forced pharmaceutical companies to pay him or else he would no longer procure their products).

[10] PMDA (n 2).

[11] MHLW, Iryoyo iyakuhin no hanbai joho teikyo katsudo ni kansuru gaidorainn (Guidelines for Sales Information Provision Activities for Medical Drugs), 25 September 2008.

[12] Rinsho shiken ho (Clinical Trials Act), Act No. 16 of 2009, as last amended by Act No. 63 of 2019.

prohibit donations. The scope of disclosure is also limited, as exemplified by the fact that entertainment expenses need not be disclosed [13].

5.3.1.3   Competition and Consumer Laws and Fair Competition Code

The Antimonopoly Act (AMA)[13] prohibits unfair trade practices (Article 19). Enticing customers by using unfair profits is designated as such by the Japan Fair Trade Commission ([JFTC] General Designation, Paragraph 9). The regulation is based on the policy that competition in the market should be merit-based, and soliciting sales by offering gifts and other benefits unrelated to the value of the goods and services themselves is contrary to fair competition. This provision is enforced primarily by the JFTC, which issues only cease-and-desist orders in the event of a violation (Article 20); no monetary sanctions are imposed on the violator. The JFTC may also issue warnings, which are a form of administrative guidance. A recent high-profile case is *Textbook,* in which the JFTC issued a warning to textbook publishers for making payments, giving gifts, and buying lunches and dinners for junior high and high school teachers involved in the selection of textbooks for their schools [14]. The case illustrates how the AMA and JFTC handle conflicts of interest and corruption.[14]

To protect consumers, the Act on Unjustifiable Premiums and Misleading Representations[15] explicitly regulates the practice of giving gifts and providing other benefits to solicit trade. As the law ensures competition operates fairly in the marketplace, it also complements the AMA. Article 4 of the Act authorises the Prime Minister to impose restrictions on providing premiums, which could be necessary to prevent unfair customer inducement. The PM issued a public notice that prohibits pharmaceutical companies from offering premiums to medical institutions.[16] The notice also states that a gift constitutes a violation when it is 'beyond the extent considered appropriate in the light of normal commercial practice'. When a breach is found, the PM issues a stopping order under Article 7 of the Act. The law further orders business operators to implement a system to properly manage matters related to premiums (Article 27). However, no financial penalty is imposed concerning unjustifiable

---

[13] Shiteki dokusen no kinshi oyobi kosei torihiki no kakuho ni kansuru horitsu (Act on Prohibition of Private Monopolisation and Maintenance of Fair Trade (AMA)), Act No. 54 of 1947, as last amended by Act No. 45 of 2019.

[14] AMA Article 19 is unique in that it allows the competition authority to intervene in the practice even without finding serious restriction of competition. Where the same practice has serious adverse effects on competition, AMA Articles 2(5) and 3 apply and the JFTC not only orders the practice to stop (Article 7), but also orders the payment of an administrative fine (Article 7–9). However, the JFTC must first establish that the company has unfairly excluded its rivals and substantially restricted competition in the relevant market.

[15] Futo keihin rui oyobi huto hyoji boshi ho (Act Against Unjustifiable Premiums and Misleading Representations), Act No. 134 of 1962 as last amended by Act No. 16 of 2019.

[16] JFTC, Iryoyo iyakuhin gyo kokuji (Notification of Ethical Drugs Business), JFTC Notification No. 54 of 11 August 1997, as last amended by Cabinet Office Notification No. 124 of 1 April 2016.

premiums. The AMA and the Act on Unjustifiable Premiums and Misleading Representations differ from the penal code in that they apply to legal persons, including pharmaceutical companies.

The Act also provides that business operators and their associations may establish self-regulatory rules, termed the Fair Competition Code (Article 31). A self-regulatory body, called the Fair Competition Council, enforces the code. The PM and JFTC approve an entity's Fair Competition Code if the following requirements are satisfied: (i) the code is 'appropriate to prevent unfair inducement of customers and to ensure independent and reasonable choice by general consumers and fair competition among businesses'; (ii) it is 'not likely to unfairly harm the interests of general consumers and related businesses'; (iii) it is not unduly discriminatory; and (iv) participation in and withdrawal from the code is voluntary (Article 31). The approved code is then published.

In the pharmaceutical sector, the Fair Trade Council of the Ethical Pharmaceutical Drugs Marketing Industry established and operates the Fair Competition Code for prescribed medicine.[17] The Code prohibits member pharmaceutical companies from offering money or goods, invitations to travel, or support to doctors as a means of inducing them to select or purchase their products. The Council set out operational standards for the Code and notified the JFTC and the Consumer Agency. The Council further issued commentaries, which are not disclosed to the public. The operational standards state that pharmaceutical companies are allowed to give gifts of up to 5000 JPY per doctor at seminars presenting their products.[18] The standards also indicate giving gifts (including year-end and mid-year gifts) is acceptable if they are within the scope of social customs.[19] Kijima ([20]: 58) explains that an unpublished commentary clarifies gifts for birthdays and wedding anniversaries are not permitted. The unpublished commentary also states member companies are allowed to serve lunches worth up to 3000 JPY per person at seminars, and members can be served a meal at an amiable gathering of a value up to 20,000 JPY per person. Kijima ([20]: 81) indicates that 20,000 JPY (about 150 EUR) for a meal is high according to international standards; the upper limit in the United Kingdom is 75 GBP whilst it is 60 EUR in France, Germany and Italy. In the event of a breach, the Council may issue a warning, and if the member does not comply with the warning, the Council may impose a penalty of up to one million yen and expel the member (Fair Competition Code, Article 10).

---

[17] Iryoyo iyakuhin seizo hanai gyo ni okeru keihin rui no teikyo no seigen ni kansuru kosei kyoso kiyaku (Fair Competition Code Concerning Restrictions on the Provision of Premiums in the Ethical Drug Manufacturing and Sales Industry), approved by the JFTC on 10 March 1984, last revision 1 April 2016.

[18] The Fair Trade Council of the Ethical Pharmaceutical Drugs Marketing Industry, Jisha iyakuhin no koen kai to ni kansuru kijun (Operational standards for seminar on medicines of their own), notified to the JFTC on 20 January 1998, last revision 21 February 2020.

[19] Keihin rui teikyo no gensoku ni kansuru kijun (General principles relating to premiums), notified to the JFTC on 20 January 1998, last revision 11 December 2015.

The Fair Trade Council is composed of 224 members and eight branches exist throughout Japan [3]. The Council investigates suspected violations, provides preliminary guidance on consultations and carries out other activities to promote compliance, such as hosting seminars and trainings. Kijima ([20]: 73) points out that although becoming a member of the Council is meant to be voluntary, it is effectively obligatory. The Council publishes neither a list of cases in which it took measures nor the name of the violators. Meanwhile, *JIHO*, a newspaper and publisher specialising in pharmaceutical businesses, reports the announced number of cases where the Council took remedial measures was one caution and guidance in 2018, one caution in 2015, five cautions and guidance in 2014, and five cautions and guidance in 2013.[20] No case is known in which the Council imposed a monetary penalty and expulsion.[21] There are no cases in which the PM or the JFTC followed up on a code violation case and took official steps.

5.3.1.4   Japan Pharmaceutical Manufacturers Association and Academic Societies Codes

The JPMA, a trade association of pharmaceutical companies, also established a Code of Practice, which states, 'Member companies shall conduct themselves according to high ethical standards without limiting themselves to mere compliance with the Fair Competition Code'. The JPMA also promulgated the *Transparency Guidelines for the Relationship between Corporate Activities and Medical Institutions* [61], which requires member companies disclose the status of research funding, donations, manuscript fees, congratulations and condolences, and food and drink provisions on its website. Having discovered that disclosure based on these guidelines is not standardised in terms of format and content [51], the *Waseda Chronicle* assembled the information and, as noted earlier, established a database through which a citizen can find out who gets how much and from which companies.[22]

Academic societies in the field of medicine also set out guidelines related to conflicts of interest and ethical rules. For example, the Research Ethics Committee of the Japanese Federation of Medical Societies [43] states that researchers should not be involved in corporate sales promotion activities. In addition, the Society of

---

[20] Jijo Nikkan Yakgyo, Database, News clips, 24 May 2019, 27 May 2016, 22 May 2015 and 22 May 2014. Several cases became known through newspapers, including Warnings against Novartis (Mainichi, 28 August 2014, 28); e (Yomiuri, 15 December 2001, 19); Guidance to Aventis Pharma (Yomiuri, 30 October 2003, 39); Warning to Eli Lilly Japan (Yomiuri, 10 April 2001, 22); Warning to Kyowa Hakko (Asahi, 11 January 2001, 18); Warning to Kyowa Hakko (Asahi, 21 August 1998, 37); Warning to Zeria Pharmaceutical (Nikkei, 16 November 1994, 38); etoToyama Chemical (Nikkei Sangyo, 2 March 1993, 14).

[21] Asahi, 12 May 2001, 33 explains there had been no case where the Council imposed a monetary penalty or expelled the member company at that time. This is the latest information that the author could find in the newspaper archives relating to the issue.

[22] Waseda Chronicle, Seiyaku kaisha to ishi: money database (Pharmaceutical companies and doctors: Money Database), < https://db.wasedachronicle.org/ >

Internal Medicine Related Associations [58] established guidelines on conflicts of interest and requires its members to disclose whether they have received benefits from companies.

5.3.1.5 Other Strategies for Discouraging Profiteering

The Pharmaceutical Affairs Subcommittee of the MHLW Pharmaceutical Affairs and Food Sanitation Council [27] prohibits committee members from participating in deliberations once she or he has received payments above five million JPY per year from the pharmaceutical company manufacturing the relevant medicinal product or its competitor, and members must not vote if they have received more than 500,000 JPY from either of the companies. The subcommittee conducts examinations of applications for drug approval, re-evaluations and any other deliberations carried out in consultation with the MHLW. The rule is contingent on members' self-reporting, and in 2015, it was revealed that eight members had failed to make disclosures, resulting in their resignation [53]. Sawano et al. [53] reveals instances of undisclosed payments still existed after the event.

5.3.2 The Need to Strengthen Regulations

The situation described above indicates the need to revise the regulatory system to make it stronger. Most doctors work in private clinics and hospitals, so they are not covered by anti-bribery rules. Even if they are bribed, it is only the individual, either an employee or a corporate official, who is punished, not the pharmaceutical company. Article 19 of the AMA and the Act on Unjustifiable Premiums and Misleading Representations, by contrast, regulate companies' practices. However, violation of these only results in a cease-and-desist order, with no financial sanctions imposed. These laws are applied across businesses by the JFTC and the Consumer Agency, and no detailed rules suitable for the doctor–pharmaceutical companies relationship exist.

This leaves most of the regulatory activities to the self-regulatory body, the Fair Competition Council, which has published detailed codes, guidelines and commentaries. Yet the commentary that outlines the concrete standards is not available to the public. The rules and standards are not only overly complicated, but it is questionable whether they are fair and effective, as exemplified by the fact that a 20,000 JPY (about 150 EUR) dinner is permitted. Such a lenient standard is understandable, as such self-regulation effectively works as a cartel amongst pharmaceutical companies. Even without ethical considerations, pharmaceutical companies hope to curtail the cutthroat gift-giving competition amongst them. Where there is virtually no mechanism to enforce their agreement to lower the promotional expenditure, a level must be established that is acceptable to the participants. Such an agreement would inevitably be different from what is needed by society.

The Council's investigation activities lack transparency. To begin with, the Council is essentially an association of pharmaceutical companies, and the consumer has no right to participate in the process of creating the Fair Competition Code.[23] Naturally, one cannot expect much from such a body. This is particularly true given the association of business operators risks an AMA violation if it imposes harsh measures on a member company arbitrarily (Articles 8 (iii) and (iv)). The same applies to the JPMA. As Kijima (2020: 72–73) notes, self-regulation based on the Fair Competition Code is a unique feature of the regulatory system in Japan. Although it is difficult to conclude the system is less effective compared to those in other jurisdictions, this chapter shows the Japanese system needs improvement.

The legal rules enforced by the MHLW, including those under the Clinical Trials Act, focus on disclosure and do not prohibit giving gifts and making payments. This is reasonable to the extent that such payments constitute fair remuneration for a service provided by a doctor or a necessary part of collaborative research activities. Blanket prohibition of such payments would inhibit innovation. However, currently the scope of mandatory disclosure is too narrow. The JPMA code requires the member to disclose benefits in broad terms, but the effectiveness of such a self-regulatory strategy is limited, as discussed earlier. In general, disclosure alone is not sufficient to deter improper giving and payment [22]. The complicated and highly specialised nature of research can make it impossible for third parties to notice and establish unjustness of payment, even if it is disclosed. Clear legal rules are required that prohibit unjust gains, which could put the patients' best interests at risk and distort competition, and such rules must be vigorously enforced. The disclosure strategy has another limitation, as several studies state that it may create a false impression for the receivers that their conduct is fair because it was disclosed [23]. Outside the pharmaceutical sector, the market mechanism, coupled with mandatory disclosure, may help control the unjust relationship between service providers and their suppliers. Consumers may switch service providers when they suspect the provider is not acting in their best interest. However, when it comes to medication, the information gap is so large that it is difficult to expect patients to make a change.

Policies to strengthen regulation often encounter opposition from doctors. The JPMA had to deal with resistance from physicians when it adopted its transparency code [33]. Doctors often consider regulation unnecessary, as they believe gifts and payments do not affect their prescribing behaviour, which, as noted earlier, is questionable. The subconscious effects may be greater than they realise.

Doctors also claim that giving gifts and buying meals for trade partners are normal commercial practices in which every business operator engages. They assert that pharmaceutical companies should remain free to promote their products as they wish, as in other business sectors [10,11]. Such arguments overlook the unique nature of issuing prescriptions and the overall doctor–patient relationship. Ordinarily, it is the consumer who decides what to buy and makes a payment. The customers doing this are incentivised to make the right decisions and most are capable of doing so. This mitigates the distortive effect that premiums and other financial benefits

---

[23] Supreme Court, 14 March 1978, 32 Minshu 2 (SHUFUREN Juice)

may have. The majority of consumers would prefer better quality and low prices to unnecessary premiums. By contrast, when it comes to medication, it is the doctors who decide what is used, and a large part of the payment comes from insurance. The best prescription does not necessarily benefit the doctor, while gifts and payments from the pharmaceutical companies do. Furthermore the autonomy of the doctor tends to be greater, even when they work for hospitals, than in a conventional workplace, where the employer would notice their employees pursuing a personal interest at the expense of others and would discipline said employee. All of these characteristics can escalate the distortive effects of gifts and payments.

Another point doctors make is that restrictive rules deter innovation by making it difficult to form a productive relationship between doctors and pharmaceutical companies [17]. If the laws merely prohibited unjust enrichment and required disclosure, they would not deter collaboration and effective interaction. That being said, the administrative cost to monitor may, in fact, burden these activities. Although the social gains from stricter regulation may outweigh the losses caused by such unintended consequences, policy makers should be mindful of such possibilities and design a regulatory strategy that will reduce the cost of compliance. Standardisation and national databases would help reduce such costs and facilitate the use of disclosed data [2].

To make such regulations effective, it is vital to create a means by which the members of the community can expect that a majority will comply with them. Otherwise, the company would expect to lose sales to rivals if it does not give a gift and so would not stop giving gifts and money to doctors (Fisman and Golden [6]: 4–12). The actions of the majority also affect social norms, which in turn reinforce individuals' beliefs and affect their behaviour (Fisman and Golden [6]: 163). It is crucial to eradicate the expectation and social norm that honesty does not pay.

5.4 Redesigning Regulations

Having confirmed the need for stronger regulation of the doctor–pharmaceutical company relationship, I will now discuss the policy directions Japan should follow. I argue that it is necessary to change the relevant parties' expectations about how others would behave, and that due care must be taken not to complicate collaborations that would spur innovation. The first step in redesigning regulation is to identify the relevant actors, which are pharmaceutical companies and their employees, doctors and their hospitals or universities, regulatory bodies, and patients in the pharmaceutical sector. Of these, the role of the patient is limited due to the lack of ability and incentive to monitor unjust gifts and payments. Therefore, the discussion focuses on the remaining actors.

5.4.1 Pharmaceutical Companies

Given that the widespread practice of paying and giving gifts to doctors potentially harms society, generally applicable anti-bribery rules should be implemented. Doctors' roles do not differ a great deal, irrespective of whether the institute they work for is public or private, so such rules should apply to all doctors who prescribe medication covered by public insurance. The legal rules should address pharmaceutical companies, not individuals, as companies profit from promotional activities. Because the managers of the companies tend to be better positioned to set up a system to ensure their officers and employees comply with the rules, making the company accountable for misbehaviour is also an efficient way to implement effective compliance systems internally. Unless the company has an incentive to abide by the rules, the employees will be placed under conflicting requirements: one from serious anti-bribery rules and the other from their employers pressuring them to promote drugs through any means, even bribery. Given that reputational harm is difficult to apply in the pharmaceutical sector, the pecuniary penalty imposed upon violating companies must be substantial enough to have deterrent effects.

However, the payment of remuneration to doctors for genuinely needed services should not be prohibited. The same holds for the provision of money, materials and services needed for collaborative or commissioned research activities. Yet pharmaceutical companies and doctors may disguise illegal payments by calling them fair remuneration. Stringent disclosure rules are necessary to detect such behaviour. The law, not the self-regulatory system, should ensure pharmaceutical companies broadly disclose payments and other gifts. Easy access to disclosed information is necessary for patients, citizens, journalists, researchers and regulators. The items and forms of disclosure need to be standardised, and a national database should be run by the government.

5.4.2 Doctors and Hospitals

As discussed earlier, exempting doctors that work for private hospitals and clinics makes little sense. Most medical institutions in Japan are private and doctors should be subject to the same anti-bribery rules as long as their services are covered by public insurance. They should also adhere to broad disclosure rules. Although disclosure alone is insufficient, it can help the general public and law enforcement detect abnormalities and can have a deterrent effect on doctors, even if to a limited extent [1, 46, 47].

The salient issue arises when a doctor not only treats patients, but does so with the intent of producing a research outcome (Rodwin [44]: 16). These doctors already have conflicts of interest, which may worsen when pharmaceutical companies, who want to develop and promote new drugs, are involved in the process of research. At the same time, doctors cannot and should not be prevented from conducting research, either through collaboration with pharmaceutical companies or by obtaining funding from them. This makes disclosure vital. Although the Clinical Trials Act has already implemented a mandatory disclosure system, the scope of compulsory disclosure needs to be broadened.

Complicated situations make it impossible to resolve the issue through a simple set of legal rules. Raising awareness and providing education and training is essential to ensure compliance. Although detailing specific rules that would apply to a variety of situations would be both time-consuming and ineffective, communicating abstract principles alone would also be unhelpful. Education and training should be presented in an interactive format so doctors themselves can apply the principles and legal rules in a variety of situations. The comprehensive educational curriculum proposed by Mukohara et al. [30], which stresses interactive learning and small group discussions, would be helpful.

5.4.3 Regulatory Bodies and Policy Makers

The MHLW regulates the pharmaceutical and medical service sectors on a day-to-day basis and often issues orders to take remedial measures when it finds unsafe products. Although these efforts would help its enforcement of the law in relation to payment and gift-giving practices, they may be insufficient as the inspection method would differ. The safety of goods and services is easier to discern; if they do not satisfy specific standards, the MHLW can detect a violation. The conclusion is straightforward, and once the MHLW notices an abnormality, the suspects and other relevant parties cooperate with the MHLW in fact finding. By contrast, judging the unjustness of a payment may not be as clear as identifying unsafe products, and the regulator may need to establish the true nature of the payment by inspecting internal documents and communications between doctors and pharmaceutical companies, who may not readily cooperate when they think that they may escape liability if the regulator fails to collect sufficient evidence. This raises questions as to whether the MHLW is well-equipped to regulate the sector or if other governmental agencies regularly involved in such inspections might be better placed to do so, or whether the MHLW should develop the expertise and human resources to carry out such inspections.

Regulators and policy makers must have the right incentives to pursue policies beneficial to patients and society. This is particularly challenging in the pharmaceutical sector, where doctors, pharmacists and pharmaceutical companies belong to powerful lobbying associations. Academic institutes may have less political influence, but they routinely help the MHLW with policy making and assessment. This implies that input must be sought from patients, consumers and other participants. Ensuring access to information related to policy making and background facts for journalists and health policy researchers is also critical.

5.5 Conclusions

In Japan, the legal rules governing pharmaceutical companies giving gifts and payments to doctors are lenient and ineffective. This chapter examines the current state of doctor–pharmaceutical company relationships and regulations and provides direction for the future.

Notably, I did not discuss the role of pharmacists. Under the current system, the influence of pharmacists on prescribing is so limited that they do not appear to play any role in ensuring the interest of patients and the general public. This is regrettable given pharmacists are drug experts and have the potential to monitor and correct the behaviour of doctors. For example, they should be able to monitor and advise on use of more than five medicines (polypharmacy) and give advice on whether an alternative to a particular prescribed medication exists. Independent pharmacists are professionals who can advocate for the interests of patients, who lack expertise. Yet unjust solicitation will always occur, and perhaps pharmaceutical companies would start giving more to pharmacies if they gain more influence.[24] However, pharmacists might still play a key role in mitigating conflicts of interest. It is worth assessing whether this manner of allocating authority and responsibility is optimal from a socioeconomic perspective.

Acknowledgements I would like to express my sincere gratitude to Dr Joseph Pozsgai-Alvarez, Osaka University, for his valuable advice, which prompted me to research the issue.

References

1. Chao, M., & Larkin, I. (2021). Regulating conflicts of interest in medicine through public disclosure: Evidence from a physician payments sunshine law. *Management Science*. https://doi.org/doi.org/10.1287/mnsc.2020.3940.
2. Dunn, A. G., Coiera, E., Mandl, K. D., & Bourgeois, F. T. (2016). Conflict of interest disclosure in biomedical research: A review of current practices, biases, and the role of public registries in improving transparency. *Research Integrity and Peer Review*. https://doi.org/doi.org/10.1186/s41073-016-0006-7.
3. Fair Trade Council of the Ethical Pharmaceutical Drugs Marketing Industry. (2018). Kotorikyo gaido (About the Fair Trade Council). http://www.iyakuhin-koutorikyo.org/index.php?action_download=true&kiji_type=1&file_type=2&file_id=2109. Accessed 21 May 2021.
4. Fair Trade Council of the Medical Devices Industry. (2021). Iyakukikigyo kosei kyoyaku ihan jian ni tsuite (On violation of the fair competition code). https://www.jftc-mdi.jp/data/topic_data/2021/277/21032511105295024.pdf. Accessed 1 May 2021.
5. Financial System Subcommittee of the Ministry of Finance. (2019). Shakai hosho ni tsuite: sanko shiryo (On social security: Reference materials). https://www.mof.go.jp/about_mof/councils/fiscal_system_council/sub-of_fiscal_system/proceedings/material/zaiseia310423/02.pdf. Accessed 1 May 2021.
6. Fisman, R., & Golden, M. A. (2017). *Corruption: What everyone needs to know*. OUP.

---

[24] Fujii et al. [7] show pharmacists are, in fact, receiving stationery and lunches at seminars hosted by pharmaceutical companies.

7. Fujii, M., Kikuchi, K., Okada, M., Watanabe, M., & Chonan, K. (2014). Yakuzaishi no rikei sohan no kanosei ni kansuru anketo chosa (A questionnaire survey about potential conflict of interest in pharmacist practice). *Japanese Journal of Social Pharmacy, 33*(2), 67–72.
8. Goupil, B., Balusson, F., Naudet, F., Esvan, M., Bastian, B., Chapron, A., et al. (2019). Association between gifts from pharmaceutical companies to French general practitioners and their drug prescribing patterns in 2016: Retrospective study using the French transparency in healthcare and national health data system databases. *BMJ*. https://doi.org/10.1136/bmj.l6015.
9. Harada, K., Ozaki, A., Saito, H., Sawano, T., Yamamoto, K., Murayama, A., et al. (2021). Financial payments made by pharmaceutical companies to the authors of Japanese hematology clinical practice guidelines between 2016 and 2017. *Health Policy, 125*(3), 320–326. https://doi.org/org/10.1016/j.healthpol.2020.12.005.
10. Hashimoto, Y. (2020a). Ishi to seiyaku kigyo no moral ni shitagaeba yoi, setumei ga hyomen teki (Just follow the morals of the doctors and the pharmaceutical companies: The explanations are superficial). *Iryo ishin*. https://www.m3.com/news/iryoishin/714716.
11. Hashimoto, Y. (2020b). Kajo na settai yameru beki, Sorenari no settai ukeru beki (Excessive entertainment should be stopped: Entertainment should be accepted so long as it is reasonable). *Iryo ishin*. https://www.m3.com/news/iryoishin/714724.
12. Hayashi, H. (2019). Kusuri ni matsuwaru okane no hanashi: seiyaku kaisha no obento (Medication and money: Lunches provided by pharmaceutical companies). Chunichi Shimbun. https://plus.chunichi.co.jp/blog/gifu-pharm/article/286/8921/.
13. Ito, T., Aoki, K., Hanai, Y., Dohi, I., Kijima, Y., & Otoguro, Y. (2019). *Seiyaku kigyo ni okeru konpuraiansu no jitsu gen* (Compliance at pharmaceutical companies). Tokyo: Yakuji Nippou.
14. Japan Fair Trade Commission. (2016). The JFTC issued warnings to nine textbook publishers. https://www.jftc.go.jp/en/pressreleases/yearly-2016/July/160706.html.
15. Japan Society for the Promotion of Science. (2021). Research fellowships for young scientists. https://www.jsps.go.jp/english/e-pd/index.html.
16. Japan Pharmaceutical Manufacturers Association. (2019). Kusuri to seiyaku sangyo ni kansuru seikatsusha ishiki chosa (Survey of ordinary citizens' views on medicine and the pharmaceutical industry). http://www.jpma.or.jp/about/issue/gratis/survey/pdf/13_all.pdf.
17. Japanese Association of Medical Sciences, Conflict of Interest (COI) Committee. (2014). Heisei 26 nenndo nihon igakukai rieki sohan anketo chosa hokokusyo (JAMS 2014 survey report on COI). https://jams.med.or.jp/coi/houkoku_h26.pdf.
18. Katz, D., Caplan, A. L., & Merz, J. F. (2003). All gifts large and small: Toward an understanding of the ethics of pharmaceutical industry gift-giving. *The American Journal of Bioethics, 3*(3), 39–46. https://doi.org/10.1162/15265160360706552.
19. Kida, F., Murayama, A., Saito, H., Ozaki, A., Shimada, Y., & Tanimoto, T. (2021). Pharmaceutical company payments to authors of the Japanese clinical practice guidelines for hepatitis C treatment. *Liver International, 41*, 464–469. https://doi.org/10.1111/liv.14761.
20. Kjima, Y. (2021). *Iryoyo iyakuhin riekikyoyo zoshuwai kisei handbook* (Handbook of Japanese regulations of transfer of value and bribery to healthcare professionals). Tokyo: Yakuji Nippou.
21. Kobashi, Y., Watanabe, M., Kimura, H., Higuchi, A., & Ozaki, A. (2019). Are pharmaceutical company payments incentivising malpractice in Japanese physicians? *International Journal of Health Policy and Management, 8*(10), 627–628. https://doi.org/10.15171/ijhpm.2019.60.
22. Lexchin, J., & Fugh, A. (2021). A ray of sunshine: Transparency in physician-industry relationships is not enough. *Journal of General Internal Medicine*. https://doi.org/doi.org/10.1007/s11606-021-06657-0.
23. Loewenstein, G., Sah, S., & Cain, D. M. (2012). The unintended consequences of conflict of interest disclosure. *JAMA, 307*(7), 669–670. https://doi.org/10.1001/jama.2012.154.
24. MHLW. (2019). Shinryo hoshu kaitei kekka kensho bukai karano hokoku: Chuo syakai hoken iryo kyogikai dai 433 sokai 2019 (Report from the committee assessing outcomes from the revision of the medical payment system at the Central Social Insurance Medical Council 433rd assembly).
25. MHLW. (2020a). Reiwa gannen do iyakuhin iryokiki sangyo jitttai chosa: yotobetsu iyakuhin uriagedaka no jokyo (FY 2019 statistics for the pharmaceutical and medical device industry:

Status of drug sales by application). https://www.e-stat.go.jp/stat-search/files?page=1&toukei=00450152&tstat=000001034412.

26. MHLW. (2020b). Reiwa gannen do iryo shisetsu (dotai) chosa, byoin hokoku no gaikyo (FY 2019 overview of the medical facilities and hospital reports). https://www.mhlw.go.jp/toukei/saikin/hw/iryosd/19/dl/02sisetu01.pdf. Accessed 1 May 2021.

27. Ministry of Health, Labour and Welfare (MHLW). (2008). Yakuji bunnka kai shingi sanka kitei (Regulations on participation to deliverables at the pharmaceutical affairs subcommittee).

28. Mitchell, A. P., Trivedi, N. U., Gennarelli, R. L., Chimonas, S., Tabatabai, S. M., Goldberg, J., et al. (2021). Are financial payments from the pharmaceutical industry associated with physician prescribing? A systematic review. *Annals of Internal Medicine, 174*(3), 353–361. https://doi.org/doi.org/10.7326/M20-5665.

29. Morar, N., & Washington, N. (2016). Implicit cognition and gifts: How does social psychology help us think differently about medical practice? *Hastings Center Report, 46*(3), 33–43. https://doi.org/10.1002/hast.588.

30. Mukohara, K., Morimoto, T., Itoh, T., et al. (2020). A proposal for educational curriculum on conflicts of interest from undergraduate through postgraduate and continuing health professions education. *Igaku Kyoiku, 51*(4), 445–449.

31. Nagaoka, S. (2019). *Drug discovery in Japan*. Springer.

32. Nakai, K., Kawahara, A., Kamei, M., & Kurata, N. (2018). Evaluation of new reimbursement fee for care of pharmacists in Japan. *Pharmacy & Pharmacology International Journal, 6*(4), 313–318. https://doi.org/10.15406/ppij.2018.06.00194.

33. Nikkan, Y. (2013). COI Semegiau rieki sohan mondai I: Surechigau seiyaku gyokai to iryokai (Conflicts of Interest I: Pharmaceutical industry and medical communities at odds). https://nk.jiho.jp/article/p-1226572674519.

34. Nippon.com. (2021). The highly educated working poor: Debt common among Japan's Graduate Students. https://www.nippon.com/en/japan-data/h01063/.

35. Niwa, H. (2014). Bento kurai de shoho ha kawari masen (Lunches do not affect prescriptions). Nikkei Medical. https://medical.nikkeibp.co.jp/leaf/mem/pub/series/1000research/201410/538942.html.

36. Normile, D. (2013). Tampered data cast shadow on drug trial. *Science, 341*(6143), 223. https://doi.org/10.1126/science.341.6143.223.

37. Normile, D. (2014). Faulty drug trials tarnish Japan's clinical research. *Science, 345*(6192), 17. https://doi.org/10.1126/science.345.6192.17.

38. Ohara, H. (1994). *Iryoyo iyakuhin shijo no kyoso koxo* (Competition in the ethical pharmaceutical market). Tokyo: Covendo.

39. Ozaki, A. (2018). Conflict of interest and the create-X Trial in the New England Journal of Medicine. *Science and Engineering Ethics, 24*, 1809–1811. https://doi.org/10.1007/s11948-017-9966-3.

40. Ozaki, A., Saito, H., Senoo, Y., Sawano, T., Shimada, Y., Kobashi, Y., et al. (2020). Overview and transparency of non-research payments to healthcare organizations and healthcare professionals from pharmaceutical companies in Japan: Analysis of payment data in 2016. *Health Policy, 124*(7), 727–735. https://doi.org/10.1016/j.healthpol.2020.03.011.

41. Posner, R. (1975). The social costs of monopoly and regulation. *Journal of Political Economy, 83*(4), 807–828.

42. Pozsgai, J. (2020). The abuse of entrusted power for private gain: Meaning, nature and theoretical evolution. *Crime, Law, and Social Change, 74*, 433–455. https://doi.org/doi.org/10.1007/s10611-020-09903-4.

43. Research Ethics Committee of the Japanese Federation of Medical Societies. (2017). Wagakuni no igaku kenkyusha rinri ni kansuru genjo bunseki to shinrai kaihuku ni mukete (Analysis of the current state of ethics of medical researchers in Japan: Toward the restoration of trust).

44. Rodwin, M. A. (2011). *Conflicts of interest and the future of medicine: The United States, France, and Japan*. OUP.

45. Sah, S., & Fugh, A. (2013). Physicians under the influence: Social psychology and industry marketing strategies. *Journal of Law, Medicine, & Ethics, 41*(3), 665–672. https://doi.org/10.1111/jlme.12076.

46. Sah, S., & Loewenstein, G. (2014). Nothing to declare: Mandatory and voluntary disclosure leads advisors to avoid conflicts of interest. *Psychological Science, 25*(2), 575–584. https://doi.org/10.1177/0956797613511824.
47. Sah, S. (2019). Conflict of interest disclosure as a reminder of professional norms: Clients first! *Organizational Behavior and Human Decision Processes, 154*, 62–79. https://doi.org/doi.org/10.1016/j.obhdp.2019.07.005.
48. Saito, S., Maeno, T., Miyata, Y., & Maeno, T. (2018). Follow-up survey of Japanese medical students' interactions with the pharmaceutical industry. *PLoS ONE, 13*(11), e0206543. https://doi.org/10.1371/journal.pone.0206543.
49. Saito, S., Maeno, T., Miyata, Y., & Maeno, T. (2018). Medical students' attitudes toward interactions with the pharmaceutical industry: A national survey in Japan. *BMC Medical Education, 18*, 286. https://doi.org/10.1186/s12909-018-1394-9.
50. Saito, S., Mukohara, K., & Bito, S. (2010). Japanese practicing physicians' relationships with pharmaceutical representatives: A national survey. *PLoS ONE, 5*(8), e12193. https://doi.org/10.1371/journal.pone.0012193.
51. Saito, H., Ozaki, A., & Kobayashi, Y. (2019). Pharmaceutical company payments to executive board members of professional medical associations in Japan. *JAMA Internal Medicine, 179*(4), 578–580. https://doi.org/10.1001/jamainternmed.2018.7283.
52. Saito, H., Ozaki, A., Sawano, T., Shimada, Y., Yamamoto, K., Suzuki, Y., et al. (2020). Pharmaceutical company payments to the professors of orthopaedic surgery departments in Japan. *The Journal of Bone and Joint Surgery, 102*(9), e39. https://doi.org/10.2106/JBJS.19.01005.
53. Sawano, T., Ozaki, A., & Saito, H. (2020). Pharmaceutical company payments to Japanese government drug regulation committee members. *Clinical Pharmacology & Therapeutics, 108*, 1049–1054. https://doi.org/10.1002/cpt.1892ada.
54. Sawano, T., Ozaki, A., Saito, H., Shimada, Y., & Tanimoto, T. (2019). Payments from pharmaceutical companies to authors involved in the valsartan scandal in Japan. *JAMA Network Open, 2*(5), e193817. https://doi.org/10.1001/jamanetworkopen.2019.3817.
55. Science Council of Japan (Clinical Application Committee). (2020). Senkoi boshu siring niyoru kenkyuryoku teika ni kansuru kinkyu teigen (Urgent recommendations regarding the decline in research capabilities due to the limitation on recruitment of major doctors).
56. Senoo, Y., Saito, H., Ozaki, A., Sawano, T., Shimada, Y., Yamamoto, K., et al. (2021). Pharmaceutical company payments to authors of the Japanese guidelines for the management of hypertension. *Medicine, 100*(12), e24816. https://doi.org/10.1097/MD.0000000000024816.
57. Shigeno, A. (2020). Seiyaku MR: Denshika de sakugen no nami (Medical representative: Digitalisation and the wave of reduction). Nikkei Sangyo Shimbun 9.
58. Society of Internal Medicine Related Associations. (2017). Igakukei kenkyu no reiki sohan ni kansuru kyotsu shishin (Policy of conflict of interest in medical research). Last amended April 2020. https://www.naika.or.jp/jsim_wp/wp-content/uploads/2020/04/coi_kaitei2020_4.pdf.
59. Takeuchi, R. (2018). *Gaishikei seiyaku kigyo no shinka shi* (Evolutionary history of foreign-affiliated pharmaceutical enterprise: Social capital and business development in Japan). Tokyo: Chuo Keizai.
60. Tejima, Y. (2020). *Ishi kanjya kankei to ho kihan* (The relationship between doctors, patients, and the law). Tokyo: Shinzan.
61. The Japan Pharmaceutical Manufacturers Association (2018). *The Transparency Guidelines for the Relationship between Corporate Activities and Medical Institutions.* https://www.jpma.or.jp/english/code/transparency_guideline/eki4g60000003klkatt/transparency_gl_intro_2018.pdf/
62. Yamamoto, K., Murayama, A., Ozaki, A., Saito, H., Sawano, T., & Tanimoto, T. (2021). Financial conflicts of interest between pharmaceutical companies and the authors of urology clinical practice guidelines in Japan. *International Urogynecology Journal, 32*, 443–451. https://doi.org/10.1007/s00192-020-04547-3.
63. Yonemura, S. (2016). *Ijijo kogi* (Lectures on medical law). Tokyo: Nihon hyoron.

Part II
The Japanese Antimonopoly Act and Its Relation to the Pharmaceutical Industry

Chapter 6
Antimonopoly Act and Its Application to the Pharmaceutical Industry in Japan

Akira Negishi

Abstract This chapter provides an overview of the Antimonopoly Act (AMA), clarifies its characteristics and examines AMA cases in the pharmaceutical sector. The AMA aims to promote fair and free competition and the democratic and healthy development of the national economy as well as to secure the interests of the general public. To this end, it prohibits private monopolisation, unreasonable restraints on trade and unfair trade practices, and regulates business combinations. The AMA is enforced primarily by the Japan Fair Trade Commission, an independent administrative body. Meanwhile, the Act on Securing Quality, Efficacy and Safety of Pharmaceuticals and Medical Devices (PMD Act) gives the Ministry of Health, Labour and Welfare (MHLW) the authority to approve and grant licenses for the manufacture and sale of pharmaceutical products. Under the Health Insurance Act, the MHLW sets National Health Insurance Price List, which determines not only the cost, but also the medicines that can be used for treatment under the universal health insurance system. The MHLW also issues administrative guidance. As such, the pharmaceutical sector is heavily regulated. Despite such regulations, intense competition exists in the sector, and the number of AMA cases is increasing.

Keywords Antimonopoly act · Pharmaceutical industry · Unilateral conduct · Cartel · Merger

6.1 Introduction

The Ministry of Health, Labour, and Welfare (MHLW) has the authority to approve the manufacture and sale of pharmaceutical products in Japan under Articles 12 and 14 of the Act on Securing Quality, Efficacy and Safety of Pharmaceuticals and Medical Devices (PMD Act).[1] In addition, Japan has a public medical insurance system based on the universal health insurance principle, and the types and prices

A. Negishi (✉)
Graduate School of Law, Kobe University, Kobe, Japan
e-mail: negishi@wine.ocn.ne.jp

[1] Act No. 145 of 1960, as last amended by Act No. 37 of 2019.

© The Author(s), under exclusive license to Springer Nature Singapore Pte Ltd. 2022
A. Negishi et al. (eds.), *Competition Law and Policy in the Japanese Pharmaceutical Sector*, Kobe University Monograph Series in Social Science Research,
https://doi.org/10.1007/978-981-16-7814-1_6

of prescribed medicine are regulated under Article 76 of the Health Insurance Act.[2] The MHLW frequently provides administrative guidance on issues for which the law does not give authority expressly to the MHLW. Such activities include the MHLW practice known as 'patent linkage', through which the MHLW approves a generic drug only after they confirm it does not infringe on a patent of the original drugs. This is a means to ensure the steady supply of the generic drugs after approval. MHLW intervention in the business activities of the pharmaceutical sector creates a highly regulated market; therefore, the Antimonopoly Act (AMA)[3] has seen few pharmaceutical cases. However, companies compete in the sector within the limits set by the MHLW, particularly in relation to research and development (R&D), patent registration, and the manufacturing and sales of pharmaceutical products. As the pharmaceutical sector becomes more important, the number of AMA cases is gradually increasing. In this chapter, I first outline the AMA and explain its unique features. This is followed by an examination of AMA cases from the pharmaceutical sector.

6.2   Regulation Under the AMA

The AMA, modelled on US Antitrust Law, was enacted in 1947 at the height of post-World War II economic measures, such as dismantling large conglomerates, called *zaibatsu*, and the dissolution of the excessive economic power held by certain companies. Although the AMA was intended to be the 'economic constitution' of Japan, neither the government nor its citizens welcomed it because they believed the United States unilaterally imposed the law after winning World War II. They also believed the AMA was not compatible with the state-led, or the state-business collaborative, economic system in Japan existed since the Meiji era (1868–1912). The AMA seemed alien to Japanese society, which traditionally values harmony and morality. Since then, the AMA has undergone many changes and has followed a considerably different path than that of US Antitrust Law. Now, both the government and citizens recognise the AMA as encompassing the basic principles underlying a free-market economy and its rulings play a significant role in Japan.

The AMA states that its purpose is to promote fair and free competition while protecting the interests of general consumers and promoting the democratic and robust development of the national economy (Article 1). To achieve these goals, the AMA prohibits private monopolisation (Arts 2(5) and 3), unreasonable restraint of trade (Arts 2(6) and 3), and unfair trade practices (UTP) (Arts 2(9) and 19) while regulating business combinations, such as mergers and acquisitions (Arts 10–16). The prohibition on UTP is designed to prevent substantial restriction of competition and other various practices, including concerted refusal to deal, discriminatory pricing, unfair low prices, resale price maintenance, exclusive trading, tie-in sales

---

[2] Act No. 70 of 1922, as last amended by Act No. 40 of 2020.

[3] Act No. 54 of 1947, as last amended by Act No. 45 of 2019.

and conditional transactions (Arts 2(9)(i)–(vi)). When the AMA was first enacted, it was modelled on Article 5 of the US Federal Trade Commission Act[4] and prohibited unfair competition methods rather than UTP. However, the 1953 amendment changed the wording to address UTP. The regulation of the abuse of superior bargaining position (ASBP) was also added at the same time (Arts 2(9)(v) and 19). The regulation of ASBP is a significant component of the AMA, and its use as a tool to confront dominant digital platforms is becoming increasingly vital.

The AMA is enforced by the Japan Fair Trade Commission (JFTC) (Article 27). The JFTC is an independent collegial administrative body composed of a chairman and four members (Arts 28–29). The organisation is modelled after the US Federal Trade Commission. The JFTC opens an investigation when they suspect an AMA violation. If such a violation is found, the JFTC issues a cease-and-desist order (Article 7) and an order to pay civil fines called *kachokin* (a surcharge) (Arts 7-2–7-9, 20-2–20-7). The level of surcharge is set at 1–10% of the transaction value affected by violations incurred during the designated period. The percentage applied depends on the type of violation. Business entities dissatisfied with these orders may appeal to the Tokyo District Court and request their cancellation (Arts 77 and 85). Another mechanism to resolve the case is the commitment procedure. Under this, if the JFTC suspects a business entity has committed an AMA violation, the entity voluntarily plans a set of measures to resolve the issue and, upon approval, produces an agreement with the JFTC to implement those plans (Arts 48-2–48-9). The commitment procedure was introduced to implement the Trans-Pacific Partnership (TPP) Agreement and the Comprehensive and Progressive Agreement for Trans-Pacific Partnership, which is known as the TPP11 Agreement. The new AMA provisions came into force on 30 December 2018, when the TPP11 Agreement became effective. After plans are approved, the JFTC publishes a document outlining the suspected violations, the planned measures to resolve them and other necessary matters. The JFTC also clarifies that it has not determined that a violation of the AMA occurred. If the commitment plan is not implemented by the business entity, the JFTC cancels its approval, conducts a formal investigation and issues cease-and-desist and surcharge payment orders (Art 48-5).

Private monopolisation and unreasonable restraint of trade are subject to criminal penalties (Arts 89 and 96). Only after the JFTC files an accusation can a public prosecutor sue offenders. Criminal accusations and punishment are limited to cartel and bid-rigging cases in practice and are rarely imposed. Even when the court sentence calls for imprisonment, a suspended sentence is always arranged.

Private parties can file injunctions in relation to UTP (Article 24) while those harmed by conduct linked to private monopolisation, unreasonable restraint of trade or UTP may claim damages against violators, as such an action constitutes a tort under Article 709 of the Civil Code.[5] Furthermore, claims for damages may be brought under the AMA once the cease-and-desist order issued by the JFTC is final and the claimant does not need to prove negligence by the offender (AMA Arts 25 and 26).

---

[4] 15 U.S.C. 45.

[5] Act No. 89 of 1896, as last amended by Act No. 34 of 2019.

Additionally, a contract that violates the AMA is generally deemed to constitute a violation of public order and morals and becomes void under Article 90 of the Civil Code. The number of civil lawsuits is gradually increasing, although it remains small.

The AMA does not expressly state that its provisions are applicable extraterritorially. However, on 12 December 2017, the Supreme Court clarified in *Cathode-ray Tube Price Cartel* that extraterritorial application is possible where a practice committed by a foreign business entity abroad causes an anticompetitive effect in the Japanese market.[6]

One characteristic of the AMA is the lack of an effective enforcement system. The surcharge system exists but does not impose sanctions; rather, it deprives companies of their unfair gains by levying a charge similar to the amount obtained through their violations, but the amount of fines is low. Additionally, criminal penalties for individuals are limited to imprisonment of up to five years, while those for corporations (judicial persons) are limited to 500 million JYP (approximately 4.7 million USD). The JFTC rarely files criminal accusations. The sanctions for non-compliance with JFTC investigations are also weak: imprisonment of up to one year or a fine of up to 3 million JYP (Art 94). At the time of writing, the sanctions have never been applied. In practice, however, business entities comply with the order issued by the JFTC in the process of investigation and, once the investigation is completed and the cease-and-desist order and surcharge payment order are issued, they do not breach these orders. The number of appeals against these orders is limited. The JFTC often issues alerts and warnings when it suspect a company is violating the AMA. Although the alerts and warnings are merely administrative guidance, and compliance with them is not mandatory, business entities rarely breach such guidance. The newly introduced commitment procedure lacks a mechanism to ensure formal compliance. However, business entities are expected to follow the planned measures. This demonstrates the AMA is effective overall in the sense that the business entities do as they are told by the JFTC.

6.3 Private Monopolisation Cases Relating to Pharmaceutical Products

6.3.1 Private Monopolisation

Private monopolisation, prohibited under AMA Article 3, occurs when one or more business entities exclude or control other business entities and substantially restrict competition in a "particular field of trade" (hereinafter, 'market') contrary to the public interest (Article 2(5)). Where a violation is found, the JFTC issues a cease-and-desist order and a surcharge payment order. In case of exclusion, the fine is 6%

---

[6] 64 Shinketsu-shu 401 *(Cathode-ray Tube Price Cartel)*.

of sales during the period of violation, and 10% of the sales amount during the said period in the case of control.

The JFTC adopted the *AMA Guidelines for Exclusion-type Private Monopoly* on 28 October 2009. According to the guidelines, the JFTC should prioritise investigations where the market share of the goods or services supplied by the concerned business entity is approximately 50% or more after the commencement of the concerned practice. Additionally, the JFTC prioritises investigations of cases where the impact on the life of Japanese citizens is considered substantial given the size of the market, the scope of business activities performed by business entities, the characteristics of the goods and other relevant factors. The guidelines list four categories as typical exclusionary conduct: (i) setting the price below cost (ii) exclusive dealing, (iii) tie-in sales and (iv)refusal to deal and other discriminatory treatment. Substantial restriction of competition is necessary to determine a case of *private monopolisation*, explained in the guidelines as the establishment, maintenance or enhancement of market power as a result of lessening competition, in which a business entity controls the price, quality, quantity and other trading conditions freely of their own will. The definition was adapted from the Tokyo High Court Judgement in *NTT East* on 29 May 2005.[7]

6.3.2 Nordion, an Exclusion-Type Private Monopolisation Case

In *Nordion* (JFTC Recommendation Decision 3 September 1998),[8] the exclusion of competitors through requirement contracts is found to be an exclusion-type private monopolisation. The violator, Nordion, is a manufacturer of radioactive isotope molybdenum 99 (hereinafter 'M99') with its head office in Ontario, Canada. It ranked first worldwide in its sector and had a substantial market share in the production and sales of M99. In Japan, Nordion sold its products to Nihon Medi-Physics and Daiichi Radio, which used M99 to produce technetium 99 hereinafter, 'T99'). Nihon Medi-Physics and Daiichi Radio were the only companies in Japan that manufactured T99. It is impossible to produce T99 without M99.

Nordion concluded a requirement contract with Nihon Medi-Physics at its Tokyo headquarters on 6 August 1996, under which the latter was to acquire and use M99 exclusively from Nordion for ten years. Daiichi Radio, on the other hand, hesitated because the M99 price set by Nordion was high and, at the time, Daiichi was negotiating with another foreign company. However, Daiichi was concerned it would suffer a disadvantage in trading conditions if it did not accept the offer by Nordion. Thus, Daiichi concluded a ten-year exclusive purchase agreement with Nordion on 27 August 1996 at Daiichi's Tokyo headquarters. As a result, competitors manufacturing and selling M99 were unable to sell to Nihon Medi-Physics and Daiichi Radio.

---

[7] 56-II Shinketsu-shu 262 *(NTT East).*

[8] 45 Shinketsu-shu 148 *(Nordion).*

Upon the commencement of the JFTC investigation, Nordion modified its contracts with Nihon Medi-Physics and Daiichi Radio and removed the exclusiornay contract terms. The JFTC concluded that Nordion restricted competition in the M99 market in Japan through this exclusionary practice. The action was, therefore, considered a private monopolisation under Article 2(5), and thus, in violation of Article 3 of the AMA. The JFTC ordered Nordion to (i) notify Nihon Medi-Physics and Daiichi Radio that it had ceased to impose the requirement contract and would not impose such a requirement in the future and (ii) would not prevent buyers of M99 from purchasing it from other companies. The JFTC did not order Nordion to pay a surcharge, as the JFTC was not authorised to do so under the AMA at that time.

6.3.3 Nihon Medi-Physics, a Private Monopolisation Commitment Case

In *Nihon Medi-Physics*, the JFTC did not find an AMA violation. Instead, the JFTC opted for fast-track resolution through the commitment procedure, under which Nihon Medi-Physics, which was suspected of violating the AMA, pledged to address the JFTC's concerns (Arts 48-2–48-9). In 2005, Medi-Physics sold fludeoxyglucose (hereinafter, 'FDG'), a drug used to detect cancer cells, for the first time in Japan and dominated the market. However, in 2014, Fujifilm commenced manufacturing and sales of FDG and entered the market. Medi-Physics was suspected of hindering Fujifilm's business activity by (i) pressuring FDG-administration equipment developers not to develop equipment used with Fujifilm drugs; (ii) once equipment capable of handling Fujifilm FDG was developed, lying to hospitals by saying that the equipment could not be used for that type of drug; and (iii) eliminating low-price Fujifilm products by telling FDG wholesalers that Medi-Physics would not sell them its products if they bought from Fujifilm.

After conducting an on-site inspection of Medi-Physics on suspicion of private monopolisation in June 2018, the JFTC issued a notice for a commitment procedure on 15 January 2020. The JFTC stated the said conduct would fall under private monopolisation as stipulated in Article 2(5) of the AMA as well as General Designation Paragraph 14 (unfair interference with a competitor's business transaction [Art 48-2]). Medi-Physics submitted its commitment plan to the JFTC stating (i) the Medi-Physics board of directors would confirm it was engaged in the suspected conduct and resolved not to engage in the same conduct in the future; (ii) Medi-Physics would inform its trading partners and employees of the said measures; (iii) Medi-Physics would establish and implement AMA compliance programmes for employees and officers involved in FDG transactions; and (iv) Medi-Physics would report to the JFTC regarding how the measures would be implemented. The JFTC approved the commitment plan on 11 March 2020 as it met the two required conditions: the planned measures were sufficient to eliminate the practice under suspicion, and the JFTC expected that the plan would be implemented without fail (Art 48-3, para 3) [8]. Although the JFTC does not have the ability to compel Medi-Physics to implement the plan, it is expected it will do so.

6.4 Unreasonable Restraint of Trade (Cartel) Cases Related to Pharmaceutical Products

6.4.1 Unreasonable Restraint of Trade

Unreasonable restraint of trade is the substantial restriction of competition in a particular field of trade carried out through an agreement contrary to the public interest (Article 2(6)), which is prohibited by Article 3 of the AMA. Unreasonable restraint of trade is subject to a JFTC cease-and-desist order and a surcharge payment order, under which companies are required to surrender 10% of their sales made during the violation period. The surcharge may be reduced or fully exempted under the *leniency system*, whereby the first applicant before the JFTC commences the investigation is exempted from the surcharge payment order in full. The level of surcharge for the second and subsequent applicants is reduced by 5–20% depending on the order of application and further by 20–40% depending on the degree of cooperation with the JFTC during the investigation.

The language of Article 2(6) requires substantial restriction of competition in a particular field of trade, and contrary to public interest, must be found to have occurred in order to hold a cartel in violation of the AMA. The JFTC, however, deems that price cartels, bid rigging, and certain other conduct is generally unlawful as long as an agreement to initiate such a cartel or bid rigging is found. This agreement is crucial in determining whether the business entity is engaged in unreasonable restraint of trade. Agreements are often substantiated by indirect evidence, such as prior information exchange on prices or bid rigging, parallel behaviour and subsequent information exchange to ensure that the agreement is effectively implemented by participants.

6.4.2 National Health Insurance (NHI) Drug Price List and Revisions

Medical drugs must be listed in the National Health Insurance (NHI) Drug Price Standard published by the MHLW [9], to be used for insured medical care under Article 76 of the Health Insurance Act. The price of medical drugs is determined by the drug price list for each brand, considering the average cost per unit incurred by the medical institution and the pharmacy supplying the drug. On the other hand, the sales prices of pharmaceutical companies to wholesalers, medical institutions and pharmacies are determined through market competition, and the price is normally below the standard drug price. The MHLW regularly conducts surveys to determine market prices and revises prices based on the outcome.

6.4.3 Generic Lanthanum Carbonate OD Tablets Price Cartel

The *Generic Lanthanum Carbonate OD Tablets* case was the first cartel case involving generic manufacturers. Nippon Chemiphar and Koa Isei participated in a price cartel involving the drug, which is used to treat hyperphosphatemia. On 20 July 2018, Nippon Chemiphar commissioned Koa Isei to manufacture all lanthanum carbonate OD tablets so that Nippon Chemiphar could sell under its own brand. At the same time, Chemiphar notified Koa Isei of the wholesale price Chemiphar would charge and requested that Koa Isei set its price with reference to Chemiphar's prices. Koa Isei met Chemiphar's requests and replied that they would set the price accordingly in early August 2018. The two companies thus agreed that their price would be the price set forth and announced by Chemiphar on 20 July 2018. Based on the agreement, Koa Isei sold generic lanthanum carbonate OD tablets to wholesalers at the stated price. Meanwhile, although Chemiphar was to sell the tablets to wholesalers at the same price, Koa Isei did not provide a sufficient number of tablets for Chemiphar to supply them consistently, so the latter did not sell the drug.

On 24 October 2018, Chemiphar filed a leniency application with the JFTC and instructed Chemiphar's sales personnel not to communicate with other companies to determine the wholesale price of generic lanthanum OD tablets.

The JFTC determined that the agreement between the two companies substantially restricted competition in the field of sales of generic lanthanum carbonate OD tablets in Japan, which was contrary to the public interest. Considering that Koa Isei had not cancelled the agreement voluntarily, the JFTC issued a cease-and-desist order for future actions on 4 June 2019.[9] The JFTC ordered the board of directors of Koa Isei to confirm the agreement was null and void; that Koa Isei would not engage in information exchange with other companies regarding the wholesale price of generic lanthanum carbonate OD tablets; that Koa Isei would notify Chemiphar of this fact; that Koa Isei would ensure this was known to its employees and wholesalers; and that Koa Isei would not determine the wholesale price of the tablets in concert with other companies in future. The JFTC also ordered Koa Isei to pay a surcharge of 1.37 million JPY. Meanwhile, the JFTC did not issue any order to Chemiphar because they had applied for leniency before the JFTC commenced its investigation.

---

[9] 66 Shinketsu-shu 283 *(Koa Isei)*.

6.4.4 Original Drug Calvin Tablets Price Fixing Cartel

This case focused on a tablet containing bevantolol hydrochloride as the active ingredient sold with the 'Calvin' trademark and used to improve hypertension symptoms. These Calvin tablets had been listed in the NHI Drug Price List as a generic drug since 26 May 1995, and the price was revised in April 2014, April 2016 and April 2018. Nippon Chemiphar and Torii Pharmaceutical engaged in a price-fixing cartel involving the wholesale price of Calvin tablets for which the MHLW's price revision was expected.

While Chemiphar and Torii regularly exchanged information involving the wholesale price of they Calvin tablets' newest revision, they agreed to coordinate the wholesale price of Calvin tablets by 5 May 2014 at the latest. They hosted a meeting when the price revision became due, in which sales department managers participated. Each company sold Calvin tablets to wholesalers at the same, or almost the same, wholesale price.

On 24 January 2019, Chemiphar applied for leniency to the JFTC, instructed Chemiphar's sales personnel not to discuss the wholesale price of Calvin tablets with Torii and set wholesale prices accordingly. Since then, the agreement has effectively disappeared.

The JFTC found that Chemiphar and Torii agreed to match the wholesale prices of Calvin tablets and therefore substantially restricted competition in Japan, contrary to the public interest, thus violating Article 3 by engaging in an unreasonable restraint of trade stipulated in Article 2(6) of the AMA. Although the violation ceased, Torii did not comply voluntarily. The JFTC issued a cease-and-desist and surcharge payment order on 5 March 2020 to Torii, and ordered it to confirm the agreement had ceased and Torii would not engage in information exchange with other companies regarding the wholesale price of Calvin tablets; that Torii would notify Chemiphar, wholesalers and its employees of this fact; and that Torii would establish a system to ensure they complied with the AMA.[10] The JFTC also ordered Torii to pay a surcharge of 2.87 million JPY. Meanwhile, because Chemiphar had applied for leniency before the JFTC began its investigation, no order was issued to Chemiphar.[11]

---

[10] 66 Shinketsu-shu 335 *(Calvin Tablets)*.

[11] On 30 June 2021, after completion of the draft, the Tokyo District Court ruled that four major pharmaceutical wholesalers had engaged in unreasonable restraint of trade by participating in bid rigging for the supply of pharmaceuticals to 57 hospitals operated nationwide by the Organization for Promotion of Regional Medical Functions. Three companies were each fined 250 million JPY and each of the seven former executives were handed a suspended sentence of 18 months in prison. The fourth company involved was the first to file a leniency application with the JFTC before the commencement the investigation, meaning the company would not be accused of such practice. See JFTC, JFTC Policy on Criminal Accusation and Compulsory Investigation of Criminal Cases Regarding Antimonopoly Violations (7 October 2005, as last amended 16 December 2020).

6.5 Unfair Trade Practices Related to Pharmaceutical Products

6.5.1 Unfair Trade Practices (UTP)

The UTP prohibited under Article 19 is a practice likely to distort fair competition (Art 2(9)(i)–vi)) and meant to prevent substantial restriction of competition, which under Articles 2(5) and 2(6) defines private monopolisation and unreasonable trade restraint. One set of UTPs is stipulated by the AMA, while others are designated under the 'General Designation' (GD) or other designating notices by the JFTC.[12] Under the AMA, UTP is subject to a JFTC cease-and-desist order and surcharge payment order. Only the cease-and-desist order may be issued for the practices falling under GD.

Statutory UTP includes concerted refusal to supply (Art 2(9)(i)), discriminatory pricing (Art 2(9)(ii)), unfair low-price setting (Art 2(9)(iii)), resale price maintenance (RPM) (Art 2(9)(iv)) and ASBP (Art 2(9)(v)). UTP designated by the JFTC includes tie-in sales (GD Para 10), exclusive dealing (GD Para 11), conditional dealing (GD Para 12) and interference with a competitor's transaction (GD Para 14). While any UTP is likely to impede fair competition, the manner of doing so differs depending on the type of practice. RPM and conditional dealing are unlawful in that they artificially maintain high prices. Concerted refusal to deal, unfair low prices, tie-in sales and exclusive dealing are unlawful when they cause foreclosure. Finally, ASBP violates the AMA where it undermines the foundation of free competition by depriving the other party of the ability to carry out the transaction freely using its own judgment.

The surcharge levied is 3% of sales during the violation period for concerted refusal to supply, discriminatory pricing, unfair low pricing and RPM, and 1% of the transaction amount for ASBP. The surcharge is levied only when the violation is repeated within ten years, except in the case of ASBP, where a surcharged is issued upon the first violation.

6.5.2 Cooper Vision Japan Contact Lenses and Suspected UTPs

In *Cooper Vision Contact Lenses*, the JFTC did not find a formal AMA violation; rather, as in *Nihon Medi-Physics*, the JFTC opted for fast-track resolution through the commitment procedure under which Cooper Vision Japan, suspected of violating the AMA, committed to addressing the concerns (Arts 48-2–48-9).

Cooper required retailers not to display the selling price of Cooper's daily disposable contact lenses and two-week disposable lenses in advertisements. Cooper also

---

[12] JFTC Public Notice No. 15 of 18 June 1982, as last amended by JFTC Public Notice No. 18 of 28 October 2009.

required retailers not to sell Cooper contact lenses online to users with a prescription issued by medical doctors that identify the product name, standard, validity period and other information needed to provide the right contact lenses to users.

The JFTC suspected these instructions constituted conditional trading under GD Paragraph 12, and thus violated Article 19 of the AMA. Paragraph 12 provides that trading with another party on conditions that unjustly restrict any trade between the said party and its other transacting party or other business activities of the said party is considered UTP. In response to the notice issued by the JFTC on 13 March 2020, Cooper submitted the following commitment plan: (i) the board of directors whould admit to the suspected practice that it had ceased and that Cooper would not engage in the same conduct for three years; (ii) Cooper would notify retailers and sales agents of the resolution and ensure users and employees were in compliance; (iii) Cooper would not engage in similar practices in future; (iv) Cooper would establish a system to ensure compliance with the AMA when sales activities of Cooper contact lenses were involved; (v) Cooper must report to the JFTC the implementation of the measures stated in (i), (ii) and (iv); and (vi) Cooper would report to the JFTC the implementation of the measures stated in (iii) and (iv) for three years. The JFTC approved the commitment plan on 4 June 2020 as it met the two conditions: the planned measures were sufficient to eliminate suspicious practices, and the JFTC expected the plan to be implemented (Article 48-3, Para 3) [7]. Although the JFTC cannot compel Cooper to implement such measures, Cooper is expected to do so.

6.5.3 Regulation of ASBP and Violations of the Subcontract Act Relating to Pharmaceutical Business

6.5.3.1 Prohibition of ASBP Under the AMA and the Subcontract Act

ASBP, a type of statutory designated UTP that falls under the AMA, occurs when a company takes advantage of a superior bargaining position and hold it over their trading partners to unfairly—in light of normal business practices—set, modify or implement transaction conditions disadvantageous to that party. Disadvantageous practices include requiring the purchase or use of particular goods or facilities, the requirement of contributions such as sponsorship fees and employee dispatch, refusal of receipt, return of goods, payment delays, and unilateral price determination (particularly, price determination that is unfairly low).

The Subcontract Act[13] supplements the AMA. Its purpose is to ensure the fairness of business-to-business transactions where subcontracting takes place. The provisions are applied when a procuring company ('parent company') with capital of more than 300 million JPY outsources manufacturing to a subcontractor with capital of 300 million JPY or less, and other cases stipulated under Articles 2(7) and 2(8) of the Subcontract Act. The Act obliges the parent company to deliver a document to

---

[13] Act No. 120 of 1956, as last amended by Act No. 51 of 10 June 2009.

subcontractors, including the amount of the subcontracting price, the payment date and the payment method. The Act also prohibits the parent company from delaying payment, refusing to receive goods, reducing the subcontract price or returning goods the parent company receives where there is no justification to do so based on the subcontractor's actions.

In a case where any of the above practices is found, the JFTC recommends the parent company receive the goods or pay the price in full promptly or otherwise terminate disadvantageous treatment and take the necessary action to correct it. JFTC recommendations are issued only as administrative guidance, and compliance with the recommendations cannot be enforced. However, in no case has the parent company not followed the recommendation, despite the large number of recommendations issued for violating the Subcontract Act.

6.5.3.2 JFTC Survey on Transactions Between Suppliers and Large-Scale Retailers

Most ASBP cases investigated by the JFTC have been against large-scale retailers, while the JFTC conducts fact-finding surveys in various sectors. In the latest survey report published on 31 January 2018, the JFTC lists problematic practices that may constitute ASBPs when large-scale retailers carry them out against their suppliers [4]. The list includes requiring the purchase or use of particular goods or services; requiring suppliers to make payments in the name of, for example, a sponsor; requiring employee dispatch; refusal of receipt; returning goods; late payments; price reductions; and unilateral determination of price (suppressing purchase prices in particular). The surveyed large-scale retailers included drugstores, home supply centres, discount stores, specialised retail stores, supermarkets, department stores, and convenience stores. According to the report, the prevalence of problematic practices was highest amongst drugstores.

Drugstores sell snacks, groceries, health and beauty-related products, and over-the-counter medications. The survey reveals that drugstores engaged in returning goods substantially more often than other types of retailers. At the JFTC hearing, the suppliers reported that drugstores believe it is acceptable to return goods if they cannot sell them. The suppliers stated that these returns cause them to lose profits, but that they cannot reject the returned goods because drugstores are known to terminate purchase agreements if they do. Furthermore, the JFTC heard that pharmaceutical products are customarily returned, and the drugstores force the suppliers to accept this custom for other goods. Drugstores also engage in other types of problematic practices, such as requiring the suppliers to make payments such as sponsorship fees and to dispatch employees to retailers' shops.

Based on the survey results, the JFTC requested drugstores: (i) provide conditions for returning goods in a provision agreement formed with suppliers and to return goods in compliance with such conditions when necessary; (ii) clarify the direct profit the supplier obtains through payments and to request these only to the extent that such profit will accrue; and (iii) to agree on the conditions for the dispatch of employees in advance with the supplier and bear the associated costs. It is assumed that drugstores are now largely compliant with these JFTC guidelines.

6.5.3.3 Violation of a Subcontract Act by Nid

Nid is a wholesaler with a head office in Tokyo that sells items such as pharmaceuticals, cosmetics and groceries and has 60 million JPY in capital. Nid outsourced the manufacturing of its products to subcontractors with 10 million JPY or less in capital. The JFTC found that from October 2014 to December 2017, Nid effectively reduced the price to be paid to 28 subcontractors by requiring payment of sponsorship fees, which were collected to secure funds for rebates paid to retailers; fees paid by subcontractors to list the products on the website operated by Nid (called a 'Plus one fee') and bank transfer fees. This lowered the price paid by approximately 115 million JPY. On 23 February 2017, the JFTC issued the following recommendations to Nid: (i) pay the difference in price to the subcontractors promptly; (ii) discuss their actions with their board of directors and confirm they violated the Subcontract Act, and that Nid would not engage in such acts in the future unless there were no grounds on which to blame subcontractors; (iii) take necessary measures to establish a system to ensure that Nid would not violate the Subcontract Act in future, including training personnel in charge of procurement; (iv) certify that officers and employees understand these measures; (v) inform subcontractors of the measures taken; and (vi)to report to the JFTC on the measures taken without delay [3]. The JFTC recommendations are only administrative guidance, and compliance is voluntarily. However, Nid took measures as recommended by the JFTC.

6.6 Two Business Combination Cases from the Pharmaceutical Sector

6.6.1 Business Combination Regulation

Business combination under the AMA refers to share acquisitions (Art 10), mergers (Art 15), business transfers (Art 16), and other actions that combine business entities provided in Chapter 4 of the AMA. The AMA prohibits such business combinations where competition in a particular field of trade is likely to be substantially restricted. To ensure the JFTC can effectively examine business combinations, companies are obliged to notify the JFTC of the business combination plan in advance when the size of the company exceeds a certain amount. If one party is a company with more than 200 billion JPY in domestic sales while the other sells more than 50 billion JPY, notification is generally required. Even when an entity's size is small enough to avoid JFTC notification, such a business combination may be prohibited if it is likely to substantially restrict competition in the relevant market.

Generally, business combinations are prohibited until 30 days after the date of receipt of the notification by the JFTC (Art 10 (8)). The JFTC conducts the first review within that period (Art 10 (9)). If the JFTC considers it necessary to carry out a more detailed examination, it may extend the prohibition period for 90 days to carry out a second examination (Art 10 (13)).

According to the JFTC *Business Combination Guidelines* (originally published 31 May 2004 and last amended 17 December 2019), in a particular field of trade, both the goods or services market and geographical markets are defined considering demand substitutability, although supply substitutability is taken into account when necessary. The guidelines also clarify that the likelihood of *substantial restriction of competition* means that a business combination is likely to create a situation where a company or companies determine the price and other trade conditions to a certain extent. Furthermore, for each horizontal, vertical or conglomerate business combination, the guidelines explain the factors considered when determining whether the business combination will cause restriction of competition through unilateral or coordinated effects. The safe harbour standard, which is thought to indicate that it is unlikely that such an effect is caused, is also set out in the guidelines.

6.6.2 Takeda's Acquisition of Shire

Takeda, a pharmaceutical company headquartered in Japan, planned to acquire all the voting shares of Shire, a pharmaceutical company headquartered in Ireland. The plan was reviewed in light of Article 10 of the AMA.

Considering demand substitutability, the relevant product markets are defined as intravenous polyvalent immunoglobulin preparations and anti-integrin inhibitors for moderate to severe ulcerative colitis or Crohn's disease. The geographical market is defined as Japan because both Takeda and Shire are capable of supplying medical drugs across the country and its medical institutions, and other buyers can procure the drugs at equivalent prices from manufacturers located throughout Japan, and because MHLW approval is necessary to sell medical drugs in Japan. Both Takeda and Shire operate in Japan and, thus, compete with each other, making this a horizontal combination.

Takeda's market share in intravenous polyvalent immunoglobulin preparations is approximately 35%, while Shire's is 0–5%. Thus, their total share is about 35%. Post-combination, they would be ranked second in the field. The post-combination Herfindahl–Hirschman Index (HHI) was expected to be approximately 3700, with an increase of approximately 30. This is within the JFTC safe harbour standard. If a post-combination HHI exceeds 2500 but the increase is 150 or less, the business combination is not considered a competition concern. Therefore, the JFTC concluded the business combination would not present any competitive concern in the market.

Neither Takeda nor Shire began selling anti-integrin inhibitors. Thus, their positions in the market were unknown. However, several competitors conducting clinical trials suggested that at least a few would launch their products, exerting competitive pressure over Takeda and Shire. In addition, multiple bio-pharmacy products with basically the same efficacy as anti-integrin inhibitors had already been launched, and more were expected. The products constituted a neighbouring market, which exerts competitive pressure over the relevant market. The JFTC thus concluded that there was no likelihood that the business combination would cause substantial restrictions in the market [5]. Notably, Takeda's acquisition of Shire was approved by the European Commission under EU merger regulations [2].

6.6.3 M3's Acquisition of Nihon Ultmark

M3, an operator of a drug information platform, acquired all voting stocks in Nihon Ultmark, a provider of a medical information database (MID) service in 2019. Ultmark's turnover was less than 5 billion JPY, and prior notification was not mandatory. However, the JFTC believed that competition concerns existed and reviewed the acquisition in light of Article 10 of the AMA.

The M3 drug information platform is an online platform that provides doctors with information relating to advertisements and the proper use of medical drugs, while the MID is a database that collects medical institution data and information on the doctors working there. The Ultmark MID is widely used and recognised as the de facto standard by pharmaceutical companies and drug information platforms in Japan. The JFTC deemed that the particular fields of trade were drug information platforms and MID, considering demand and supply substitutability. For both services, the fees did not differ across the nation. The JFTC thus defined the geographical market as Japan.

The acquisition constituted a vertical business combination through which a downstream drug information platform operator, M3, acquired an upstream company, Ultmark, which provides MID. It also took the form of a conglomerate merger, as pharmaceutical companies were the likely buyers of both the M3 drug information platform and Ultmark MID. The JFTC determined the acquisition would cause competitive concern in both vertical and conglomerate aspects by foreclosing rivals.

The JFTC was concerned about the vertical agreement because if Ultmark stopped providing its widely used MID to M3 competitors or began to deal with them in a disadvantageous way, it would have an exclusionary effect on the drug information platform. On the other hand, if Ultmark provided MID service to M3 competitors, Ultmark would gain access to M3 rivals' confidential business information and share it with M3, which might use such information to its advantage, disadvantaging M3 competitor drug information platform entities in the downstream market.

To address this concern, M3 and Ultmark proposed remedial measures. Ultmark would not refuse to provide its MID to competitors, and would not discriminate against users in relation to price or other trade conditions and Ultmark would be prohibited from disclosing confidential information obtained from M3 competitors to M3 officers and employees.

The JFTC was also worried that with a conglomerate combination, Ultmark might insist that pharmaceutical companies using its MID also use the drug information platform provided by M3, or prohibit MID users from using drug information platforms operated by competitors of M3. The JFTC was concerned that Ultmark might offer a discount on MID to buyers using the M3 platform. These practices were likely to have an exclusionary effect by prompting users to buy both MID and drug information platform services and foreclosing M3 competitors in the drug information platform market.

To address these concerns, the companies again offered to undergo remedial measures. Ultmark would not insist that pharmaceutical companies buy the M3 drug information platform service or prohibit them from using services provided by M3 competitors. It also would not discount or set favourable conditions regarding content, quality or other services related to its MID if MID users switched to the M3 platform.

Furthermore, Ultmark also offered to ensure that a legal group would monitor the state of compliance with the measures yearly for five years, that it would continue reporting to the JFTC for five years and that the company would meet the JFTC requirement to provide information indefinitely.

The JFTC concluded that if these measures were implemented, competition among drug information platforms would not be restricted. M3's acquisition of all voting stock of Ultmark was carried out as planned [6].

6.7   Pharmaceutical Product Price Regulation Under the AMA

The prices of drugs covered by medical insurance are regulated by the MHLW, which publishes and revises the NHI Drug Price List. However, the list price only covers sales to patients. Drug manufacturers and distributors may thus charge unreasonably high prices when they sell drugs to distributors or medical institutions. Furthermore, as the MHLW does not regulate the price of drugs not covered by medical insurance, drug manufacturers and distributors can freely set exorbitantly high prices.

The AMA is designed to protect market mechanisms through the elimination of anticompetitive practices, and it generally does not intervene in price setting in business-to-business transactions. However, exceptional circumstances under which the setting of high prices may constitute ASBP (Art 2(9)(v)), a statutory UTP.

Article 2(9)(v)(c) provides that, in light of normal business practices, leveraging the superior bargaining position a business entity has over its trading partners to set, modify or implement a transaction condition disadvantageous to the party is a UTP. As such, the practice of setting unfairly high prices for drugs could be considered an ASBP violation. However, to date, there has been no instance in which the AMA has been applied to such a case.

The JFTC *ASBP Guidelines* (originally published on 30 November 2010 and amended on 16 June 2017) state that where the business entity with a superior bargaining position over another party unilaterally sets extremely high prices and it is inevitable that the other party will accept such a requirement given the adverse effect refusing may have on future transactions, such a practice is deemed an unfair disadvantage in light of normal business customs and thus constitutes an ASBP. However, the guidelines permit the JFTC to consider various factors, including the way the price is set and whether sufficient discussion between parties preceded such a price setting.

The JFTC addressed a price increase by a business entity with a dominant position in *TEPCO* in 2012, in which the JFTC found that such an increase may constitute an unlawful ASBP [1]. For customers in liberalised markets who were buying electricity of 50 kilowatts or more, TEPCO accounted for most of the supply in the area. The TEPCO supply area encompassed Tokyo, Shizuoka and seven other prefectures. Customers' business operations would have been severely hindered if they could not continue purchasing electricity from TEPCO. Therefore, these customers could not reject TEPCO's prices even when the conditions were significantly unfavourable. Thus, TEPCO was deemed to have a superior bargaining position over its customers.

TEPCO unilaterally raised the price of electricity on 1 April 2012, despite concluding contracts between January and March 2012 that prohibited price increases without consent during the contract period. Furthermore, for customers who consumed less than 500 kW of electricity, TEPCO issued a written statement that they were deemed to have given consent to such a price increase unless they objected to it.

The JFTC issued a written alert that TEPCO's practices may amount to an ASBP and violation of Article 19 of the AMA and told TEPCO not to engage in such practices in future. The JFTC advised that they should disclose sufficient information justifying the price increase and sufficiently inform customers prior to raising electricity prices.

References

1. Endo, M., Yamashita, T., & Yago, Y. (2012). Tokyo denryoku kabushiki kaisha ni taisuru dokusen kinshi ho ihan higi jiken no shori ni tsuite [On *TEPCO*]. *Kosei Torihiki, 743*, 80–82.
2. European Commission. (2020). Mergers: Commission waives the commitments made by Takeda to obtain clearance of its acquisition of Shire. 28 May 2020. https://ec.europa.eu/commission/presscorner/detail/en/IP_20_967.
3. JFTC. (2017). Kabushiki kaisha Nid ni taisuru kankoku ni tsuite (On Recommendations to Nid). 23 February 2017. https://www.jftc.go.jp/houdou/pressrelease/h29/feb/170223.html.
4. JFTC. (2018). Daikibo kouri gyosha tono torihiki ni kansuru nonyu gyosha ni taisuru jittai chosa (Results of survey on trading between large-scale retailers and suppliers). 31 January 2018. https://www.jftc.go.jp/houdou/pressrelease/h30/jan/180131.html.
5. JFTC. (2019a). Heisei 30 nenndo ni okeru shuyo na kigyo ketsugo jirei (Major business combination cases in fiscal year 2018 (FY2018) business combinations report). https://www.jftc.go.jp/dk/kiketsu/jirei/30nendo.html. Accessed 4 November 2020.

6. JFTC. (2019b). M3 kabushiki kaisha ni yoru kabushiki kaisha nihon arutomaku no kabushiki shutoku ni kansuru shinnsa kekka ni tsuite (On M3's acquisition of Nihon Ultmark). 24 October 2019. https://www.jftc.go.jp/houdou/pressrelease/2019/oct/191024m3.html.
7. JFTC. (2020a). Approval of the Commitment Plan submitted by Cooper Vision Japan, Inc. 4 June 2020. https://www.jftc.go.jp/en/pressreleases/yearly-2020/June/200604.html.
8. JFTC. (2020b). Approval of the Commitment Plan submitted by Nihon Medi-Physics Co., Ltd. 12 March 2020. https://www.jftc.go.jp/en/pressreleases/yearly-2020/March/200312.html.
9. MHLW. (2020). Yakka kijun syusai hinnmoku risuto oyobi kohatsu iyakuhinn ni kansuru joho ni tsuite (Reiwa 2 nenn 8 gatsu 26 nichi tekiyo) (On Drug Price List [Effective from 26 August 2020]). https://www.mhlw.go.jp/topics/2020/04/tp20200401-01.html.

Chapter 7
Horizontal Cooperation and Alliances Amongst Pharmaceutical Companies and the Japanese Antimonopoly Act

Shingo Seryo

Abstract The Japanese Antimonopoly Act (AMA) has not been widely enforced when horizontal agreements concerning Japanese pharmaceutical companies are involved. The application of the AMA to horizontal agreements between businesses is concentrated on hard-core cartels such as price agreements made between competitors. The manufacture and sale of pharmaceuticals are regulated by the government. Yet alliances between pharmaceutical companies related to research and development, manufacturing and sales could fall under the AMA. Agencies have published reports related to such horizontal alliances. These provide clues for understanding and analysing anti-competitive effects and law enforcement regarding horizontal alliances between pharmaceutical companies under the AMA. This chapter presents the status and analytical framework of AMA enforcement of horizontal alliances between pharmaceutical companies using reports, guidelines and consultation cases published by the Japan Fair Trade Commission.

Keywords Pharmaceutical industry · Competition law · Cartel · Horizontal alliance · Co-marketing · Co-promotion

7.1 Introduction

This chapter examines the status of regulations on horizontal business alliances between pharmaceutical companies under the Japanese Antimonopoly Act (AMA). These horizontal alliances include consortia or joint ventures between competitors and the related agreements needed for their execution such as co-marketing. It does not address joint conduct between competitors, or *hard-core restraints*. These agreements involve price, quantity and other important competitive characteristics, in which competitors engage with no purpose or effect other than to restrict competition. Vertical restrictions and unilateral actions are also not considered.

S. Seryo (✉)
Faculty of Law and Graduate School of Law, Doshisha University, Kyoto, Japan
e-mail: sseryo@mail.doshisha.ac.jp

© The Author(s), under exclusive license to Springer Nature Singapore Pte Ltd. 2022   109
A. Negishi et al. (eds.), *Competition Law and Policy in the Japanese Pharmaceutical Sector*, Kobe University Monograph Series in Social Science Research,
https://doi.org/10.1007/978-981-16-7814-1_7

The remainder of this chapter begins with Section 2, which provides an overview of the major AMA provisions that apply to horizontal business alliances. Section 3 considers the treatment of horizontal business alliances under the AMA and reviews cases handled by the Japan Fair Trade Commission (JFTC) and related documents, such as guidelines and study group reports. These reveal the current state of the AMA regulation analysis framework for horizontal business alliances in pharmaceutical companies and the pharmaceutical industry. Section 4 summarises the analysis framework used to apply the AMA to major types of horizontal alliances, with reference to past consultation cases. Finally, Section 5 presents a comprehensive AMA enforcement policy relative to the JFTC's guidelines and reports.

7.2 AMA Provisions Regarding Business Alliances

Article 2(6) defines *unreasonable restraint of trade* as:

> mutually restricting or conducting business activities in such a manner as to fix, maintain, or increase prices, or to limit production, technology, products, facilities, or customers or suppliers, thereby causing, contrary to the public interest, a substantial restraint of competition in any particular field of trade.

Article 3 of the AMA covers private monopolisation and unreasonable restraint of trade. This chapter focuses on prohibitions on unreasonable restraint of trade, which is often referred as the second part of Article 3. Technically, the prohibitions could be applied to vertical restraints, but court decisions in the 1950s limited the scope of this provision to agreements amongst competitors. Case law and JFTC practices reveal that JFTC enforcement of unreasonable restraint of trade focuses on horizontal agreements amongst competitors, especially those involving serious or *hard-core cartels*. It is difficult to find formal cases of horizontal, non-hard-core cartels investigated by the JFTC.

Article 8 was enacted to regulate trade association activities that created anticompetitive effects in entrepreneurial markets. It also prohibits decisions or behaviours that involve engaging in any act that falls under paragraphs (i)–(v) of the Article:

(i)   substantially restraining competition in any particular field of trade,
(ii)   entering into an international agreement or an international contract as provided in Article 6,
(iii) limiting the present or future number of enterprises in any particular field of business,
(iv)   unjustly restricting the functions or activities of the constituent
(v)   enterprise (meaning an enterprise who is a member of the trade association; the same applies hereinafter),
(vi)   inducing an enterprise to employ such an act as falls under unfair trade.

It forbids trade associations from allowing entrepreneurs to exhibit anticompetitive behaviours as defined by Article 8, including engaging with hard-core cartels or in horizontal agreements.

Article 19 states an entrepreneur must not employ unfair trade practices. These practices are defined in Article 2(9), which outlines a range of discriminatory, restrictive or coercive behaviours that tend to impede fair competition. Article 19 primarily regulates vertical restraints, including tying, resale price maintenance and exclusive dealing. It also covers certain types of horizontal behaviours and concerted refusals to deal.

The difference between unfair trade practices and unreasonable restraint of trade depends on the degree of anticompetitive effect. Article 3 requires a substantial restraint of competition in any particular field of trade as an anticompetitive effect, while Article 19 requires the anticompetitive effect tend to impede fair competition. The finding of a substantial restraint of competition signifies the establishment, maintenance or strengthening of market power. Meanwhile, the tendency to impede competition through unfair trade practices addresses behaviours with weaker competitive effects than those of unreasonable restraint of trade or private monopolisation.

Articles 3 and 19 diverge in their sanctions. Generally, sanctions under Article 3 (unreasonable restraint of trade) are the most stringent, depending on the gravity of the anticompetitive effects. Therefore this chapter focuses on the application of Article 3 (unreasonable restraint of trade).

7.3 Sample Cases Involving Pharmaceuticals

Few cases exist in which the JFTC has formally applied the AMA to issue measures that affect pharmaceutical companies' horizontal joint activities. Those that do involve hard-core cartels. Cartel behaviours are a result of industry trade association decisions. In Europe and the United States recent cases have involved reverse payment agreements between branded and generic drug companies; Japan has no formal cases of such agreements. In Japan, pharmaceutical companies actively engage in business as well as strategic alliances; the latter emulate the format and content of horizontal cooperation agreements. Certain horizontal agreements raise concerns about competition. Based on relatively active AMA enforcement of horizontal hard-core agreements in Japan, pharmaceutical companies need to be aware of the risks involved in forming business alliances and take steps to mitigate them if necessary, or in fact possible.

The JFTC established a consultation system to improve the transparency of legal operations and increase the predictability of AMA application. The system responds to questions regarding whether an act violates the AMA's provisions and sets the procedure for what follows if so. On several cases, the JFTC expressed its views using this consultation system.

7.3.1 Recent JFTC Horizontal Cartel Cases

7.3.1.1 Generic Lanthanum Carbonate OD Tablets

In *Koa Isei*,[1] Nippon Chemiphar decided to outsource the production of all generic lanthanum carbonate OD tablets[2] to Koa Isei. On 20 June 2014, Koa Isei and Nippon Chemiphar mutually confirmed the generic lanthanum carbonate OD tablets would not be sold at a low price. On 20 July 2018, Nippon Chemiphar sent Koa Isei information regarding the wholesale price of the tablets that Koa Isei would produce for Nippon Chemipher to sell as its own brand, and it requested that Koa Isei match that price when setting the wholesale price of Koa Isei branded tablets. In early August, in response to this request, Koa Isei replied that it would set the wholesale price of the tablets that it manufactured and sold according to the price requested by Nippon Chemipher. The two companies agreed that by early August 2018 at the latest, the wholesale price of the generic lanthanum carbonate OD tablets would be set at the price that Nippon Chemiphar sent to Koa Isei on 20 July 2018, to prevent a decline in price and increase the profits of both companies.

The JFTC determined the two companies' agreement substantially restricted competition of the sales of generic lanthanum carbonate OD tablets in Japan, contrary to public interest. Subsequently, the JFTC issued a cease-and-desist order and a surcharge payment order of 1.37 million JPY to Koa Isei, which had violated Article 3 (unreasonable restraint of trade) of the AMA.

7.3.1.2 Original Drug (Calvin Tablets) Price-Fixing Cartel

Torii Pharmaceutical and Nippon Chemiphar exchanged information on the wholesale price (called the 'partition price' in this case) of Calvin tablets, which was changed in accordance with the National Health Insurance (NHI) Drug Price Standard published by the Ministry of Health, Labour and Welfare (MHLW). Calvin tablets are a branded medicine used to treat high blood pressure. After 5 March 2014, when the drug price was revised, the two companies cooperated to match their wholesale prices of Calvin tablets to prevent the wholesale price from falling and to secure profits for the companies. A meeting between the managers of the two companies' sales departments resulted in an agreement that their Calvin tablets' wholesale prices would be the same, or nearly the same.

The JFTC found that by agreeing to the wholesale price, the two companies substantially restricted competition in the field regarding the sales of Calvin

---

[1] See Chapter 6, Section 4.3. JFTC cease and desist order 4th of June 2019, 66 Shinketsu-shu 283(Koa Isei).

[2] 'Generic Lanthanum Carbonate OD' is the generic drug of Lanthanum Carbonate Hydrate Orally-Disintegrating Tablets, which are used to treat hyperphosphatemia.

tablets in Japan, contrary to the public interest, and behaved as a price-fixing cartel.[3]Consequently, the JFTC issued a cease-and-desist and surcharge payment order of 2.87 million JPY to Torii Pharmaceutical, which had violated Article 3 (unreasonable restraint of trade) of the AMA.

7.3.1.3 Maintenance of Drug Prices by Trade Associatio Decisions

In *Japan Pharmaceutical Manufacturers Association (JPMA)*,[4] the influential trade association asked its member entrepreneurs not to respond to requests for price reductions, with the aim of preventing them from lowering prices on the pharmaceutical products they manufacture and sell.

Pharmaceutical companies deliver their drugs to medical institutions such as hospitals through wholesalers. They set the wholesale price higher than the actual selling price. The wholesaler negotiates with medical institutions on the retail price. The wholesaler then reports the negotiated individual prices to the pharmaceutical company. In response to the reported individual price, the pharmaceutical company determines the price for shipping to the wholesaler.

Pharmaceutical companies have used discount compensation systems, or adjustments, to reduce wholesale selling prices to levels commensurate with reported retail prices. Medical institution purchase pricing for drugs is regulated by the drug's standard price as established by the Ministry of Health and Welfare.,[5] with regular review. When a drug's standard price decreases, medical institutions, amongst others, can act through a slide-down request, asking wholesalers and pharmaceutical companies to reduce purchase prices.

The JPMA received a report from its subordinate organisation that price cuts due to slide-downs would adversely affect the management of member pharmaceutical companies, and it was necessary to take measures to maintain prices. The JPMA decided that member pharmaceutical companies should not reduce prices in response to slide-down requests and should instead aim to reduce the consequent price differences caused by setting different delivery prices for the same brand for each medical institution. The JPMA demanded compliance with these measures from its member pharmaceutical companies; it simultaneously took various other actions such as discussions with pharmaceutical wholesaler associations and further explaining and promoting the measures.

The JFTC found that the JPMA unreasonably restricted member pharmaceutical companies' functions or activities by restraining their free business activities related

---

[3] JFTC cease-and-desist order 5 March 2020, 66 Shinketsu-shu 335 (Calvin Tablets). See Chapter 6, Section 4.4.

[4] JFTC recommendation decision, 30 June 1984, 30 Shinketsu-shu 35 (*Japan Pharmaceutical Manufacturers Association*).

[5] The former name for the Ministry of Health, Labour and Welfare, which changed due to organisational restructuring in 2001.

to price determinations for medical drugs, violating the provisions of Article 8 (Item 4, Paragraph 1); in response, the JFTC issued a cease-and-desist order.

7.3.2 JFTC Consultation Cases

It is difficult to find formal AMA cases addressing horizontal agreements without a hard-core cartel component. However, competitors engage in many activities to organise their businesses and cooperate through such economic behaviours as joint production, distribution and research and development activities. These sometimes risk violating the AMA. The JFTC has addressed various concerns through prior informal consultations, a service that offers advice regarding whether a specific action planned by an entity would be problematic under the AMA.

Based on JFTC advice, many amend or entirely abandon their plans. The JFTC publishes several consultation cases annually, selecting examples helpful for other entities and presenting them as case studies in an attempt to prevent AMA violations as well as to increase transparency and predictability. It is helpful for entities to review JFTC guidelines, including additional reports and the analytical framework used to address certain types of horizontal cooperation. The following sections consider these materials while examining relevant issues to clarify the AMA analysis of horizontal alliances in the pharmaceutical industry.

7.3.2.1 Cooperation to Distribute Medicine

Pharmaceutical companies A and B produce and distribute medicine; both have established sales departments to distribute medicine X to hospitals and medical institutions. In the medicine X sales market, company A has a 40% market share, and company B has 10%. Hospitals and medical institutions need a steady, prompt supply of medicine X at the time of large-scale disasters. Thus, companies A and B build a distribution alliance as a fundamental infrastructure to respond to requests for supply of medicine X. They establish a joint distribution alliance to store and distribute medicine X while maintaining independently owned distribution companies. Both companies asked the JFTC to flag any AMA-related concerns about this business plan.

The original plan included the following: (i) both companies would continue purchasing a certain volume of medicine X from each distribution company; (ii) order information from hospitals and other customers would be sent to both companies, with the distribution company nearest each customer filling the order; and (iii) both companies would take measures to block information exchanges about their sales volumes and other sensitive information through each distribution company.

The JFTC published its opinion expressing no concerns about this alliance.[6] First, the JFTC examined the agreement in light of Article 3 (unreasonable restraint of trade). The JFTC defined the relevant market as the sales market of medicine X.

Second, the JFTC noted that both companies would have an integrated market share of approximately 60% after executing their plan. A high market share leads to competitive concerns. The JFTC also considered the additional facts of this case, as the scope of this alliance is limited to distribution and storage. Analysis of the structure of cost showed that both businesses would incur only 5% of the total cost to supply this medicine. According to this analysis, price competition would continue to exist between the products provided by companies A and B.

Third, if both companies provide sales information, they could use such information to avoid fierce competition, which would create serious concerns regarding their alliance, but they intend to block such information exchanges. Provided they continuously implement such remedies, that particular concern would never be realised.

The JFTC notified the related parties that the joint distribution scheme would not restrain market competition for medicine X, and therefore would not violate the AMA. The JFTC explains that the lack of such violation is due to (i) the alliance being limited only to storage and distribution, and (ii) the parties continuously blocking sensitive sales information from one another.

7.3.2.2 Joint Purchasing and Utilising of Pharmaceutical Compounds for Research and Development

Another JFTC case involved a consortium for the joint purchasing and utilisation of pharmaceutical compounds used in the research and development (R&D) of certain new medicines established by ten pharmaceutical companies.[7]

Each domestic pharmaceutical company has its own storage 'library' in order to accumulate certain compounds, many of which they need. It is crucial for pharmaceutical companies to have many compounds in their libraries to develop new medicines. Further, many domestic pharmaceutical companies take various steps to research and develop new medicines:

1. Purchasing certain compounds used in the R&D of new medicines from domestic or foreign compound manufacturers;
2. Selecting appropriate compounds from many candidates with the assumption that these compounds will have an effect on or increase efficacy of the targeted medicines (basic research);
3. Creating structured compounds designed with unknown features to be safer and more effective than known compounds based on the selected appropriate compounds in Step 2 (applied research); and

---

[6] JFTC (2005), Case 4.

[7] JFTC (2020), Case 4.

4. Examining newly created compounds to conduct R&D for practical utilisation
    of new medicines.

The planned consortium would not only purchase certain compounds, but also
jointly manage public libraries, available to the ten domestic pharmaceutical member
companies with no charges. These libraries' storage would include space for the joint
purchase of certain compounds. Member pharmaceutical companies are not limited
in what they can purchase, as they can also buy certain compounds independently
and use other libraries, including their own. The volume of the planned consortium
libraries was estimated at approximately 10% of the total volume of the libraries of
all domestic pharmaceutical companies.

The estimated ratio of volume purchased by this planned consortium would be *de
minimis* in the Japanese market because many firms in various industries use specific
compounds. Further, only a small ratio of shared costs from using the planned consortium would figure into the total cost to produce new medicines, because member
companies could use the consortium's resources at an earlier basic research stage.
The ten member companies would never have an obligation to make their research
results known to the consortium itself or other members as a consequence of utilising the public libraries. Additionally, they could take measures to block information
exchanges about the use of certain compounds from the libraries to avoid information-
sharing. There would be no restrictions placed on any company joining or exiting
this consortium; non-member pharmaceutical companies could also use these public
libraries if they paid the required fees.

The JFTC's published opinion expresses no concern about the planned consortium. First, the JFTC examined the plan under Article 3 (unreasonable restraint
of trade), with the two relevant markets defined as the purchase (input) market of
certain compounds and the production and sales market for medicine in Japan. The
purchase market would include many purchasers other than the planned consortium
and pharmaceutical companies, with the consortium occupying a small percentage
of purchases. These factors—including the number of competitors and the market
share—led the JFTC to conclude that the plan does not substantially restrain trade
in a particular market and therefore does not violate AMA regulations.

Next, the JFTC examined the consortium's competitive effect in the medicines'
production and distribution markets and pointed out the following factors:

- The ten member companies have no obligation to disclose the results of their
  research to the consortium and its other member companies through the use of
  the libraries. Each member company would continue to research and develop its
  own medicines independently.
- The estimated number of specific compounds in the planned libraries for joint use
  is 10% of the total volume of those compounds held by all pharmaceutical companies. The consortium members are not restricted to buying certain compounds and
  can use other compound libraries.
- This scheme would create blocking measures for sharing information with the
  planned consortium regarding the use of certain compounds.

- The agreement would have minimal effects on medicine pricing given the small ratio of shared to total costs from using the planned consortium to produce new medicines, because member companies use the consortium's resources at the basic research stage.

The JFTC determined that elements of the plan involving competition issues are of no concern, and concluded that this planned joint purchasing and utilising of pharmaceutical compounds for R&D did not conflict with the AMA.[8]

7.3.3 Co-Promotion and Co-Marketing

7.3.3.1 Co-Marketing

Co-marketing is a joint marketing alliance or cooperation between two (or more) pharmaceutical companies to sell the same medicine; each party uses its own distribution network for sales, with various co-marketing patterns.[9]

The major types of sales are single- and multi-branding sales. In single branding, one entity obtains manufacturing and marketing approval and sells its products to others. Medicines are distributed with the same brand name through individual companies' sales networks. In contrast, with multi-branding sales, each company obtains manufacturing and marketing approval and sells products with different brand names through their own sales networks. Certain parties add joint R&D activities with the intent to sell the resulting medicines jointly through co-marketing arrangements.

Single-brand sales can improve product recognition for customers and patients and increase market share at an early stage. Both parties keep their own brands. On the other hand, with multi-brand sales it is easy for all parties to forge their own path in product promotion and sales activities. In both cases, partner companies can strengthen their own product pipelines. However, it tends to be difficult to improve brand value and synergy with multi-branding sales.

7.3.3.2 Co-Promotion

Co-promotion involves joint sales-promotion activities between two (or more) pharmaceutical companies that sell the same medicine under the same brand name.[10] Normally, only one party has the authorisation to produce and sell the medicine; only authorised parties can produce and distribute the medicine through medical distributors. Both companies can provide information about the medicine to hospitals and pharmacies and conduct other promotional activities. The authorised party

---

[8] JFTC (2020), Case 4.

[9] Japan In-House Lawyer Association (ed) (2019), 108–111.

[10] Japan In-House Lawyer Association (ed) (2019), 108–110.

would earn all profits from medicine sales, but the other would receive loyalty or compensation payments from the joint sales-promotion activities.

Co-promotion benefits both parties. The authorised party could compensate for a shortage of medical representatives (MRs) or enlarge its sales or share in new markets in addition to the already advantageous markets reached through co-promotion schemes. The party without authorisation could earn new profits in the targeted medicine market, because it could avoid a lot of additional investment required to research and develop new medicines for entry into the targeted market, thus reaping extra profits simply by using its existing promotional resources.

Another type of co-promotion involves the authorised party selling the authorised medicine to another party, which supplies the drug to its medical distributors. The authorised party does not handle the medicine after production. A non-authorised party would be the sole source supplying these distributors. Both parties would engage in co-promotion activities under this relationship, and co-promotion agreements seldom have serious anticompetitive effects.

7.3.3.3   The JFTC Consultation Case

The JFTC addressed one consultation case[11] in which pharmaceutical company A developed a new medicine α and was to begin production and sales in pharmaceutical market X. Company A was required to provide appropriate information to customers and patients and to implement a market survey examining the efficacy and adverse effects of the drug after marketing it under the Pharmaceutical Affairs Law to allow new products to penetrate market X. Many MRs were needed to sufficiently realise these activities; however, company A did not have these resources. Therefore, company A decided to align with pharmaceutical company B, which already developed and sold its medicine in market X.

The agreement included co-promotion and co-marketing provisions implemented to increase sales channels by supplying the new medicine α to company B, and to obtain the cooperation of its MRs. While approximately ten manufacturers had already entered pharmaceutical market X, companies A and B were the fourth- and fifth-largest manufacturers in market X, respectively, with other highly influential pharmaceutical companies holding a market share of over 70%.

When launching the sale of a medical drug, a pharmaceutical company's MRs explain its efficacy to medical institutions, and the medical institutions decide which drugs to purchase based on that information. The companies decided to divide their MR activities to improve efficiency given their role in providing new drug information to medical institutions:

- The target is medical institutions with 100 beds or more—approximately 5,500 institutions;

---

[11] JFTC (2004), Case 3.

- If the MRs of each company have been allocated to the same medical institution, both companies will coordinate their MRs appropriately;
- The allocation period is one year from the release date; and
- Neither company will instruct wholesalers regarding specific sales destination.

The JFTC focused on one problem: allocating the medical institutions between companies A and B for their MRs' activities to provide the information of a new medical drug at the time it goes on sale. The JFTC analysed the allocation provisions under AMA Article 19, the unfair trade practices clause. Hindering price competition and maintaining prices by restricting sales allocations to business partners are considered unfair trading practices, as trading on restrictive terms violates the AMA. Subsequently, the JFTC explained that a problem occurs when it hinders price competition between wholesalers and maintains prices by allocating the medical institutions between the MRs of companies A and B.

However, in this case, MRs are sent out to explain a new drug's efficacy, among other traits, in order to promote it. In addition, companies A and B are not involved in each other's sales activities. Even if they divide the MRs' active relationships with medical institutions, the prices are unlikely to be maintained, and it is not considered that any problem exists under the AMA.

Joint sales and promotional activities in this case were implemented through a horizontal cooperation agreement. However, the JFTC's evaluation does not address the cooperation agreement itself. The JFTC concerned the arrangement to divide MRs to conduct sales promotions at medical institutions, as well the second aspect of the previously described alliance analysis framework.

The second feature of this case is that the medical institutions' allocation arrangements were evaluated under Article 19 of the AMA, rather than Article 3. The published document does not explain why (although it implies) the allocation of medical institutions to which MRs can provide information restricts the affiliated parties' activities. In addition, the sales destinations of wholesalers—who purchase medicines from parties in the alliance and sell and deliver medicines to medical institutions—are also limited to the MR of each alliance party providing information. The restriction on the information provision to medical institutions with their respective MRs is a binding condition that restricts the activities of the wholesaler who purchases the product from the partner party and sells it to medical institutions. This vertical restraint which pharmaceutical companies place on their trading partners is regulated under Article 19, which prohibits trading on restrictive terms and applies to the vertical restraints between trading partners.

Another reason why the use of Article 19 might be appropriate is because the case had a rather weak anticompetitive effect; the allocation of medical institutions to which MRs provide information does not directly limit important competitive factors, such as price and quantity. Further, parties hold a weak market share and position in the relevant market. Article 3 regulates cases with high anticompetitive effects, and thus is not appropriate for this case.

Finally, the JFTC emphasises that MRs are allocated to allow for the early penetration of new drugs by explaining their efficacy, and rapid new drug penetration could create fierce competition in market X. This is a substantial pro-competitive effect of this alliance.

7.4 General Analytical Framework of the AMA in Business Alliances

The JFTC has addressed other various types of horizontal cooperation under prior consultation, including R&D, sales, purchasing, production, logistics, technology and standardisation. This section summarises the characteristics as observed from the consultation cases.

7.4.1 Horizontal Production Alliances

Examples of horizontal production alliances exist wherein production occurs through competitors sharing production facilities. This happens for a variety of reasons: one of the partners has disposed of its own facilities; the companies' production bases are far from each other; customers are in areas located within competitors' production bases, and competitors called 'original equipment manufacturers' (OEMs) supply products to each other to reduce transportation or other costs; one of the partners receives full or partial OEM supply from competitors instead of using in-house production; or competitors share a variety of products and supplies through OEMs.

The JFTC has examined many OEM cases under prior consultation to consider their impact on the relationship between partners. The following factors influence JFTC attitudes dealing with OEM cases, with the total market impact also evaluated when competition between the partners is restricted: market share and the parties' position in the relevant (almost objected product sales) market; standardisation of cost structure; information exchange and sharing; existence or absence of powerful competitors; possibility of coordinated production volumes; competitive pressure from imports; and nascent markets increasing consumers' benefits.

7.4.2 Horizontal Sales Alliances

Examples of horizontal sales alliances include cases where competitors with sales bases in more remote areas supplement their sales networks by covering for or entrusting sales to one other. Competitors share sales operations, such as negotiations with customers, and jointly conduct sales-promotion activities, such as the advertising and marketing of products and advertisements, which can include planning for prizes.

Generally, sales alliances can have a pro-competitive effect, as the mutual supplementation of distribution networks and reduced time to enter new markets lead to decreased costs. However, integrated decision-making involving important modes of competition, such as sales prices, should be weighed carefully in case the alliance verges into hardcore-cartel territory. Further, there must be assessment as to whether the likelihood of competitive risks is too great, as such cartels often use horizontal sales as implementation tools.

The product sales market is typically defined as the most relevant, in addition to being a target of alliances. The JFTC's past consultation cases have considered the aspects of joint decision-making regarding price, service content and other business activities related to the implementation of sales alliances. In certain cases, limiting the duration of the alliance as well as its area was crucial in the evaluation.

7.4.3   Horizontal Purchase Alliances

Examples of horizontal purchase alliances include cases of joint purchasing of inputs (e.g., raw materials) amongst competitors and joint negotiations of purchasing conditions with suppliers. Purchasing alliances should have pro-competitive effects due to their decreased costs, which realise economies of scale through increased quantities of purchased units. Alternatively, partners must consider the following problems that may arise, in order to avoid purchasing cartels and the exclusion of competitors when dominance occurs in the purchasing market, input exclusion, unreasonable restraint of trade and restrictions on competition between alliance partners in the sales market.

7.4.4   Horizontal R&D Alliances

In horizontal R&D alliances, businesses with competitive relationships in the product market form joint organisations to conduct R&D activities that not only improve products or create substitute products, but also improve or develop R&D technology using the products. Other cases of such alliances include the sharing of R&D amongst partners, as well as those in which one partner provides funds and another partner conducts R&D. Such R&D efforts should have pro-competitive effects by decreasing R&D costs—diversifying risk or shortening the risk period—and mutually supplementing technology between enterprises in different fields.

The JFTC focuses on the following points that may lead to competition concerns. First, cases sometimes involve substantial restraint of competition due to joint activities exceeding the permitted range and development of substitute products; the exclusion of enterprises from the market given restrictions on participating in joint R&D; and arrangements that impose unfair restraints on business activities associated with the implementation of joint R&D.

Two markets are defined as relevant: the technology market, in which technology is an outcome of R&D; and the product market, which involves sales of products manufactured using this technology. The JFTC evaluates the market share, the rankings of participants in the relevant market, the scope and duration of such alliances and the factors specific to joint R&D efforts. These include the nature of the research under affiliation—whether basic, development-based or applied—and the need for collaboration. In addition to the alliance itself, the JFTC examines the various arrangements associated with implementing the alliance and restrictions on the use of the results.

7.5 JFTC Enforcement Policies Regarding Horizontal Cooperation

No comprehensive guidelines or guidance exist regarding horizontal cooperation in the AMA, such as the European Union's guidelines for the assessment of horizontal cooperation agreements or the United States' antitrust guidelines for collaborations among competitors. JFTC guidelines include enforcement policies and the interpretation of provisions related to the AMA on horizontal cooperation agreements. These guidelines involve mergers and acquisitions (M&A), joint R&D projects, the use of intellectual property, standardisation, patent pool arrangements, distribution systems and business practices.[12]

One of study groups at the Competition Policy Research Centre,[13] supported by the JFTC, issued a report (the study group report) on horizontal cooperation[14] that summarised consultation cases and other materials to understand the AMA's analytical framework and treatment of such issues. The JFTC's attitude toward horizontal cooperation can be found in its enforcement practice of M&A and hardcore cartels. The study group report observed that horizontal cooperation has aspects both shared with and different from those of mergers. Horizontal cooperation typically integrates decision-making and actions amongst related parties to a certain degree, whilst mergers integrate them almost perfectly. Horizontal cooperation agreements unite participants for a specific action, but provide substantial room for cooperation partners to continue acting independently outside the agreement.

---

[12] JFTC (2004) M&A Guidelines, JFTC (1993) Joint Research and Development Guidelines, JFTC (2007) the Use of Intellectual Property Guidelines, JFTC (2005) Guidelines on Standardisation and Patent Pool Arrangements, Secretary General of the JFTC (1991) Guidelines concerning Distribution System and Business Practices.

[13] The Competition Policy Research Centre (CPRC) aims to build and improve functional, sustainable cooperative platforms between intellectual resources of outside researchers and practitioners and staff members of the JFTC to reinforce the theoretical foundation on which antitrust laws operate. Further, it plans, proposes, and evaluates competition policies from medium- and long-term perspectives as well as from the perspective that such platforms should be used to enforce measures for current issues.

[14] JFTC & CPRC (2019).

The JFTC examination of horizontal cooperation is two-fold. First, it looks at the extent and scope of the competitive effect that the integration of business activities amongst parties would have on the relevant markets. On the one hand, the JFTC estimates the competitive effects of the integration itself in relevant markets, and on the other hand, it considers the possibility of facilitating coordinated action in the relevant markets. Second, the JFTC must evaluate incidental or ancillary arrangements that restrict either party's business activities, unilaterally or mutually, and lead anticompetitive effects to eliminate or avoid competition in relevant or related markets.

The JFTC's analysis under prior consultation is influenced by the existence of illegality, based on current or retrospective action in the current market; therefore, cases are typically subject to regulation primarily under Article 3 (unreasonable restraint of trade) of the AMA. In this evaluation, the JFTC uses a similar framework as for a merger analysis—especially horizontal merger analysis— to estimate competitive effects related to the integration of business activities amongst parties (the first aspect as previously discussed). Therefore, it is appropriate to take into account the consideration and factors of the JFTC M&A guidelines and merger cases. In addition to this framework, it is also necessary to determine a means to evaluate incidental arrangements of horizontal cooperation agreements, for the previously mentioned second aspect, sometimes called an 'ancillary restraint' analysis.

The JFTC has taken a harsh attitude towards hardcore cartels, which account for almost all formal cases under Article 3 (unreasonable restraint of trade). However, it has never implemented prudent, detailed analyses of hardcore cartel cases. The first step should be to ensure that a horizontal cooperation agreement does not meet the standard of a hardcore cartel, which does not have beneficial aspects other than for those involved. The framework and factors considered for horizontal cooperation differ from that of hardcore cartels. JFTC enforcement policy uses a case-by-case or 'rule-of-reason' approach to horizontal cooperation agreements, which have beneficial aspects beyond those for an object or effect of restraint from competition. Most of the time, the JFTC accepts the existence of pro-competitive effects or neutrality to competition in horizontal cooperation.

A detailed examination by the JFTC reveals several situations in which horizontal cooperation might have anticompetitive effects. In many cases, the JFTC appears to focus on the price and quantity effects that could result from the parties' business integration if a horizontal business alliance were implemented. In doing so, a common consideration involves determining the aspects of business integration that influence business decision-making: specifically, whether decision-making is integrated for competitively important factors, such as a product's cost, price, quality or quantity.

If the integration of decision-making is approved for such factors, the JFTC reviews their influence on the competition between the parties, given the degree of cost-structure standardisation of the products and businesses to be integrated, as well as the contents of any information exchanges and information-sharing. This analysis reveals the degree to which the alliance affects any competitive relationship between the parties. In many cases, the duration of the alliance is also considered as an additional factor peculiar to the business alliance, which differs from mergers.

If the JFTC perceives that the competition among alliance parties will be significantly limited by integration, it proceeds to analyse the impact of horizontal cooperation agreements on competition in relevant markets. The basic analytical framework for the next stage is similar to that used in its review of mergers; the process and factors are included in the JFTC's M&A guidelines.[15]

The JFTC separates and explains the analysis of the unilateral and anticompetitive effects of coordinated action in its M&A guidelines. In past consultation cases, it has focused on the unilateral effects of horizontal cooperation agreements. However, the possibility of a coordinated effect cannot be excluded. The study group report also analysed the coordinated effects in detail.

The JFTC also evaluates arrangements that unilaterally or mutually restrict the business activities of each partner associated with the alliance's implementation whilst also considering the examination's results. The following four types of arrangements are most likely to be found[16]:

- An act in which one party unfairly imposes unfavourable conditions on the other party (e.g., abuse of superior bargaining position). An act that requires only certain participants to disclose technological information of the partners in joint R&D, and that would result in an unfair disadvantage for the partners that are obliged to disclose such information.
- An act in which one party unfairly restrains the business activities of another party (e.g., trading on restrictive terms). The act of requiring the transfer of improved inventions etc. of the outcomes amongst the joint R&D alliance partners to another party, or imposing an obligation on another party to grant an exclusive licence.
- The act of arranging the sales price, sales area or customers etc. of the product between the alliance partners (unreasonable restraint of trade). An act that mutually restricts the price, quantity or other considerations of the product in joint R&D conducted between businesses with a competitive relationship in the product market.
- An act in which a partner excludes a person other than the alliance partners (e.g., private monopolisation, concerted refusal to trade). An act restricting participation of specific businesses without justifiable reason in cases where without participation in standardisation activities, it would be difficult to develop and produce products that adopt the established standards, creating a risk of those businesses being excluded from the market.

As each arrangement is treated under each applicable provision based on an analysis of its form and its impact on competition, the analysis method differs for each case. The JFTC accepts that an arrangement's pro-competitive effects should be evaluated considering its rationality in the cases not including hardcore restriction, and that consideration should be given as to whether other, less restrictive alternatives exist.

---

[15] JFTC M&A Guidelines (2004).

[16] JFTC & CPRC (2019) Part 5. 3. C.

References

1. Japan In-House Lawyer Association (ed). (2019). Q & A de wakaru gyousyubetuhoumu iyakuhinn/iryoukiki. Cyuou Keizaisya.
2. JFTC & CPRC (Competition Policy Research Center). (2019). Report of study group on business alliances. https://www.theJFTC.go.jp/en/pressreleases/yearly-2019/July/190710-3.pdf
3. JFTC. (2004). Dokkusen kinsihou ni kansuru soudann jireisyu (Heisei 14 nenn 1 gatu kara 16 nenn 3 gatu) [Consultation Cases Related to the Antimonopoly Act (From Jan. 2002 to Mar. 2004)].
4. JFTC. (2005). Dokkusen kinsihou ni kansuru soudann jireisyu (Heisei 16 nenndo) [Consultation Cases Related to the Antimonopoly Act (FY 2004)].
5. JFTC. (2020). Dokkusen kinsihou ni kansuru soudann jireisyu (Reiwa 1 nenndo) [Consultation Cases Related to the Antimonopoly Act (FY 2019)] https://www.jftc.go.jp/houdou/pressrelease/2020/jun/r1soudanjireihontai.pdf
6. JFTC. (2004.) Guidelines to application of the Antimonopoly Act concerning review of business combination Revised December 17, 2019. https://www.jftc.go.jp/en/legislation_gls/imonopoly_guidelines_files/191217GL.pdf
7. JFTC. (1993). Guidelines concerning joint research and development under the Antimonopoly Act. https://www.jftc.go.jp/en/legislation_gls/imonopoly_guidelines_files/jointresearch.pdf
8. JFTC. (2007) .Guidelines for the use of intellectual property under the Antimonopoly Act. https://www.jftc.go.jp/en/legislation_gls/imonopoly_guidelines_files/IPGL_Frand.pdf
9. JFTC. (2005). Guidelines on standardisation and patent pool arrangements. https://www.jftc.go.jp/en/legislation_gls/imonopoly_guidelines_files/Patent_Pool.pdf
10. Secretary General of the JFTC. (1991). Guidelines concerning distribution system and business practices under the Antimonopoly Act, Revised June 16, 2017. https://www.theJFTC.go.jp/en/legislation_gls/210122.pdf

Chapter 8
Merger Regulations in the Japanese Pharmaceutical Industry

Kuninobu Takeda

Abstract Although there have been no formal merger cases in Japan since 1973, the Japan Fair Trade Commission (JFTC) publishes around 10–13 unofficial cases each year. These usually include at least one case from the pharmaceutical industry. This chapter reviews cases where the JFTC seems to have conducted a characteristic analysis. For example, the JFTC usually delineates a product market starting with the ATC (Anatomical Therapeutic Chemical Classification) Level 3 in the pharmaceutical manufacturing industry and does not consider the so-called innovation market. It is true the JFTC cares about the disappearance of incentives for research and development (R&D). However, its concern is not just a decrease in R&D investment or channels, but an impact on competition in a specific market. I will then summarise general problems with JFTC merger regulation. Many of the published cases are standardised, and that the process of analysis and the basis of judgment are unclear. In response to such criticisms, in recent cases the JFTC uses an economic analysis and publishes its findings in more detail. However, there remain other problems such that the JFTC relies heavily on behavioural remedies rather than structural ones, even in horizontal mergers.

Keywords Merger regulation · Business combinations · Innovation market · Pharmaceutical distribution market · Remedies

8.1 Introduction

Chapter 4 of the Antimonopoly Act (AMA) prohibits the acquisition or possession of the shares of a company (AMA art 10), interlocking directorates (AMA art 13), shareholding by a person other than a company (AMA art 14) or a merger of companies (AMA art 15), joint incorporation-type split or absorption-type split (AMA art 15–2), joint share transfer (AMA art 15–3), or acquisition of businesses (AMA art 16) (hereinafter collectively referred to as 'business combination'), where it creates

K. Takeda (✉)
Graduate School of Law and Politics, Osaka University, Toyonaka, Osaka, Japan
e-mail: takeda@law.osaka-u.ac.jp

© The Author(s), under exclusive license to Springer Nature Singapore Pte Ltd. 2022   127
A. Negishi et al. (eds.), *Competition Law and Policy in the Japanese Pharmaceutical Sector*, Kobe University Monograph Series in Social Science Research,
https://doi.org/10.1007/978-981-16-7814-1_8

a business combination that may substantially restrain competition in any particular field of trade, or where a business combination is created through an unfair trade practice.

To review whether the effect of a business combination may substantially restrain competition in any particular field of trade, the Japan Fair Trade Commission (JFTC) clarifies the underlying principles in its Guidelines to Application of the Antimonopoly Act concerning Review of Business Combination (2004, revised 2019) (hereinafter referred to as the 'Business Combinations Guidelines'), and it releases summaries of the review of certain cases in which notifications or other submissions were accepted, as a reference for operators intending to create or evaluate a business combination plan. There have been no formal cases related to business combinations since Hiroshima Electric Railway and Hiroshima Bus Case[1] in 1973 (1: 133). Although there has been no formal case in decades, information can be obtained about JFTC practice from the published summaries. Around 10–13 business combination cases are announced every year by the JFTC. Usually, one pharmaceutical industry case. The 'pharmaceutical industry' refers to a pharmaceutical manufacturing industry, a pharmaceutical wholesale industry, and/or a pharmaceutical retail industry.

In the following study, I review cases in which the JFTC appears to have conducted a characteristic analysis. Through these case studies, I clarify the problems of business combination regulation in the Japanese pharmaceutical industry. I then summarise the general problems with JFTC business combination regulations. Among the informal cases discussed in this paper, recent ones are translated in English as 'Major Business Combination Cases' on the JFTC website (https://www.jftc.go.jp/en/index.html). The content of the cases published in English matches those published in Japanese. We can know JFTC practice only from those informal cases. But the degree of publicity of those cases is not always sufficient for ex-post analysis in comparison to that of those in the European Union or United States.

8.2 Cases in the Pharmaceutical Manufacturing Industry

8.2.1 Published Cases

The Japanese pharmaceutical market is the third-largest in the world. However, the market growth rate is less than 0% per year, the lowest amongst developed countries. Research and development (R&D) costs for pharmaceuticals are soaring, and the probability of success in developing a new medicine is declining. Large sums of money are required to expand research facilities, increase the number of researchers and introduce new technologies. To increase funds and human resources, mergers and acquisitions (M&A) often occur.

---

[1] 20 Shinketsu-shu 62 (*Hiroshima Electric Railway and Hiroshima Bus*)

Of the published cases related to the pharmaceutical manufacturing industry, a few business combinations involve Japanese companies: (i) Astellas Pharma Case (FY2004 Case7), (ii) Daiichi Sankyo Case (FY2005 Case4), (iii) Mitsubishi Tanabe Pharma Case (FY2007 Case 2), (iv) Kyowa Kirin Case (FY2008 Case 1) and (v) Takeda and Shire Case (FY2018 Case 3). In addition, (vi) Novartis and Glaxo-SmithKline Case (FY2014 Case 4), (vii) Sanofi Group and Boehringer Ingelheim Case (FY2016 Case 4) and (viii) Bristol-Myers Squibb and Celgene Case (FY2019 Case 1) are related to business combination between foreign companies.

Of these, the most detailed and typical JFTC appears in Kyowa Kirin Case (FY2008 Case 1) and Novartis and GlaxoSmithKline Case (FY2014 Case 4), which are horizontal business combination cases in the pharmaceutical industry. I will review the JFTC analysis of those cases.

8.2.2 Kyowa Kirin Case (FY 2008 Case 1)

8.2.2.1 Outline of the Case

In this business combination case between the Kirin Group and the Kyowa Hakko Group, the recombinant human granulocyte colony-stimulating factor preparation (G-CSF), a biopharmaceutica, is one of the relevant products defined by the JFTC. In Japan, the only manufacturers of G-CSF were Company A and the two companies concerned. The merger of these two companies meant they dominated 60% of the market share and ranked first in the field. The entry of follow-on biopharmaceuticals (biosimilars) is difficult due to clinical trial know-how, development costs and technological capabilities required for development and manufacturing. Certain antibiotics have the same effect as G-CSF but do not provide the restraining power equivalent to that of the original drugs. Doctors have the right to prescribe medicinal drugs. They have no incentive to choose affordable medicines. Therefore, there is little competitive pressure from users to reduce the price of G-CSF. Before the business combination, Kyowa Hakko's products had lower prices than the other two products. The JFTC determined the business combination could lead to the disappearance of Kyowa Hakko's products, which would lead to higher prices in the market.

8.2.2.2 Analysis

Relevant market definition

In this case, the market is defined by the JFTC based on the function and utility of the drug. The JFTC uses the ATC, which groups pharmaceutical products based on their therapeutic indications, instead of examining the functions and utilities of the relevant drugs. First, it checked ATC Classification Level 3 and assumed products with different functions and utilities were included. So, it narrowly checked Level 4. It excluded products that were not substitutable with each other at Level 4. As a result, the relevant product market was defined as G-CSF. The delineation of the relevant product market, which starts with ATC Level 3, is the JFTC's established method for business combination regulation in the pharmaceutical industry.

Similarly, Mitsubishi Tanabe Pharma Case (FY2007 Case 2), is an example of excluding non-interchangeable products from Level 4. The JFTC practice of defining the market, which starts from ATC-related commodities, is basically the same as that of the EU Commission. The EU Commission also first reviews therapeutic interchangeability using ATC Levels and then considers price restraint (2; 3: 248–250).

Japan is defined as the relevant geographic market. Due to marketing approval procedures, markets are not defined across national borders. In many cases, the JFTC points out the sale of pharmaceutical products in Japan requires the approval of the Ministry of Health, Labour and Welfare (MHLW). The Bristol-Myers Squibb and Celgene Case (FY2019 Case 1) is an example. Even for pipeline products, the relevant geographic market is limited to Japan.

8.2.2.3   Position of the Parties and Conditions of Competing Enterprises

After market delineation, market share and market concentration are calculated. In this case, where there was fierce competition between the companies concerned before the business combination, and where the product of one of the parties (Kyowa Hakko) was characterised by a competitive price, the JFTC found that competition problems might occur regardless of the increase in market share. Therefore, the JFTC was concerned the disappearance of that low-price product would cause competitive problems.

In other cases, the JFTC may focus on large market share to narrow down cases. For example, in the Daiichi Sankyo Case (FY2005 Case 4), it identified relevant products as those in which the companies concerned had a market share of 10% or more after the combination, and companies that had a market share of 1% or more. In other cases the JFTC found no concern after determining that the business combination created no increased market share. For example, in the Unicharm and Shiseido Case (FY2005 Case 1), the market share and ranking after the merger was 65% (the largest in the market), but because the increase in market share was very small, the JFTC found no competitive issue.

After calculating the market share of the companies concerned, the existence of 'influential competitors' is often confirmed. In the Bristol-Myers Squibb and Celgene Case (FY2019 Case 1), the companies concerned were ranked first (a market share of 55%), but the JFTC determined two leading competitors held a market share of 15%. In previously published cases, if a competitor's market share is 10%, it is considered a strong competitor. For example, in the Astellas Pharma Case (FY2004 Case 7), the JFTC decided competitors with a market share of 10% had supply capacity. On the other hand, in the Mitsubishi Tanabe Pharma Case (FY2007 Case 2), the market share of competitors is less than 5%, so it was not evaluated as a leading competitor.

However, there are doubts about such formal criteria only focusing on market share (4: 43).

8.2.2.4 Entry

In this case, the JFTC explains the difficulty of entry for new compounds. Usually, it takes about 9–17 years from the start of the search for a new compound to the birth of a drug. The cost, per ingredient, of developing a drug amounts to 50 billion JPY. On the other hand, generic drugs have a much smaller burden due to decreased R&D costs and development period. Approval is usually obtained within 1–2 years of application. The preparation period for generic drugs before launch is 2–3 years.

The JFTC states that once the patent period expired, the period and cost from R&D of generic products to launch were less than those from the entry of the original product. The relevant product in this case is a biopharmaceutical. Follow-on biopharmaceuticals cannot be manufactured in exactly the same way as the originals, unlike ordinary chemically synthesised drugs containing low molecular weight compounds; this is due to the instability and complex chemical structure of the active. Generic bio-pharmaceuticals lacking the exact same active ingredient but with the same efficacy and effect are called biosimilars. They are classified as a new category, different from originals and generics. Biosimilars are not widespread in Japan, and only 15 have been approved by the MHLW.[2]

In other cases, the JFTC evaluates the product at the Phase III clinical stage as a potential entrant. When considering the disappearance of potential competition, the JFTC focuses on whether the drug is in the Phase III clinical stage or not. There is a distinction between prescription pharmaceuticals and over-the-counter drugs because of differences in the legal framework, distribution, rules for reimbursement, and so on. However, the JFTC believes competition might take place between them. Sanofi Boehringer Ingelheim (FY2016 Case 4) is an example in which the JFTC evaluated entry pressure due to the possibility of converting medical drugs to over-the-counter drugs.

8.2.3 Novartis and GlaxoSmithKline Case (FY2014 Case 4)

8.2.3.1 Outline of the Case

In this case, the Novartis Group sought to take over the anti-cancer drug product-related business from the GlaxoSmithKline Group (GSK). Of the molecular-targeted therapies classified as 'protein kinase inhibitors antineoplastic agents' (L1H) at ATC Level 3, Novartis was conducting R&D of α and β (Phase III clinical trial stage), and GSK was conducting R&D of γ and δ (preparation stage for manufacturing and

---

[2] https://www.biosimilar.jp/biosimilar_list.html (last accessed 27 June 2021).

marketing approval application after Phase III clinical trial stage), respectively. All products are for B-RAF mutation-positive advanced melanoma and are likely to be used widely in medical institutions after they have been approved for sale.

The status of the companies concerned was unknown because none of the companies' products had been put on the market. No company in Japan was approved to manufacture and sell L1H drug for the indication of B-RAF mutation-positive advanced melanoma. However, one company had applied for approval prior to the companies concerned. Because this product was also expected to be launched with high probability, it was expected there would be a certain amount of competitive pressure on the products of the companies concerned. In addition, there were currently several companies conducting R&D in the Phase III clinical trial stage, which would exert competitive pressure as they were likely to be launched in time. Furthermore, four other companies were conducting R&D in the Phase I or II clinical trial stages. The JFTC ruled that the business combination would not substantially limit competition because multiple competitors currently being developed would create a considerable amount of competitive pressure.

8.2.3.2   Analysis

In this case, the business combination between potential competitors was a problem. Competition authorities can predict the probability of new entries more accurately in the pharmaceutical industry than in other industries, in that information about pipeline products can be reliably obtained. Therefore, even if the new drug development process is not close to market, it is theoretically possible to regulate a business combination that would eliminate the pipeline in the clinical Phase I or Phase II stages. However, under Japan's business combination regulations, the effect on the product or service market must be proven, and the timespan of entry analysis is two years. On the other hand, during the period of the new drug development process in Japan, clinical trials (Phase I to Phase III) are three years, and then one to two years are needed for marketing approval. In short, new drugs considered potential competition will naturally be in the advanced stage after Phase III. This is in contrast to the EU Commission's analysis of innovation markets on pharmaceutical mergers. For example, in Novartis and GlaxoSmithKline Oncology (COMP/M.7559), the EU Commission found that after the transaction, Novartis risked stopping the ongoing development of two innovative pipeline drugs for skin and ovarian cancer [5].

In Japanese practice, the so-called innovation market is not considered. Only product markets, service markets and technology trading markets, in which specific products, services, or technology are or will actually be traded, are included. The disappearance of potential competition will not become an AMA concern until the impact on those related markets is recognised. The JFTC revised the Business Combinations Guidelines in 2019, mainly with digital platform operators in mind.

The method of analysis regarding business combination for companies conducting research and development was clarified[3]:

> If each party is engaged in the research and development of competitive goods or services, the JFTC will determine the effects of the relevant business combination on competition in consideration of the actual condition of such research and development.
>
> For instance, suppose a case where one of the parties supplies certain goods or services (α) to the market and the other party is engaged in the research and development of certain other goods or services (β) that compete with α. If β is found to be highly competitive with α after β is supplied to the relevant market, then the relevant business combination will greatly affect competition compared to a situation in which α and β are found not to be highly competitive, because the combination will cause the competition between α and β that would be realised were it not for the combination to decrease. And, when β of the other party is expected to be highly competitive with α, after it is supplied to the relevant market, a business combination between the two parties is deemed likely to cause the other party to be less willing to be dedicated to research and development, thereby greatly affecting competition between the two parties compared to a situation in which α and β are expected not to be highly competitive. In the same manner, if the two parties are mutually engaged in the research and development of competing goods and services, the JFTC will determine how a business combination between the two parties will affect competition. In particular, it will consider the possibility of extinction of competition between the goods or services that are provided by the two parties because of business combination or parties' diminished dedication to research and development.

The Business Combinations Guidelines mention the disappearance of incentives for R&D. However, the case is confined to such a situation 'when the degree of competition is expected to be high' between α and β.[4] Therefore, the problem is not just a decrease in R&D investment or a decrease in R&D channels, but an impact on competition in the precise product market. In the *Guidelines under the Antimonopoly Act on Joint Research and Development*, the JFTC states the effect of reducing competition will be minor if the total market share of the parties in the product market is 20% or less.[5] Furthermore, when the impact on the technology trading market cannot be determined based on the market share in the product market, the JFTC states that the competitive effect will be minor if there are four or more parties with alternative technologies other than the companies concerned.[6]

---

[3] Business Combinations Guidelines, PART IV.2 (1) F.

[4] Id.

[5] Guidelines Concerning Joint Research and Development under the Antimonopoly Act (1993, revised 2017), Part II. (1) [2].

[6] Guidelines for the Use of Intellectual Property under the Antimonopoly Act (2007, revised 2016), Part II. (5).

8.3   Cases in the Pharmaceutical Wholesale and Retail Industry

8.3.1   Cases

There are many published cases of business combinations related to the pharmaceutical retail and distribution industry: (i) Hayashi and OAK Case (FY1997 case 5), (ii) Valeo and Hoshi Ito Case (FY1998 Case 5), (iii) Sanseido, Kuraya and Tokyo Iyakuhin Case (FY1999 Case 11), (iv) Suzuken and Okinawayakuhin Case (FY2004 Case 2), (v) Mediceo Paltac Holdings and Kobashou Case (FY2007 Case10), (vi) Alfresa Holdings and Tampei Nakata Case (FY2010 Case9), (vii) Medipal Holdings and JCR Pharma Case (FY2017 Case1) and (viii) Matsumotokiyoshi and Cocokarafine Case (FY2019 Case 9). Through Alfresa Holdings and Tampei Nakata Case (FY2010 Case 9), I review the JFTC analytical method for horizontal business combinations in the over-the-counter (OTC) drug wholesale business, and through Medipal Holdings and JCR Pharma Case (FY2017 Case 1), I identify the JFTC analytical method for vertical business combinations between pharmaceutical manufacturers and distributors.

8.3.2   Alfresa Holdings and Tampei Nakata Case (FY2010 Case 9)

8.3.2.1   Outline of the Case

Alfresa Holdings, a wholesaler of OTC drugs, attempted to acquire Tampei Nakata, who operated the same type of business, as a subsidiary. Wholesalers operate in regional blocks, but many small retailers procure only from wholesalers in the prefecture where their stores were located. Therefore, 10 regional blocks and 47 prefectures were defined as geographical markets. The market share of the parties in each regional block varied from 25% (Kyushu block) to 55% (Okinawa block). Some prefectures did not fit the safe harbour criteria under which no anticompetitive effect is deemed to occur. However, in each of these markets, several strong competitors with market shares exceeding 10% had sufficient supply capacity. Additionally, a wide variety of rebates were used in the distribution process of OTC drugs, so it was difficult for each wholesaler to predict the price and trading conditions of others. Furthermore, the profit margins in the market were very low, there was competitive pressure from drug manufacturers to sell directly to retailers, and Tampei Nakata's business was failing. Considering the above factors in a comprehensive manner, the JFTC concluded merger did not restrict competition.

8.3.2.2 Analysis

In this case, the relevant geographic markets were defined by 10 regional blocks in Japan, and the 47 prefectures overlapped in those blocks due to different groups of consumers. On the one hand, drugstore chains procure from wholesalers from a wide geographic area. On the other hand, local pharmacies and small drugstores procure only from wholesalers with distribution bases in the prefecture where their stores are located. In the Mediceo Paltac Holdings and Kobashou Case (FY 2007 Case 10), another business combination case between OTC drug wholesalers, the relevant markets were defined in the same manner, as nine regional blocks with 47 prefectures. The Business Combinations Guidelines generally allow for such overlapping markets. There are many cases of business combinations of local banks in which the relevant geographic markets are delineated for each region within a prefecture, as well as for the prefecture as a whole.

In this case, direct sales from a pharmaceutical manufacturer to a retailer were evaluated as a pro-competitive effect. In the case of business combinations between wholesalers, direct sales to retailers are considered a pro-competitive effect in neighbouring markets. The JFTC also evaluated the financial condition of one party. In many published cases, the financial conditions, such as whether the business performance of part of the company group or the business section in question are poor, are considered when examining the business ability of the company group.

8.3.3 Medipal Holdings and JCR Pharma Case (FY2017 Case 1)

8.3.3.1 Outline of the Case

Medipal Holdings, a wholesaler of prescription pharmaceuticals, attempted to acquire the voting rights of JCR Pharma, a manufacturer and distributor of prescription biopharmaceuticals. This is an example of a vertical business combination, as JCR Pharma develops, manufactures and sells many biopharmaceuticals. By referring to the Kyowa Kirin Case (FY2008 Case1), amongst others, the JFTC used ATC Level 3 as a starting point to define the relevant product market. As a result, 'anterior pituitary hormone and analogues (H1A)' in ATC Level 3 and 'drugs for anaemia in premature infants' were identified as the product markets. These are upstream markets. JCR Pharma had the third-largest share the H1A market, at 20% and the second-largest market share of the anaemia for premature infants drugs, at 30%. The JFTC defined the downstream product market as a 'prescription drug wholesale business' and the geographic market as 'each prefecture'. Because Medipal Holdings Group had a sales office in every prefecture, the JFTC examined the impact of this case in each. Medipal Holdings' market share ranged from about 15% to about 50% in the 23 prefectures that did not fall under the safe harbour criteria.

According to the JFTC, JCR Pharma did not have the ability to restrict competition through input foreclosure, which occurs from denial of supply or so, in the H1A and drugs for anaemia in the premature infant markets. Medipal Holdings also did not have the ability to restrict competition through customer foreclosure. Theoretically, Medipal Holdings' dealings with manufacturers (aside from JCR Pharma) could lead to concerted action between JCR Pharma and its competitors as a result of JCR Pharma obtaining information on competitors' selling prices. However, prescription drug manufacturers provided rebates and allowances to distributors, and it was difficult to ascertain the real selling prices. Therefore, the JFTC concluded that the business combination would not restrict competition either in the upstream or downstream markets.

8.3.3.2 Analysis

In the 2019 amendments to the Business Combination Guidelines, the JFTC explains its approach to vertical business combinations and conglomerate business combinations.[7] This was mainly intended for business combinations involving digital platforms. In the pharmaceutical industry, the M3 and Nihon Ultmarc Case (FY2019 Case 1) involved a vertical business combination in which a platform has a restrictive effect on competition (1: 64). The contents of this case are described in chapter 6 (Prof. Negishi), para 6.3. Nihon Ultmarc had a dominant position in the business of providing medical databases (MDB), an upstream product market. Through the business combination, the parties had the ability and incentive to refuse to provide the database to competitors in downstream market. Therefore, the parties proposed they would no longer inhibit supply and would prohibit discriminatory treatment as remedies for dispelling foreclosure concerns.

In this case, the JFTC did not find concerted action through the means of obtaining confidential information. This was due to the uncertainty of the real transaction price as made unclear by the rebates. Similar market uncertainty is seen in other cases, such as the Mitsubishi Tanabe Pharma Case (FY 2007 Case 2). On the other hand, in the above-mentioned M3 and Nihon Ultmarc Case (FY2019 Case 1), the exclusion of competitors through the acquisition of confidential information was an issue. If M3 obtained any commercial confidential information about any of its competitors through Nihon Ultmarc and used such information to its advantage, competitors would suffer.

8.4 Remedies

The Business Combinations Guidelines state that even if the effect of a business combination is to substantially restrain competition in a particular field of trade, this

---

[7] Business Combinations Guidelines, PART V, VI.

may be remedied by certain appropriate measures taken by the company group. In many published cases, the JFTC found no restriction on competition based on the proposed remedies(6: 690; 7: 67). The Business Combination Guidelines state that the most effective measures to resolve the problem are those that create a new independent competitor or strengthen the competition so effective checks and balances exist. They also require the remedies should, in principle, be structural measures, such as the transfer of a business. In the Mitsubishi Tanabe Pharma case (FY 2007 Case 2), such a structural remedy was proposed by the parties and reviewed by the JFTC. The JFTC determined the remedies a third-party pharmaceutical company would need to successfully seek the manufacturing approval (including trademark) of related products, and stated the agreement should be concluded before the merger. In the Kyowa Kirin Case (FY 2008 Case 1), the transfer of a business was accepted as a remedy. In addition, in the Mediceo Paltac Holdings and Kobashou Case (FY 2007 Case 10), the creation of a strong competitor, by reducing the percentage of voting rights held and termination of interlocking directorates, was found acceptable.

On the other hand, in the M3 and Nihon Ultmarc Case (FY2019 Case 1), a vertical business combination, the parties proposed behavioural remedies. According to the Business Combination Guidelines, a rapidly changing market structure due to technological innovations could allow for certain types of behavioural measures.[8] Although a certain rationale exists for using behavioural remedies in vertical or conglomerate business combinations as the Business Combination Guidelines say, the JFTC tends to use behavioural remedies rather than structural remedies, even in horizontal business combinations. This practice has been criticised as too permissive [8, 9].

8.5   Conclusion

Above, I discuss representative cases of business combinations in the pharmaceutical industry and outline the typical JFTC analysis. JFTC practice clarifies the anticompetitive effect of the merger should be recognised for the precise product market. The elimination of competition between pipeline products below Level 3 is outside AMA regulation. This contrasts with the practices of foreign competition authorities concerned with the termination of an R&D program or the reduction of innovation capabilities for unmet patient needs.

The content of the published cases takes comprehensive consideration of each of the factors listed in the Business Combinations Guidelines. Issues with the guidelines include that they are standardised or formal, the process of analysis and the basis of judgment leading to the decision regarding substantial restriction on competition is unclear, and the objectivity of the examination results is questionable. One possible resolution would be to introduce economic analysis, and the probability of restricting competition should be shown quantitatively in order to ensure objectivity in examinations.

---

[8] Business Combinations Guidelines, Part VII.1.

In response to such criticisms and suggestions, in recent cases the JFTC uses an economic analysis and publishes its finding in more detail. In the Matsumotokiyoshi and Cocokarafine Case (FY2019 Case 9), which involved a business combination between drugstores, the JFTC conducted an economic analysis to evaluate whether the company group would stop competing in price and if the gross margin rate of its stores would rise as a result and reduce the number of drugstore groups in geographic areas where the company group's stores exist. It also considered whether stores in other business categories, including supermarkets and discount stores, were working competitively against the company group and bringing down the gross margin rate of the company group's stores.

There is no specific prior notification threshold for mergers in the pharmaceutical industry. Therefore, the business combination of a pharmaceutical company with a new drug that currently has no sales but is likely to generate significant sales in the future may not be notified to the JFTC. To identify business combinations that currently escape regulation, the JFTC announced a new policy looking at the value of the transaction instead of sales. The guidelines state:

> Regarding notification-free business combination plans, when the total consideration for the acquisition exceeds 40 billion yen, and the notification-free business combination plan is expected to affect domestic consumers, such as satisfying one of the specific cases, it is recommended that the parties having the notification-free business combination plan consult the JFTC.[9]

References

1. Wakui, M. (2019). Antimonopoly law: Competition law and policy in Japan.
2. Have, F. T., Martinez, J. T., & Demertzi, E. (2016). The European Commission's Pharmaceutical merger control practice: An overview of the state of play. *World Competition, 39*(1), 85–118.
3. Figueroa, P., & Guerrero, A. (2019). EU law of competition and trade in the pharmaceutical sector. Edward Elgar Publishing
4. Takeda, K. (2012). Kigyou ketsugou kisei niokeru teiryouteki hyouka to teiseiteki hyouka (Quantitative and qualitative evidence in merger regulation). *The Annual of the Japan Association of Economic Law, 2012*, 42–61.
5. Iren Mirabile et al. (2015). Protecting the drugs of tomorrow: Competition and innovation in healthcare, Competition Merger Brief 2/2015.
6. Hayashii, S. (2011). Kigyou ketugou kisei (Merger regulation), Shoji Houmu, Tokyo.
7. Kurita, M. (2012). Zikkouteki na kigyoukisei seido no kakuritu ni muketa kadai (Institutional problems of merger review under the AMA: The quest for an effective regime). *The Annual of the Japan Association of Economic Law, 2012*, 62–79.
8. Tahira, M. (2020). Kigyou ketsugou kisei niokeru sinsa to tetsuzuki no arikata (How does merger control work in Japan?). *The Annual of the Japan Association of Economic Law, 2020*, 50–63.
9. Vande Walle, S. (2021). Digital Platform ziken ni okeru mondai kaishou soti to Kakuyaku soti no zikkousei (Competition law and digital platforms: Are remedies and commitments effective?). The Annual of the Japan Association of Economic Law 2021.

---

[9] Policies Concerning Procedures of Review of Business Combination (2011, revised 2019), 6(2).

Chapter 9
Pay-For-Delay Agreements in Japan

Naoko Mariyama

Abstract Pay-for-delay agreements are attracting attention amongst the global antitrust community; however, no official pay-for-delay agreement case has been found in Japan to date. The reason could be the absence of a system that facilitates the detection of such agreements in Japan. Pay-for-delay agreements involve brand-name drug manufacturers paying a substantial sum of money (or other value) to generic manufacturers in return for their delaying the generic entry to the market, usually as a form of settlement for a patent infringement lawsuit. Such agreements are likely made everywhere in the world. This chapter addresses the difficulty of detecting such agreements and the possibility they might have been made in the past or may be made in the future in Japan, based on Japanese regulations and related cases. It also explains the regulation of pay-for-delay agreements under the Japanese Antimonopoly Act, which is similar to EU and US regulations. The chapter demonstrates Japanese regulations and cumulative cases have sufficient competency to address and prevent possible pay-for-delay agreements in Japan.

Keywords Pay-for-delay · Scope of the patent · Reverse payment · Pharmaceutical · Patent linkage

9.1 Introduction

Pay-for-delay agreements, also known as reverse payment settlements, have been greatly considered in the global antitrust community. These agreements have been used to settle patent infringement litigation between brand-name drug manufacturers (hereinafter, originators) and generic manufacturers, with the originators paying to delay a generic drug introduction to the market. Although these agreements are considered a legitimate means to settle costly lawsuits, they can also be viewed as anticompetitive agreements that restrict competition amongst potential competitors.

This chapter is based on Gallasch and Mariyama [4]

N. Mariyama (✉)
Undergraduate School of Law, Tokai University, Hiratsuka, Kanagawa, Japan
e-mail: mariyama@tokai-u.jp

Cases involving pay-for-delay agreements have occurred in the European Union, the United States and other countries, where the legitimacy of such agreements has been questioned. Japan currently lack an official record of cases involving pay-for-delay agreements. In this chapter, the possibility that such agreements have been made or will be made in Japan is considered alongside their potential regulations.

The following briefly overviews pay-for-delay agreements and the current legal standards governing them in the European Union and the United States, where extensive enforcement and analyses of pay-for-delay agreements have been conducted over the past two decades. Relevant literature from these countries is foundational for regulating pay-for-delay agreements in Japan. Furthermore, I consider whether pay-for-delay agreements have been made in Japan and outline Japanese pharmaceutical industry regulations and the Antimonopoly Act (AMA)[1] as they relate to pay-for-delay agreements. Finally, I conclude by discussing how these agreements might be regulated under the AMA in future.

9.2   Pay-For-Delay Agreements Outside Japan

9.2.1   Pay-For-Delay Agreements

Pay-for-delay agreements are used to settle patent litigation between originators and generic manufacturers. When a generic manufacturer enters or attempts to enter the pharmaceutical market, the originator holding a valid patent for the drug typically files an infringement lawsuit against the generic manufacturer. If the originator loses the case, it also loses enormous profits. To deter such a risk, originators may enter into a pay-for-delay settlement agreement with the generic manufacturer. A *pay-for-delay agreement* typically involves a generic manufacturer delaying introducing its drug to the market in return for significant payments from the originator. These agreements enable generic manufacturers to earn as much money as they would have if they had entered the market at the desired date, and the originator to continue earning profits on a drug without generic competition. This deal is often mutually beneficial; however, patients and national health insurance systems, which are funded by taxpayers, lose. Such agreements raise concerns because they restrict competition between originators and generics. They could be considered a classic example of a per se illegal restraint of trade.[2]

However, it has been argued that 'absent sham litigation or fraud in obtaining the patent, a reverse payment settlement is immune from antitrust attack so long as its anticompetitive effects fall within the scope of the exclusionary potential of the

---

[1] Act No. 54 of 1947, as last amended by Act No. 45 of 2019.

[2] Louisiana Wholesale Drug Co. v. Hoechst Marion Roussel, Inc. (In re Cardizem CD Antitrust Litigation), 332 F.3d 896, 908 (6th Cir. 2003).

patent'.[3] Patents permit patentees the right to exclude others; therefore, a pay-for-delay agreement is lawful if the agreement falls within the scope of the patent. The question is whether these agreements restrict competition beyond the exclusionary zone of the patent.[4] Pay-for-delay agreements usually delay generic entry until the patent at issue expires. This suggests that because such agreements do not extend beyond the scope of the patent, they should be legal. However, this scope of the patent test has been rejected by the US Supreme Court and the Court of Justice of the European Union (CJEU),[5] as described below.

9.2.2 Pay-For-Delay Agreements in the United States

The Hatch–Waxman Act, formally known as the Drug Price Competition and Patent Term Restoration Act,[6] provides the regulatory context of pay-for-delay agreements in the United States. The Hatch–Waxman Act

> [S]trikes a balance between two potentially competing policy interests, inducing the pioneering and development of pharmaceutical formulations and methods and facilitating efficient transition to a market with low-cost, generic copies of those pioneering inventions at the close of a patent term.[7]

The Act requires a prospective generic entrant to assure the Food and Drug Administration (FDA) its product will not infringe on the originator's patent. The generic manufacturer can either certify that the originator's patent is invalid or that it will not be infringed by the manufacture, use or sale of the generic drug.[8] The generic manufacturer must notify the originator of the certification.[9] The Hatch–Waxman Act encourages patent challenges by granting the first generic challenger 180 days of generic exclusivity from the day of generic entry.[10] During this term, no other generics are allowed to enter the market.[11]

The Supreme Court decision in *Actavis* is considered the most important ruling involving pay-for-delay agreements in the United States. The *Actavis* ruling established the applicable legal standards. First, it rejected the *scope of the patent test*[12]:

---

[3] F.T.C. v. Watson Pharm., Inc., 677 F.3d 1298, 1312 (11th Cir. 2012).

[4] In re Ciprofloxacin Hydrochloride Antitrust Litigation, 544 F. 3d 1323, 1333 (Fed Cir. 2008).

[5] FTC v. Actavis, Inc., 133 S. Ct. 2223, 2231; Case C—307/18, Generics (UK) Ltd. and others v CMA [2020] ECLI:EU:C:2020:52, para 81.

[6] Drug Price Competition and Patent Term Restoration Act, Pub. L. No. 98–417, 98 Stat. 1585 (1984) (codified as amended in sections of 21 U.S.C. and 35 U.S.C.).

[7] Novo Nordisk A/S v. Caraco Pharmaceutical Labs, Ltd., 601 F.3d 1359, 1360 [Fed Cir. 2010].

[8] 21 U.S.C. § 355(j)(2)(A) (vii)(IV).

[9] 21 U.S.C. § 355(j)(2)(B) (iii).

[10] 21 U.S.C. § 355(j)(5)(B)(iv).

[11] 21 U.S.C. § 355(j)(5)(B)(iv).

[12] Actavis 2231.

According to this test, as long as the anticompetitive effects of a pay-for-delay agreement fell within the scope of the patent's exclusionary potential, the agreement is immune from antitrust attack.[13] Several circuit courts allowed the test,[14] while others did not,[15] and academics and practitioners disputed the scope of the patent test regarding pay-for-delay agreements. The US Supreme Court ended the argument by stating, 'It would be incongruous to determine antitrust legality by measuring the settlement's anticompetitive effects solely against patent law policy, and not against procompetitive antitrust policies as well'.[16]

Second, the Court ruled that pay-for-delay agreements are subject to a rule of reason rather than a quick-look approach.[17] It held the *quick-look approach* is only appropriate when 'an observer with even a rudimentary understanding of economics could conclude that the arrangements in question would have an anticompetitive effect on customers and markets and that reverse payment settlements do not meet this criterion'.[18] It follows that the *rule of reason* would be applied to pay-for-delay agreements.

Third, the Supreme Court provided guidance for lower courts to apply the rule of reason in pay-for-delay cases. It quoted eminent antitrust scholars and showed, 'There is always something of a sliding scale in appraising reasonableness, and as such, the quality of proof required should vary with the circumstances'.[19] The opinion also states that a large and unexplained payment can 'provide a workable surrogate for a patent's weakness, all without forcing a court to conduct a detailed exploration of the validity of the patent itself' and the likely anticompetitive effects of a pay-for-delay agreement depend on its size and scale in relation to the payor's anticipated future litigation costs and other services.[20]

Moreover, the Court rejected the idea of using a risk-aversion claim as a justification for pay-for-delay agreements. It can be argued that originators pay a large amount of money to generic competitors to avoid losing infringement lawsuits, even if the chance of losing is small. According to the Supreme Court, '[T]he payment (if otherwise unexplained) likely seeks to prevent the risk of competition. And, as we have said, that consequence constitutes the relevant anticompetitive harm'.[21]

---

[13] Actavis 2225.

[14] See e.g. Schering Plough Corp. v FTC, 402 F.3d 1056, 1076 (11th Cir. 2005); Arkansas Carpenters Health & Welfare Fund v Bayer AG, 604 F.3d 98, 104 (2nd Cir. 2010); FTC v Watson Pharmaceuticals, Inc., et al., 677 F.3d 1298, 1312(11th Cir. 2012).

[15] In re K-Dur Antitrust Litigation, 686 F.3d 197, 218 (3rd Cir. 2012).

[16] Actavis 2231.

[17] Actavis 2237.

[18] Id.

[19] Id.

[20] Actavis 2236–37. This opinion is clearly ignored in In re Wellbutrin XL Antitrust Litigation Indirect Purchaser Class, 868 F.3d 132 (3rd Cir. 2017). In the case, the Third Circuit required the generic manufacturer to prove the patent was either invalid or not infringed, which the Actavis Court did not require.

[21] Actavis 2236.

Based on this judgment, notable scholars created the *Actavis inference test*. Under this test, if an originator pays more than its avoided litigation costs plus service fees to the generic company threatening entry and the generic company agrees to delay entry into the market, then such a large and unexplained payment is made to delay generic entry and is considered anticompetitive (see [1]: 18,[2]: 1,[3]: 589).

After *Actavis*, pay-for-delay agreements involving non-monetary compensation from the originator to generic manufactures emerged. (see [13]: 965). Several courts[22] attempted to limit the scope of the *Actavis* judgment to a 'cash payment' and to allow non-monetary reverse payment agreement to preserve a viable path for litigants to resolve patent disputes.[23] However, these judgments have been overturned on appeal,[24] as substance is prioritised over form.[25] In these cases, the originator agrees not to sell its authorised generic drug in return for delaying the generic entry. Authorised generic drugs are generic drugs sold by originators, which do not need FDA generic approval and would be the competitor of the first-file generic drug. If an originator launches its authorised generic drug, it can keep some of its profits. On the other hand, if an originator gives up selling its authorised generic drug, generic manufactures can make more profit. Accordingly, an agreement by an originator not to launch its authorised generic drug is a way to transfer value from the originator to a generic manufacture. The *Actavis* test extends to pay-for-delay agreements involving not launching authorised generic drugs in return for delaying generic entry.

9.2.3 Pay-For-Delay Agreements in the European Union

Only three pay-for-delay agreement cases have been litigated in European Union courts. One of the cases is a General Court (GC) case,[26] which is under appeal, while the others are a CJEU case[27] and a preliminary ruling by the CJEU on a case from the Competition Appeal Tribunal (UK).[28] The difference in the number of cases between the United States and the European Union is explained by regulatory variances. The European Union lacks an equivalent law to the US Hatch–Waxman

---

[22] See e.g. In re Loestrin 24 FE Antitrust Litigation, 45 F. Supp. 3d 180 (D.R.I. 2014); Lamictal Direct Purchaser Antitrust Litigation v All Direct Purchaser Action (In re Lamictal Direct Purchaser Antitrust Litigation), 18 F. Supp. 3d 560 (D.N.J. 2014).

[23] In re Losterin 2014 192.

[24] In re Loestrin 24 FE Antitrust Litigation, 814 F.3d 538, (1st Cir. 2016); King Drug Co v Smithkline Beecham Corp. 791 F.3d 388 (3rd Cir. 2015).

[25] In re Loestrin 2016 550.

[26] T-691/14 Servier v Commission, ECLI:EU: T:2018:922.

[27] Cases C-586/16 P Sun Pharmaceutical Industries and Ranbaxy (UK) v Commission, ECLI:EU:C:2021:241; C-588/16 P Generics (UK) v Commission, ECLI:EU:C:2021:242; C-591/16 P Lundbeck v Commission, ECLI:EU:C:2021:243; C-601/16 P Arrow Group and Arrow Generics v Commission, ECLI:EU:C:2021:244; C-611/16 P Xellia Pharmaceuticals and Alpharma v Commission, ECLI:EU:C:2021:245; C-614/16 P Merck v Commission, ECLI:EU:C:2021:246.

[28] Case C-307/18—Generics (UK) and Others v CMA, ECLI:EU:C:2020:52.

Act, which facilitates pay-for-delay agreements. The Act encourages generics to challenge patents and enter pharmaceutical markets by granting a 180-day exclusivity period during which the FDA will not approve subsequent generic applications, making it easier for originators to pay the first generic manufacturer and share the profits. The Act enables an originator and a generic manufacturer to create a duopoly; without this kind of regulation, originators would prevent generic entry by buying out every generic manufacturer that announces its intent to enter the market. In the European Union, originators that conclude pay-for-delay agreements enter into settlement agreements with generic manufacturers.

The first EU pay-for-delay case was *Lundbeck*, in which the European Commission found the pay-for-delay agreements at issue restricted competition by object and infringed Article 101 of the Treaty of the Functioning of the European Union (TFEU)[29]; the GC and the CJEU upheld the Commission's finding.[30] Because of their nature, restrictions on competition *by object* have such a high potential for negative effects on competition that it is unnecessary to demonstrate any actual or likely anti-competitive effects on the market for the purposes of applying Article 101(1) of the TFEU.[31] The CJEU held that pay-for-delay agreements concluded between an originator and generic manufacturers that have the effect of delaying market entry of generic medicines in exchange for value transfers from the originator to generic manufacturers cannot be considered restrictions by object in all cases.[32] The court also stated such characterisation as a restriction by object must be adopted when it is plain from examination of the agreement concerned that the transfers of value do not have any explanation other than the commercial interest of both the holder of the patent and the party allegedly infringing the patent not to engage in competition on the merits.[33] Agreements whereby competitors deliberately substitute practical cooperation between them for the risks of competition can clearly be characterised as restriction by object.[34]

Further, it must be determined whether the net gain of the transfers of value from the originator to the generic manufacturer is sufficiently large to act as an incentive to the manufacturer to refrain from entering the market and not to compete on the merits with the originator.[35] The GC judgment indicates the size of the payment could

---

[29] Case AT.39226—Lundbeck, Commission Decision of 19 June 2013.

[30] Case T 472/13 — Lundbeck v Commission, EU: T: 2016:449; Cases C-586/16 P Sun Pharmaceutical Industries and Ranbaxy (UK) v Commission, ECLI:EU:C:2021:241; C-588/16 P Generics (UK) v Commission, ECLI:EU:C:2021:242; C-591/16 P Lundbeck v Commission, ECLI:EU:C:2021:243; C-601/16 P Arrow Group and Arrow Generics v Commission, ECLI:EU:C:2021:244; C-611/16 P Xellia Pharmaceuticals and Alpharma v Commission, ECLI:EU:C:2021:245; C-614/16 P Merck v Commission, ECLI:EU:C:2021:246.

[31] European Commission, Guidance on restrictions of competition'by object' for the purpose of defining which agreements may benefit from the de minimis notice, SWD (2014) 198 final, 3.

[32] Lundbeck (CJEU), para 113; Generics (UK), para 84, 85.

[33] Lundbeck (CJEU), para 114; Generics (UK), para 87.

[34] Lundbeck (CJEU), para 114; Generics (UK), para 83.

[35] Lundbeck (CJEU) para 115; Generics (UK) para 93.

constitute an indicator of the strength of a patent, citing *Actavis*.[36] This is especially true when the amount of the pay-for-delay payment appears to correspond to the profits anticipated by the generic manufacturer if it had entered the market or to the damages which could have been paid if it had succeeded in litigation.[37] However, the CJEU states, 'There is no requirement that the net gain should necessarily be greater than the profits which manufacturers of generic medicines would have made if they had been successful in the patent proceedings'.[38]

The GC judgment cited case law to determine the justification for pay-for-delay agreements and found:

> [T]he adoption of anticompetitive behaviour may be the most cost-effective or least risky course of action for an undertaking in no way excludes the application of Article 101 TFEU. . . . particularly if that behaviour consists in paying actual or potential competitors not to enter the market and sharing with those competitors the profits resulting from the absence of generic medicinal products on that market, to the detriment of consumers, as in the present case.[39]

The avoidance of significant costs linked to litigation could be the justification for the agreement, although this was not allowed in the *Lundbeck* case because the parties did not provide adequate explanation to rationalise the agreement.[40]

As in *Actavis*, the EU courts also rejected the scope of the patent test because it often leads to the presumption that a generic drug infringes upon the originator's patent and the originator's patent is valid, whereas litigation may result in a finding of no patent infringement or even invalidation of the patent.[41] Intellectual property rights include the right to oppose infringement, but not the right to conclude agreements by which actual or potential competitors are paid not to enter the market.[42]

Generics (UK) and Others[43] was the first CJEU decision on pay-for-delay agreements. The Court found it is possible to apply Article 102 to an originator, thus using a settlement agreement to strengthen its dominant position.[44]

In *Servier v Commission*,[45] the European Commission found that Servier infringed upon Article 101 as well as Article 102 of the TFEU. In this case, Servier acquired production technology used in manufacturing the drug, as well as entering pay-for-delay settlement agreements with generic manufactures. The Commission held the agreements infringed upon Article 101 of the TFEU, and Servier's exclusionary

---

[36] Lundbeck (GC) para 353.

[37] Id paras 354 and 414.

[38] Lundbeck (CJEU) para 115.

[39] Lundbeck (GC) para 380.

[40] Id para 388.

[41] Id para 491.

[42] Lundbeck (CJEU) para 122; Lundbeck (GC) para 495.

[43] Case C-307/18—Generics (UK) and Others, ECLI:EU:C:2020:52.

[44] Id para 172.

[45] European Commission decision CASE AT.39612—Perindopril (Servier), 30/09/2016.

strategy of combining the acquisition of the technology with the settlement agreements constituted a single and continuous infringement of Article 102 of the TFEU.[46] The GC, however, did not uphold the Commission's finding on the infringement of Article 102, because the Commission failed to establish Servier's dominant position in the market, as the definition of the market was erroneous.[47]

9.2.4 Similarities Between Approaches in the European Union and the United States

The CJEU found pay-for-delay agreements cannot be restrictions by object in all cases. Such agreements must be adopted as restrictions by object if they do not have any explanation other than the commercial interest of both parties not to engage in competition on the merits.[48] On the other hand, *Actavis* adopted the rule of reason approach, while the decision showed the anticompetitive effect of reverse payment may well be assessed by examining the size of the payment along with its potential justification.[49] These approaches are similar, as the Directorate General for Competition of the European Commission commented:

> Incidentally, to those of you who are familiar with the Supreme Court's *Actavis* opinion, the factors taken into consideration by the Commission will sound familiar. Indeed, the Supreme Court looked at the same factors, in particular the size of the payment, including as compared to the expected profits of the generic producer, and the lack of any other convincing justification ([8], 9–10).

On both sides of the Atlantic, courts have held that the size of a payment may constitute an indicator of the strength of a patent.[50] They have rejected the scope of the patent test and have not allowed business risk aversion as a justification for pay-for-delay.[51] Meanwhile, they both have allowed the cost of litigation and services supplied by generics to be used as justification for payment.[52] This reveals the two systems have adopted a similar position on pay-for-delay agreements.

---

[46] T-691/14, Servier v Commission, ECLI:EU: T:2018:922, para 1625.

[47] Servier para 1621.

[48] Lundbeck (CJEU) para 113, 114.

[49] Actavis 2237.

[50] Lundbeck (GC) para 353; Actavis,2226.

[51] Lundbeck (GC) para 385, 499; Actavis 2231, 2236.

[52] Generics (UK) para 85, 86; Actavis 2236.

9.3 The Japanese Approach to Pay-For-Delay Agreements

9.3.1 Pay-For-Delay in Japan

Although no official pay-for-delay cases have been recorded in Japan, it cannot be said no such agreements have been made confidentially. It is likely it would be difficult to make pay-for-delay agreements in Japan ([11]; 19), especially considering the country has passed no legislation resembling the Hatch–Waxman Act. The Hatch–Waxman Act encourages generic manufacturers to challenge drug patents through lucrative incentivisation. The first generic manufacturer to file an approval receives a 180-day exclusivity period during which the FDA will not approve subsequent generic applications. Without this kind of regulation, so many generics would try to enter the market that originators would not be able to buy them all out. Therefore, there would be little reason for pay-for-delay to occur in jurisdictions outside the United States.

Yet pay-for-delay agreement cases occur in Europe, where no legislation similar to the Hatch–Waxman Act exists. Although without such an act, an originator may have to buy out multiple generic manufacturers to prevent their entry and maintain its monopoly, pay-for-delay agreements happen without such legislation. Technical or other barriers to entering a market may prevent many generic manufacturers from even attempting. A recent Japanese cartel case[53] between two generic manufacturers shows the number of generics entering the market can be limited even if the price was raised by a cartel (see [4]: 179).

Another possible reason for the absence of these agreements in Japan is drug price regulation ([11]; 19). Medical drug prices are regulated in Japan, and their retail prices are listed on the National Health Insurance (NHI) Drug Price Standard. This prevents drug prices from falling as far as they do in the United States, where one year after generic entry, generics sell at an 85% discount and account for 90% of the sales volume ([16]: 53).[54] Without such a significant potential drop, the originator may not have an incentive to buy out generic manufacturers; however, as in the European Union, even if generic entries do not cause as steep a fall, originators are still motivated to hinder generic entry, which causes the price to drop.[55] Therefore, pay-for-delay agreements or agreements that hinder or delay generic entry may also occur in Japan ([11]: 19). These features may function as an 'accelerant', but are by no means a fundamental requirement for pay-for-delay agreements ([4]: 175).

---

[53] Koa Isei, 66 Shinketsu-shu 283(Koa Isei).

[54] Because other generics' entry drops drug prices, the vast majority of potential profits for the first entrant materialises during the 180-day exclusivity period (Actavis 2229).

[55] 'After [the] generic's entry, the share of the generics is considered when setting the price of the originator's drug at the drug price revision'. Ministry of Health, Labour and Welfare [MHLW], Yakka santei no kijun nitsuite (Reiwa 2 nen 2gatsu 7nichi) Hohatsu, 0207 dai 1gou, [Concerning the standard for calculation of drug prices (7 February 2020), Notification No. 0207-1, issued by the director of the Health Insurance Bureau of the MHLW].

It is often believed that in Japan, people tend to obey authority, especially in regulated industries, and typically avoid engaging in unlawful actions. This may be true in a sense; however, recent cartel cases between pharmaceutical companies reveal this assumption is inaccurate, and Japanese pharmaceutical companies do sometimes engage in anticompetitive conduct.[56] As such, pay-for-delay agreements may have been made or will be made in Japan.

Authorities would find it difficult to detect pay-for-delay agreements in Japan. There is no legislation similar to the Hatch–Waxman Act or the Medicare Prescription Drug, Improvement, and Modernization Act,[57] which requires originators and generic manufacturers that conclude pharmaceutical patent settlement agreements to report them to the US FTC and the Department of Justice, and there is no sector inquiry similar to the one used in the European Union.[58] Such laws make it easy for regulating bodies in other countries to detect anticompetitive agreements. Moreover, in Japan the content of settlement agreements is not usually disclosed, and competition restricted by agreement usually remains within the scope of patents. Accordingly, even if no official pay-for-delay cases have been found, this does not necessarily mean confidential agreements do not exist in Japan; it only means they have not been discovered.

9.3.2 Pharmaceutical Regulation in Japan

Based on the premise that pay-for-delay agreements could occur in Japan, the focus turns to pharmaceutical regulation in relation to pay-for-delay agreements, as it is crucial when considering pay-for-delay regulation. The Ministry of Health, Labour and Welfare (MHLW) regulates the Japanese pharmaceutical industry in ways both similar to and different from those of the European Union and the United States. The Patent Act protects patent rights for 20 years from the date the patent application is filed,[59] which may be extended up to five years for pharmaceutical products.[60] Until this term lapses, generics cannot enter the market without infringing the patent. The prescription drug re-examination system also delays generics from entering the market. The purpose of this system is to review the safety and effects of new drugs after approval. The re-examination period lasts six to ten years from the date of approval of the drug.[61] During this period, generic manufacturers are not allowed

---

[56] Koa Isei, 66 Shinketsu-shu 283 (Koa Isei); Calvin Tablets, 66 Shinketsu-shu 335 (Calvin Tablets).

[57] Pub. L. No. 108–173 §112 (2003).

[58] European Commission reports on pharmaceutical sector inquiries and their follow up are available at https://ec.europa.eu/competition/sectors/pharmaceuticals/inquiry/index.html.

[59] Act No. 121 of 1959, as last amended by Act No. 3 of 2019, Art. 67(1).

[60] Act No. 121 of 1959, as last amended by Act No. 3 of 2019, Art. 67(2).

[61] Act No. 145 of 1960, as last amended by Act No. 63 of 2019, Art. 14–4.

to apply for manufacture and sale authorisation.[62] Afterwards, they may be granted authorisation and enter the market, even if the patent remains valid.

Japan's patent linkage system can prevent the entry of generics. Originators' patents are examined in two stages before the launching of a generic drug. Pharmaceutical manufacturers wanting to sell their drugs must obtain MHLW approval and then apply for listing on the NHI Drug Price Standard. Originators' patents are involved in both stages.

At the drug approval stage, the MHLW will not approve a generic drug if valid patents on active ingredients prevent the manufacturing of the generic drug.[63] The MHLW established this system to ensure a stable drug supply. If a generic enters the market before related patents expire and the manufacturer claims the patents are invalid or it has not infringed upon them, the originator naturally files suit against the generic manufacturer. In court, it may transpire that the patents are valid and the generic is found to have infringed. In such cases, the generic manufacturer is prohibited from manufacturing and selling the generic drug. In other words, the generic manufacturer may stop selling generic drugs, depending on court judgments. This type of uncertainty may confuse patients who take the drugs. To avoid such unpredictability, the authority does not allow generic manufacturers to manufacture and sell a generic drug until patents for the active ingredients expire.[64] This practice is not stipulated in any law, but is detailed in the MHLW notification involving the need for a stable drug supply.

Notifications are issued by agencies to advise people on specific matters, and they reflect the views of the issuing organisation. Although they generally lack legally binding effects or sanctions, they are typically followed.

According to the MHLW notification, even if patents for the indications, dosages and administrations of an originator are still valid, generic manufacturers may create a generic version of the brand-name drug with different indications, dosages and administrations. In these cases, the MHLW will approve the generic drug, except for valid patent-protected indications, dosages and administrations. Nevertheless, this does not mean there is no barrier to launching generic drugs. The manufacturer must apply for the generic to be listed on the NHI Drug Price Standard.

At the NHI price listing stage, the MHLW asks the manufacturer of a generic to discuss the possible dispute over the patent with the originator before applying for

---

[62] MHLW, Iyakuhin no shounin shinsei ni tsuite (Heisei 26nen 11gatsu 21nichi) Yakushoku-hatsu 1121 dai 2gou, [Concerning the approval of medical drugs (21 November 2014), Notification No. 1121–2, issued by the Director of Pharmaceutical and Food Safety Bureau of the MHLW].

[63] MHLW, Iryouyou Kouhatsu Iyakuhin no Yakujihoujouno Shouninn Shinsa Oyobi Yakka Shuusai ni Kakaru Iyakuhin Tokkyo no Toriatsukai ni tuite (Heisei 21nen 6gatsu 5nichi) Iseikei Hatsu 0605001gou/Yakushokushinsa Hatsu 0605014gou, [Concerning Handling of Drug Patents Pertaining to Approval of Generic Drugs Under the Pharmaceutical Affairs Law and Their NHI Price Listing (5 June 2009), Notification No. 0605014 issued by the Director of the Economic Affairs Division of the Health Policy Bureau and the Director of the Evaluation and Licensing Division of the Pharmaceutical and Food Safety Bureau of the MHLW].

[64] The notification states the MHLW does not approve drugs while the validity of a patent for active ingredients, indications, dosages and administration is disputed in court. However, several cases in which the authority approved generics despite patent validity being in dispute exist. [7] 56.

NHI drug price list registration and to apply for registration only when the manufacturer can ensure a stable supply of the drug.[65] Even if a generic manufacturer assumes its drug does not infringe upon any of the originator's patents and should be approved, the originator might disagree. At this stage, the validity and infringement of patents beyond a drug's active ingredients becomes important. After ex-ante negotiations between the originator and the generic manufacturer, the results of the discussion must be reported to the MHLW ([11]: 17).

When ex-ante negotiations do not settle the issue, the MHLW might still proceed with the price-listing procedure. In such cases, the agency asks the manufacturer of a generic to submit a letter of commitment to provide a secure supply of the drug, even if an infringement lawsuit or injunction has been filed by the originator ([11]: 17). The Ministry's main concern is maintaining a stable supply of drugs, not disputes between originators and manufacturers of generics. In certain cases, the manufacturer of a generic withdraws its application to the NHI Drug Price Standard after negotiations with the originator. The reason for the withdrawal is unknown to anyone other than the parties involved ([11]: 18). The manufacturer might believe it cannot win the infringement lawsuit, or there may be another reason to withdraw, such as a pay-for-delay agreement. The ex-ante negotiations could induce coordination between an originator and a generic manufacture, and then it could result in pay-for-delay agreements.

9.3.3 Patent Infringement Lawsuits and Settlements in Japan

It is unclear why pay-for-delay agreements have not been found in Japan. Without cases involving such agreements, it is helpful to provide an overview of the status of patent infringement lawsuits and their settlements to address this question. First, given the market size and number of patent applications and registrations, a proportion of patent infringement lawsuits filed in Japan is relatively small compared to those filed in the United States and other countries ([18]:128). This discrepancy may be may be due to the relatively low success rate of patent litigation in Japan.[66] Other potential reasons for the disparity include the claim of patent invalidation as a defence. Patent invalidation is claimed in 74% of infringement lawsuits.[67] The lower level of damages awarded in infringement lawsuits may also be a factor that

---

[65] MHLW, Kouhatsu Iyakuhin no Yakka Kijun heno Shuusai tou nituite (Hesei 24nen 2gatsu 15nichi) Iseikei Hatsu 0215 Dai 1gou, [Concerning NHI Price Listing of Generic Drugs, etc. (15th February 2012), Notification No. 0215 from the director of the Economic Affairs Division of the Health Policy Bureau of the MHLW].

[66] [9], The patentee success rate in patent infringement lawsuits was 21% from 2014 to 2019. However, in the same period, roughly 30% of infringement lawsuits end up through settlements, and around 80% of the settlements favour patentees. Therefore, by including those settlements, about 45% of infringement lawsuits actually end up in favour of patentees [6]. This number might not be so low.

[67] [6].

discourages originators from filing patent infringement lawsuits.[68] Around 80% of infringement lawsuits result in less than 100 million yen (about 1 million USD) in damages.[69] These factors may discourage patentees from filing patent infringement lawsuits.

Patent infringement lawsuits between originators and generic manufacturers are usually filed over 'weaker' patents (e.g. process patents) after 'stronger' patents (e.g. patents for active ingredients) expire ([11]: 18). This pattern follows the same trend as the European Union and the United States, where pay-for-delay agreements are often made after strong patents expire, while weak patents, which are often considered invalid or easy to circumvent, remain in effect (see [5]: 643).

Further, settlements between originators and generic manufacturers may be concluded during the course of ex-ante negotiations or infringement lawsuits. The content of settlements is typically not disclosed, and no one, except the parties involved, has knowledge of their content ([11]: 18). These factors suggest it is possible for pay-for-delay agreements to be concluded clandestinely in Japan. Overall, without legislation similar to the US Hatch–Waxman Act or the EU sectorial investigation, it may be difficult to uncover such agreements, making them lucrative for both parties.

9.4 Pay-For-Delay Under the AMA

9.4.1 Scope of the Patent Test Under the AMA

Article 21 of the AMA outlines the relationship between the Act and intellectual property (IP) law. According to the provision, the AMA does not apply to 'acts found to constitute an exercise of rights' under IP law. According to the Guidelines for the Use of Intellectual Property under the AMA, Article 21 'means that the AMA is applicable to restrictions pertaining to the use of technology that is not essentially considered to be the exercise of (IP) rights'.[70] The next paragraph states any act that may seem to be an exercise of a right cannot be 'recognisable as the exercise of the rights' provided for in Article 21 if it is found to deviate from or run counter to the intent and objectives of the IP system.[71] Because of the intent and objectives of the IP system, the effect on competition should be taken into consideration, as well as the intent and objectives inherent in IP law. Conduct that involves using IP rights primarily to restrict free and fair competition is against the intent of IP law ([12]: 399). Article 10 of the Intellectual Property Basic Act dictates, 'In promoting measures for the creation, protection, and exploitation of intellectual property, consideration

---

[68] Id.

[69] Id.

[70] [10] Part 2(1).

[71] Id.

shall be paid... to promote fair and free competition'.[72] According to Part 3(1)(i) and Part 4(2) of the guidelines, filing a lawsuit to seek an injunction against an infringer is considered an exercise of rights, and it does not normally constitute a problem. However, if such conduct is 'found to deviate from or run counter to the intent and objectives of intellectual property systems... it is not recognisable as an exercise of rights'.[73] It follows that the AMA would be applied to conduct that involves using IP rights primarily to restrict free and fair competition, as this conduct is not recognisable as an exercise of the rights.

Based on this interpretation of Article 21, the AMA is applied to pay-for-delay settlements involving large payments, which prevent the entry of generics. *Actavis* held, 'An unexplained large reverse payment itself would normally suggest that the patentee has serious doubts about the patent's survival and... the payment's objective is to maintain supra competitive prices to be shared among the patentee',[74] and 'a reverse payment, where large and unjustified, can bring with it the risk of significant anticompetitive effects'.[75] These types of pay-for-delay settlements are clearly against free and fair competition, as well as the intent and objectives of the IP system. They should not be regarded as an 'exercise of rights' under IP law. Consequently, the AMA should apply to pay-for-delay settlements that transfer large amounts of value from originators to generic manufacturers and prevent generic entry.

9.4.2 Private Monopolisation and Pay-For-Delay Agreements

Article 3 of the AMA could be applied to pay-for-delay agreements. The first paragraph, a counterpart to Sect. 2 of the Sharman Act and Article 102 of the TFEU, prohibits private monopolisation. The second paragraph of Article 3, which is a counterpart of Sect. 1 of the Sharman Act and Article 101 of the TFEU, prohibits unreasonable restraint of trade. The AMA is enforced by the Japan Fair Trade Commission (JFTC). Section 1 of the Sharman Act and Articles 101 and 102 of the TFEU have been applied to pay-for-delay agreements. Considering pay-for-delay agreements are restrictions between competitors, it seems natural to apply unreasonable restraint of trade to pay-for-delay agreements if the agreements were regulated in Japan.

The clause prohibiting private monopolisation could be applied to pay-for-delay agreements under limited circumstances; in exceptional cases, it would be appropriate to apply when originators force generic manufacturers to enter into such agreements. If an agreement involves coercion and the generic manufacturer enters the agreement unwillingly, it should be treated as private monopolisation. The AMA defines one or more enterprises excluding or controlling the business activities of

---

[72] Act No. 122 of 2002, as last amended by Act No. 63 of 2020, Art. 10.

[73] [10] Part 3(1)(i), Part 4(2).

[74] Actavis 2236.

[75] Actavis 2237.

other enterprises and substantially restricting competition in a market as an act of private monopolisation.

In *Nihon Iryoushoku Kyoukai*,[76] two companies agreed to restrict a new entrant, divide customers and fix a selling price. The JFTC found this conduct was not an unreasonable restraint of trade, but an act of private monopolisation. One of the two competitors was not treated as an offender, as the first forced the other to enter the agreement, and the agreement was far more favourable and lucrative for the one determined to be the offender ([14]: 18). The JFTC found one of the competitors had controlled the other's business activities illicitly and applied the first paragraph of Article 3.[77] If, as in this case, an originator forces a generic manufacturer to enter a pay-for-delay agreement, the agreement can be found to be a private monopolisation. Otherwise, the second paragraph of Article 3 would be applied to pay-for-delay agreements.

9.4.3 Unreasonable Restraint of Trade and Pay-For-Delay Agreements

The aforementioned experiences with pay-for-delay agreements in the European Union and the United States are a good reference to consider the application of unreasonable restraint of trade to pay-for-delay agreements. The second paragraph of Article 3 of the AMA, which prohibits unreasonable restraint of trade, could be applied to pay-for-delay agreements in Japan. An *unreasonable restraint of trade* is defined as an activity contrary to the public interest that substantially restrains competition in a market through an agreement between enterprises.[78] The issue in applying the second paragraph of Article 3 to pay-for-delay agreements is whether the conduct causes a substantial restraint of competition. According to case law,[79] a *substantial restraint of competition* enhances the market power of an enterprise or enterprises as a consequence of lessening competition, as a business entity or entities control the price, quality, quantity and other trading conditions freely and wilfully to a certain extent. In *Actavis*, an unexplained large payment in itself would normally suggest the patentee has serious doubts about the patent's survival, which indicates 'the very anticompetitive consequence that underlies the claim of antitrust

---

[76] 43 Shinketsu-shu 209 (Nihon Iryoushoku).

[77] The history of an industry can affect the case and its finding. This case involved food served to hospitalised patients. To be covered by the NHI, food must be examined and cleared by a regulatory body, the only organisation approved by the MHLW to perform this task. The body and the food company conspired to control the hospital food market, which drew public criticism. To appease the public, the body and the company invited another food company to enter the market. They asked the new entrant to agree to divide the market and sell only to a designated distributor in order to ensure their control over the distribution channel.

[78] AMA, Art. 2(6).

[79] Tokyo High Court Judgment, 29 May 2005, 56-II Shinketsu-shu 262 (NTT East).

unlawfulness'.[80] Such an unexplained large reverse payment to prevent generic entry could cause serious anticompetitive harm and establish a state in which an originator and generic manufacturer(s) can control the price, quality, quantity and other trading conditions freely and wilfully to some extent. Such an agreement would likely violate the second paragraph of Article 3, unless it is justified. Restriction of competition, despite its anticompetitive harm, may be allowed if it serves a justifiable purpose ([17]: 91). This purpose should be legitimate, and the restriction of competition must be essential to achieving this purpose for it to be justified ([17]: 91).

The European Union and the United States cases allowed payments for fair value of services or that would cover litigation costs.[81] Such payments could be allowed in Japan: if the value transfer from an originator to a generic manufacturer does not exceed litigation costs plus fair value of service, the payment would be essential for achieving a legitimate purpose(s). Such a payment would not violate the AMA; however, payment for risk aversion is unlikely to be permitted, as it is not allowed as a justification in other jurisdictions. In *Lundbeck*, the GC denied the justification of pay-for-delay settlements that were based on cost and risk:

> The fact that the adoption of anticompetitive behaviour may be the most cost-effective or least risky course of action for an undertaking in no way excludes the application of Article 101.[82]

In *Actavis*, the US Supreme Court explained:

> The owner of a particularly valuable patent might contend, of course, that even a small risk of invalidity justifies a large payment. But, be that as it may, the payment (if otherwise unexplained) likely seeks to prevent the risk of competition. And, as we have said, that consequence constitutes the relevant anticompetitive harm.[83]

In one instance involving Japanese case law on resale price maintenance, the Supreme Court held that justifications from a solely commercial or trade perspective that do not directly relate to competition cannot be approved.[84] While making pay-for-delay agreements to avoid the risk of competition is understandable from a business perspective, it should not be allowed as justification for restricting competition.

In light of the aforementioned discussion, pay-for-delay agreements should be assessed as follows. As is the case in the European Union and the United States, in Japan even if the anticompetitive effect of a pay-for-delay agreement does not extend beyond the scope of the originator's patent, the AMA should be applied. Furthermore, if an originator pays the manufacturer of a generic more than future litigation costs plus the value of services in monetary or non-monetary value in return for delaying

---

[80] Actavis 2236.

[81] Actavis 2236; Lundbeck (GC) para 390.

[82] Lundbeck (GC) para 380.

[83] Actavis 2236.

[84] Supreme Court, 10 July 1975, 29–6 Minshuu 888[Wakodo]. Although this case does not technically concern unreasonable restraint of trade but rather unfair trade practices, which are subject to another provision, it illustrates the Court's view on justification for conduct that deters competition.

the entry of a generic drug, the agreement will substantially restrict competition. Only if the agreement has a legitimate purpose and the restriction of competition resulting from the agreement is essential to achieving a legitimate purpose is it considered acceptable under the second paragraph of Article 3. Risk aversion or cost efficiency is not allowed as a justification.

9.4.4 Unfair Trade Practice and Pay-For-Delay Agreements

Generally, pay-for-delay agreements should be regulated under Article 3 of the AMA, as they significantly harm competition, as stated in previous sections. The anti-competitive effect may vary amongst the various situations in which pay-for-delay agreements are made.[85]

In certain situations, pay-for-delay agreements may be subject to provisions prohibiting unfair trade practices (AMA Article 19) rather than private monopolisation or unreasonable restraint of trade (AMA Article 3). Unfair trade practice is defined as conduct likely to distort fair competition (AMA Article 2(9)) and encompasses various types of conduct.[86] Unfair trade practice is meant to forestall the substantial restraint of competition that private monopolisation and unreasonable restraint of trade have cause,[87] as it involves less restraint on competition than private monopolisation and unreasonable restraint of trade ([15]: 183). If a pay-for-delay agreement does not restrict competition as much as substantial restraint of competition would, unfair trade practice would be applied to the agreement. For example, when one of the originators of a drug for a symptom, which could be treated by some originators' drugs, concludes a pay-for-delay agreement with the generic manufacturer(s), the agreement may constitute an unfair trade practice.[88] Because such a pay-for-delay agreement might not restrict competition substantially if there are alternative drugs to manage the symptom, but it does restrict competition to a certain extent. In such a case the JFTC may find unfair trade practice instead of unreasonable restraint of trade.

---

[85] Actavis 2237.

[86] Chapter 6, Sect. 5.1.

[87] Id.

[88] Amongst unfair trade practices, pay-for-delay agreements may constitute conditional trading. According to the Designation of Unfair Trade Practices (Fair Trade Commission Public Notice No. 15 of 18 June 1982) para 12, conditional trading is trading with another party on conditions that unjustly restrict any trade between the said party and its other transacting party or other business activities of the said party.

9.5 Conclusions

While Japan may well be a hotbed of clandestine pay-for-delay agreements, it is impossible to be certain because of the difficulties in detecting such agreements in the absence of laws such as Hatch–Waxman or intensive investigations into the pharmaceutical sector. However, if such cases are uncovered, Japanese courts and the JFTC would be able to address them under the AMA.

How pay-for-delay agreements could be handled in Japan should be similar to the methods employed in the European Union and the United States. The scope of the patent test is not likely to be allowed. Additionally, an agreement in which a value in excess of litigation costs plus the fair service value of a generic is transferred from an originator to the generic manufacturer in return for delaying its entry amounts to unreasonable restraint of trade, unless the parties of the agreement provide a justification, which must be something other than risk aversion or cost efficiency.

Although the MHLW prioritises the maintenance of a stable drug supply, a competitive pharmaceutical market is crucial for promoting innovation and public well-being. Pay-for-delay agreements could cause serious harm to patients and the National Health Insurance system. All anticompetitive conduct should be examined carefully, including pay-for-delay agreements, to ensure the pharmaceutical market remains competitive and innovative. Existing Japanese regulations and cumulative cases could be used to address pay-for-delay agreements, and these regulative tools should discourage companies from engaging in the types of pay-for-delay agreements that stifle competition in the pharmaceutical market.

References

1. Edlin, A. S., Hemphill, C. S., & Shapiro, C. (2013). Activating Actavis. *Antitrust, 28*, 16–23.
2. Edlin, A. S., Hemphill, C. S., Hovenkamp, H. J. & Shapiro, C. (2014). Actavis and error costs: A reply to critics. 2014 *The Antitrust Source* 1.
3. Edlin, A. S., Hemphill, C. S., Hovenkamp, H. J., & Shapiro, C. (2015). The Actavis inference: Theory and practice. *Rutgers Law Review, 67*, 585–635.
4. Gallasch, S., & Mariyama, N. (2020). Should pay for delay be a cause for concern in Japan? *World Competition, 43*(1), 163–184.
5. Hemphill, S., & Sampat, B. (2011). When do generics challenge drug patents? *Journal of Empirical Legal Studies, 8*, 613–649.
6. Intellectual Property High Court (2019) Tokkyoken no shingai ni kansuru soshou ni okeru toukei (Tokyo chisai Osaka chisai Hesei 26—Reiwa 1 nen) [Statistics on patent infringement lawsuits in the Tokyo District Court and Osaka District Court 2014–2019]. https://www.ip.cou rts.go.jp/vc-files/ip/2020/2019_sintoukei_h26-r1.pdf
7. Ishino, M., Kaneko, S., Shimura, M., Takei, R., Maruyama, S., et al. (2018). Nihon no Patent Linkage no Unyou Jittai Institute [Regarding implementation of patent linkage in Japan]. *Patent, 71–10*, 54–65.
8. Italianer A (2013) Competitor agreements under EU competition law. In *40th annual conference on international antitrust law and policy*, Fordham Competition Law Institute. https://ec.eur opa.eu/competition/speeches/text/sp2013_07_en.pdf

9. Japan Patent Office (2014) Shingai soshoutou ni okeru tokkyo no anteisei ni shisuru tokkyo-seido/unyoutokkyoseido/ unyou ni kansuru chousa kenkyuu houkokusho [Report on the patent system for the stability of patents in infringement lawsuits, etc.] *Chizai ken kiyou* [Institute of Intellectual Property bulletin] 23, 1–6. https://dl.ndl.go.jp/view/download/digidepo_10959417_po_h25_06.pdf?contentNo=1&alternativeNo

10. Japan Fair Trade Commission (2016) Chitekizaisan no riyou ni kansuru dokusenkinshi hou jouno shishin [Guidelines for the use of intellectual property under the Antimonopoly Act]. https://www.jftc.go.jp/en/legislation_gls/imonopoly_guidelines_files/IPGL_Frand.pdf

11. Japan Fair Trade Commission Competition Policy Research Center (2015) Iyakuhin shijou niokeru kyousou to kenkyuukaihatsu incentive—generic iyakuhin no sannyuu ga sijou ni ataeta eikyou no kenshou wo tsuujite [Competition and research and development incentives in the pharmaceutical market: Thorough examinations of the impact of the entry of generic drugs on the market]. https://www.jftc.go.jp/cprc/reports/index_files/cr-0115.pdf

12. Kanai, T., Kawahama, N. & Sensui, F. (2018). *Dokusen kinshi hou* [Antimonopoly Act] Koubundo.

13. Karas, L., Anderson, G. F., & Feldman, R. (2020). Pharmaceutical 'pay-for-delay' reexamined: A dwindling practice or a persistent problem? *Hastings Law Journal, 71*, 959–973.

14. Matsuyama, T. (1996). Iryouyou shokuhin bunya heno shitekidokusen no houtekiyou wo meguru shoronten [Issues on the application of private monopolisation on the sector of medical food] *Kousei Torihiki* 550, 12–23.

15. Negishi, A. & Funada, M. (2015). *Dokusen kinshi hou gaisetsu* [Overview of the Antimonopoly Act] Yuuhikaku.

16. Rozanski, G. (2019). The global antitrust economics conference 31 May 2019—New York University Stern School of Business verbatim transcript of oral presentations provided by concurrences without prior vetting by the speakers. https://www.concurrences.com/en/confer ences/the-global-antitrust-economics-conference-en

17. Shiraishi, T. (2016). *Dokusen kinshi hou* [Antimonopoly Act] Yuhikaku.

18. Yamaguchi, K. (2016). Japanese patent litigation and its related statistics—Current environment and future agenda *AIPPI Journal* 41(3), 128–142.

Chapter 10
No Challenge Clauses
in the Pharmaceutical Industry in Japan

Thomas K. Cheng

Abstract This chapter focuses on the use and regulation of no challenge clauses in the pharmaceutical industry in Japan. Licensing activities are prevalent in this industry. Although no direct evidence has been found on the prevalence of no challenge clauses, there are reasons to believe that these clauses are common in the licensing agreements in the industry. This gives rise to the question of whether these clauses should be regulated under competition law, and if so, how. The chapter concludes that no challenge clauses should be subject to the purview of competition law due to their potential to inflict consumer harm. There are, however, two preconditions for such harm: that the underlying patent is invalid and that the patentee possesses market power over a patented technology or product. This result indicates that no challenge clauses should only be illegal when both preconditions are met. The Japan Fair Trade Commission's approach to these clauses is largely consistent with these important theoretical insights.

Keywords No challenge clause · Patent licensing · Patent validity · Pharmaceutical industry

10.1 Introduction

Among the patent licensing practices that are subject to competition law scrutiny, no challenge clauses have received relatively little attention, both in Japan and globally. Thus far, the Japan Fair Trade Commission (JFTC) has not pursued even a single enforcement action regarding these clauses. The amount of attention received by these clauses in Japan, however, may not be commensurate with their prevalence. If the information and communications technology (ICT) industry is typical in its use of no challenge clauses, evidence suggests that they are widespread in Japan. Certainly,

T. K. Cheng (✉)
The Department of Law, University of Hong Kong, Pok Fu Lam, Hong Kong
e-mail: thomas.cheng@hku.hk

159

A. Negishi et al. (eds.), *Competition Law and Policy in the Japanese Pharmaceutical Sector*, Kobe University Monograph Series in Social Science Research,
https://doi.org/10.1007/978-981-16-7814-1_10

their prevalence may indicate their generally pro-competitive nature. Vertical distributional restraints are everywhere in the economy, and they are generally pro-competitive or at least competitively neutral. No challenge clauses, however, may cause significant consumer harm if the underlying patent is invalid and a patented technology or product possesses significant market power. These clauses hence call for some attention from the enforcers. This chapter examines licensing practices and the use of these clauses in the pharmaceutical industry in Japan and evaluates the current approach to these clauses taken by the JFTC. It concludes that the JFTC's approach may in fact be the soundest one among all the major jurisdictions of the United States (US), the European Union (EU), and China.

10.2   No Challenge Clauses

10.2.1   Overview

A no challenge clause prevents a licensee from initiating a challenge against the validity of the patent covered by a licensing agreement [1: 87]. A no challenge clause, however, does not provide patentees absolute protection from validity challenges as third parties that are not covered by the licensing agreement remain free to launch challenges [1: 87]. There are two categories of no challenge clauses. The first category covers clauses that outright prohibit validity challenges. Miller and Gal [2: 127] call these no contest clauses [2: 127]. The second category includes penalty clauses that are triggered in the event of a validity challenge. Miller and Gal [2: 131] have called these challenge penalty clauses. The distinction between the first and second categories may not necessarily be clear-cut as the penalty imposed by a challenge penalty clause can be so onerous that it effectively functions as an outright ban.[1]

10.2.2   No Challenge Clauses in Japan

There is a limited amount of information pertaining to the use of no challenge clauses in Japan, let alone specifically in the pharmaceutical sector. To the best of the author's knowledge, there has been no case in court and no enforcement action by the JFTC regarding the legality of these clauses under the Antimonopoly Act (AMA).[2] The JFTC issued a warning in the early 1980s in a case involving a licensing agreement in the pharmaceutical industry that incorporated a no challenge clause. The JFTC took the view that the clause and other provisions in the agreement may have exceeded

---

[1] Rates Technology, Inc. v. Speakeasy, Inc., 685 F.3d 163 (2d Cir. 2012).

[2] Shiteki dokusen no kinshi oyobi kosei torihiki no kakuho ni kansuru horitsu (Act on Prohibition of Private Monopolisation and Maintenance of Fair Trade (AMA)), Act No. 54 of 1947, as last amended by Act No. 45 of 2019.

the scope of the exemption for the exercise of patent rights under Article 21 of the AMA and may constitute private monopolisation and an unreasonable restraint of trade under Article 3 of the AMA.

In a more recent case, a court affirmed the enforceability of no challenge clauses contained in a settlement agreement. It held that a party that has acceded to such a clause lacks standing under the Patent Act to launch a validity challenge.[3] The practical effect of this ruling is that the breach of a no challenge clause not only results in damages but also automatically translates into specific performance as a remedy against the validity challenger. This case goes beyond the position taken by even the most pro-patent appellate court in the US.

The relative dearth of case law and decisional practice on no challenge clauses notwithstanding, there is some evidence that no challenge clauses are in fact quite common in Japan, at least in the ICT industry. A survey questionnaire was distributed in 2014 to 1000 domestic companies and research institutions that were engaged in licensing activities related to ICT [3: 2]. The corporate respondents were chosen because they had applied for patents in the relevant fields or were members of a patent pool in the industry [3: 2]. Survey results confirmed the widespread use of no challenge clauses. Just over 50% of the respondents reported that their current patent licensing agreement contained a no challenge clause [3: 37]. Meanwhile, almost 30% of them believed that such clauses were problematic [3: 37]. In particular, they asserted that these clauses forced a licensee to continue with a licensing agreement even if doubts regarding the validity of the patent existed. Further, they highlighted the significance of these clauses in a portfolio licensing agreement.

To the best of the author's knowledge, there has been no enforcement action by the JFTC or court cases on the legality of no challenge clauses under the AMA. On April 23, 1982, the JFTC did issue a warning to four pharmaceutical companies on the grounds that their licensing terms substantially restricted competition in the field of trade of metoclopramide preparations and might have violated Article 3 of the AMA [4]. The companies subject to the warning included Fujisawa Yakuhin Kogyo K. K.; Yamanouchi Pharmaceutical Co., Ltd.; Nippon Kayaku Co., Ltd.; and Teikoku Kagaku Sangyo Co., Ltd. (hereinafter referred to as Teisan).

Fujisawa Yakuhin had obtained an exclusive license from a French company for the manufacture of metoclopramide, over which the French company owned a Japanese patent. Yamanouchi Pharmaceutical, Nippon Kakayu, and Teisan subsequently launched metoclopramide products in Japan in 1971 [4]. Rather than filing an infringement action, Fujiwara Yakuhin proposed a licensing agreement to the other three companies that contained several provisions. These included an undertaking on the part of Fujisawa not to assert the patent against the other three companies, an obligation on the part of the three companies not to challenge the validity of the French company and Fujisawa's patent, a royalty of 7% of net sales to Fujisawa, a host of obligations imposed on the contracting parties that were aimed to prevent the entry of third parties, and, most importantly, a minimum price obligation for sales

---

[3] IP High Court, 19 December 2019, 2019 (gyo ke) 10,053.

of metoclopramide products to medical institutions [4]. The market entry prevention measures included refusal to license the patent to third parties. New entrants emerged later in 1971 and the contracting parties cooperated to issue warnings and file lawsuits to attempt to stop them [4].

The JFTC warning covered all the licensing restrictions in the agreement. The no challenge clause was not singled out for condemnation. But the JFTC did emphasise that the restrictions ensured that the contracting parties would not engage in any patent disputes with each other with respect to the manufacture and sale of the metoclopramide products. The JFTC noted the anticompetitive potential of the licensing provisions and only resorted to issuing a warning because there was only a short time left in the licensing agreement by the time the case was decided.

A more recent case concerning no challenge clauses was decided by the IP High Court on December 19, 2019.[4] The case did not concern the legality of no challenge clauses under the AMA but was about the impact of these clauses on a licensee's standing to launch a validity challenge under the patent law. In particular, only an interested person may file a request for a trial for patent invalidation under Article 123 (2) of the Japanese Patent Act.[5] The IP High Court ruled that a licensee subject to a no challenge clause is not an interested person for the purpose of Article 123.[6] This is because a licensee subject to a no challenge clause will be liable for damages under the licensing agreement if he or she chooses to launch a validity challenge. Therefore, a licensee is deemed not to have a legal interest in launching such a challenge under the Patent Act.

The court's reasoning is open to criticism. It is disputable whether a party that is willing to pay damages for the right to challenge a patent's validity has no legitimate legal interest to launch such a challenge. This is especially true in light of the public policy dimension of the patent system. Invalidation of a patent is not a purely private matter between the patentee and the challenger. The general public has a right to access a technology that is not subject to patent protection. Therefore, a wrongfully granted patent implicates public interest by denying the public access to the technology. If the technology is valuable and has no close substitutes, patent protection may confer market power on the technology owner, allowing her to charge supra-competitive prices. Consumers certainly have an interest in avoiding the payment of supra-competitive prices when patent protection for the technology is not justified.

Allowing a licensee to challenge a patent is doubly important because the licensee is often the party with the strongest financial interest to overturn an invalid patent.[7] Invalidation of a patent may terminate a licensee's royalty payment obligation and result in immediate savings for the licensee. The court's ruling effectively forecloses an important, and sometimes the only, source of patent validity challenges.

From the perspective of remedy, the ruling effectively granted specific performance for no challenge clauses. Although the IP High Court did not rule on the

---

[4] IP High Court, 19 December 2019, 2019 (gyo ke) 10,053 [Double eyelid forming tape].

[5] Tokkyo ho [Patent Act], Act No. 121 of 1959, as last amended by Act No. 3 of 2019, art. 123(2).

[6] Double eyelid forming tape, supra note [].

[7] Lear, Inc. v. Adkins, 395 U.S. 653, 670–71 (1969).

legality of no challenge clauses under the AMA, its ruling lends these clauses a veneer of legitimacy. There is a strong argument that no challenge clauses must be legal at least in some instances if they are so vigorously enforced by the courts. It would be indeed quite odd for a clause to enjoy the highest level of protection from patent law just to be deemed illegal across the board by competition law.

The ruling by the IP High Court sets Japanese patent law quite far apart from US patent law as far as the legality of no challenge clauses is concerned. As will be explained subsequently, some US courts have held no challenge clauses to be unenforceable if they are found in certain types of agreement. With the exception of the United States Court of Appeals for the Federal Circuit, most appellate courts in the US have been hesitant to enforce these clauses, at least under some circumstances. In sharp contrast, these clauses are an absolute bar to validity challenges under Japanese patent law.

Given the dearth of case law—the fact that Japan is a civil law jurisdiction where case law has no precedential value notwithstanding—and the fact that much of the AMA enforcement is public enforcement by the JFTC, the JFTC's attitude toward no challenge clauses becomes highly consequential. In the Guidelines for the Use of Intellectual Property, the JFTC asserts that no challenge clauses, which are translated as no-contest obligations in the English translation of the Guidelines, are generally recognised to promote competition by facilitating technology transfer and are unlikely to reduce competition directly.[8] The Guidelines stipulate that these clauses "may constitute an unfair trade practice when it is found to tend to impede fair competition by continuing rights that should be invalidated and by restricting the use of the technology associated with the said rights."[9] They further clarify that a termination-upon-challenge clause is, in principle, unlikely to constitute an unfair trade practice.

The conventional understanding of these Guidelines is that no challenge clauses would only violate the AMA if the underlying patent would otherwise be invalidated. Furthermore, such a clause would need to constitute an impediment to fair competition, which requires an effect to reduce competition[10] (which is generally known as an effect to lessen free competition).[11] Although the meaning of the clause it is not entirely clear, the safe harbour, which provides that restrictions are deemed to have a minor effect of reducing competition where the total share of entrepreneurs using the licensed technology is 20% or less, applies to no challenge clauses.[12] The JFTC will examine various factors including "the number of entrepreneurs subject

---

[8] Japan Fair Trade Commission (2016) Guidelines for the Use of Intellectual Property under the Antimonopoly Act, p. 21.

https://www.jftc.go.jp/en/legislation_gls/imonopoly_guidelines_files/IPGL_Frand.pdf. Accessed 10 June 2021. [hereinafter JFTC IPR Guidelines]

[9] Ibid.

[10] Ibid. 5–8, 15.

[11] Dokusen kinshi ho kenkyukai [AMA Study Group] (1972) Hokokusho: Fukosei na torihiki hoho ni kansuru kihon teki na kangae kata [Report: The basic approaches to unfair trade practices] (8 July 1972). Kosei torihiki 382:34–35.

[12] Ibid. 7–8, 15.

to the restriction and the level of competition between the entrepreneurs" to confirm that the clause "impede[s] the ability of the competitors and the others to compete" or "reduce[s] competition in pricing, acquiring customers and other means."[13] The reference to 20% is an indirect indication of market power on the part of the licensor in the relevant technology market. This suggests that some sort of market power is an important factor in determining the legality of no challenge clauses under the AMA.

10.2.3 No Challenge Clauses in Other Jurisdictions

10.2.3.1 The United States

No challenge clauses have been treated mostly as an issue of enforceability under US patent law. No US court seems to have ruled on the legality of these clauses under antitrust law [5: 447]. The lineage of the jurisprudence on no challenge clauses can be traced back to *Lear, Inc. v. Adkins*. The case was concerned with the doctrine of licensee estoppel, which had originated in the 1856 US Supreme Court decision in *Kinsman v. Parkhurst*.[14] The doctrine states that a licensee is deemed to have acquiesced to the validity of the patent being licensed and is estopped from challenging its validity. In *Lear*, the Supreme Court reversed its position and abandoned the doctrine of licensee estoppel. It declared that the public policy of eliminating invalid patents overrides the equitable considerations that favour the patentee:

> Surely the equities of the licensor do not weigh very heavily when they are balanced against the important public interest in permitting full and free competition in the use of ideas which are in reality a part of the public domain. Licensees may often be the only individuals with enough economic incentive to challenge the patentability of an inventor's discovery. If they are muzzled, the public may continually be required to pay tribute to would-be monopolists without need or justification. We think it plain that the technical requirements of contract doctrine must give way before the demands of the public interest in the typical situation involving the negotiation of a license after a patent has issued.[15]

Appellate courts in the US have followed *Lear's* holdings in cases involving no challenge clauses in the ensuing decades, and with varying results [6: 235–41]. The US Court of Appeals for the Federal Circuit, unsurprisingly, has taken a pro-patentee stance and allowed these clauses to be enforced under most circumstances.[16] Meanwhile, other circuits have tended to take a more conservative approach.[17] One of the key factors in the analysis is the type of agreement that incorporates the no

---

[13] Ibid. 15.

[14] Kinsman v Parkhurst, 59 U.S. 289 (1855).

[15] Lear, 395 U.S. at 670–71.

[16] Baseload Energy, Inc. v. Roberts, 619 F.3d 1357 (Fed. Cir. 2010); Flex-Foot v. CRP, 238 F.3d 1362 (Fed. Cir. 2001).

[17] Bendix Corp. v Balax, Inc., 421 F.2d 809 (7th Cir. 1970); Massillon-Cleveland-Akron Sign Co. v. Golden State Advertising Co., 444 F.2d 425 (9th Cir. 1971); Warner-Jenkinson Co. v. Allied Chemical Corp., 567 F.2d 184 (1977).

challenge clause. Courts have consistently taken a hostile attitude toward no challenge clauses found in licensing agreements.[18]

For example, in a relatively recent case, the US Court of Appeals for the Second Circuit refused to enforce a no challenge clause in a settlement agreement that was consummated before the initiation of litigation.[19] While acknowledging that "the important policy interests [favouring] the settlement of litigation *may* support a different rule with respect to no-challenge clauses in settlements entered into after the initiation of litigation,"[20] the court held that "enforcing no-challenge clauses in pre-litigation settlements would significantly undermine the 'public interest in discovering invalid patents.'"[21] Despite its reference to the initiation of litigation, the court drew the line of enforceability at discovery on the grounds that discovery would provide the parties a more informed basis to decide about settlement and would tend to indicate the existence of a genuine dispute over patent validity. The court noted that it would not enforce a no challenge clause entered into before discovery.[22]

The Second Circuit's view is not universally shared. One case pronounced that a no challenge clause is unenforceable across the board.[23] Directly contradictory to the Second Circuit's position, one court refused to enforce something akin to a no challenge clause agreed to after discovery.[24] Meanwhile, one other court was willing to enforce a no challenge clause entered into prior to discovery.[25]

In summary, the US approach to no challenge clauses focuses on somewhat arbitrary and tangential considerations, such as the timing of the agreement vis-à-vis discovery and neglects factors that go directly to the issue of consumer harm, such as a patentee's market power and the validity of a patent. This is perhaps understandable because the issue is one of enforceability under patent law and not legality under antitrust law, which would require a consideration of consumer harm.

10.2.3.2   The European Union

Unlike the US, the EU has analysed no challenge clauses under competition law and has generally adopted a hostile attitude toward them. The first EU case to feature a no challenge clause was *Windsurfing International v. Commission*.[26] In this case, the Court of Justice of the European Union (CJEU) condemned the clause at issue without examining its competitive effects, practically deeming it to be a restriction by object. The Court declared that "the public interest in ensuring an essentially free

---

[18] Bendix, 421 F2d 809; Massillon-Cleveland-Akron, 444 F2d 425; Speakeasy, 685 F3d 163.

[19] Speakeasy, 685 F3d 163.

[20] Ibid. 172.

[21] Ibid.

[22] Ibid.

[23] Massillon-Cleveland-Akron, 444 F.2d at 427.

[24] Warner-Jenkinson, 567 F.2d at 188.

[25] Baseload Energy, 619 F.3d 1357.

[26] Case C-193/83 Windsurfing International, Inc. v. Commission, 1986 ECR 611.

system of competition and therefore in the removal of a monopoly perhaps wrongly granted to the licensor must prevail over any other considerations".[27]

The CJEU toned down somewhat its hostility in *Bayer v. Süllhöfer*. In this case, the Court refused to consider these clauses as a restriction of competition by object under Article 101 (1) and instructed that "the legal and economic context" must be considered when assessing their legality.[28] Contrary to the position in the US, the CJEU held that the type of agreement in which a no challenge clause is found is irrelevant to the question of legality.[29] This different position can be attributed to the disparity between a determination of enforceability under patent law as opposed to competition law analysis. Instead, the CJEU specified two safe harbours for no challenge clauses: (1) when the license is royalty-free, which implies that the licensee suffers no competitive disadvantage from having to make royalty payments, and (2) "when the licence relates to a technically outdated process which the licensee undertaking did not use".[30]

It is didactic to also consider the European Commission's enforcement policy regarding no challenge clauses, which is arguably as important as the case law for understanding the EU position on these clauses. The Commission issued the most recent set of Technology Transfer Block Exemption Regulation (TTBER) and the accompanying guidelines in 2014. The TTBER continues to consider no challenge clauses an excluded restriction, which excludes them from the block exemption. Their legality must be assessed individually. The Guidelines state that no challenge clauses are likely to infringe Article 101(1) and unlikely to be exempted under Article 101(3) where the technology is valuable and gives a licensee a competitive advantage.[31] The Guidelines also adopt the two safe harbours enumerated in *Bayer v. Süllhöfer*.

Furthermore, the Commission amended its position on no challenge clauses in settlement agreements, acknowledging that these clauses could be restrictive of competition under some circumstances.[32] This is consistent with the Commission's approach in the *Motorola Mobility* case, in which the Commission invalidated a termination-upon-challenge clause found in a settlement agreement between Motorola and Apple on the grounds that the clause discourages Apple and other licensees from initiating validity challenges against Motorola's standard-essential patents.[33] The incidental effect of the clause is an increase in the licensees' production costs, which could be passed on to consumers.[34]

---

[27] Ibid. 664.

[28] Case 65/86, Bayer AG v. Süllhöfer, 1988 ECR 5249, 5286.

[29] Ibid.

[30] Ibid.

[31] Guidelines on the Application of Article 101 of the Treaty on the Functioning of the European Union to Technology Transfer Agreements (TTBER Guidelines), 2015 O.J. C89/3, para. 134.

[32] Ibid. art. 243.

[33] Case at 39,985-Motorola-Enforcement of GPRS Standard-Essential Patents (EC) 1/2003 of Apr. 29, 2014, art. 7, 2, http://ec.europa.eu/competition/antitrust/cases/dec-docs/39985/39985_92816.pdf.

[34] Ibid. 67–68.

10.3 Licensing in the Pharmaceutical Industry

10.3.1 Overview

Pharmaceutical companies have traditionally tended to handle the entire lifecycle of product development in-house, from R&D to commercialisation. Although many multinational pharmaceutical giants continue to do so, it has become increasingly common for some pharmaceutical companies to engage in what is known as out-licensing [7], whereby a pharmaceutical company, having developed a product, "tasks an external business partner to help bring the product to the intended markets" [8]. Out-licensing is to be distinguished from in-licensing, under which a pharmaceutical company licenses a potential drug candidate from a research institution or a biotech company for further product development [8]. Out-licensing agreements are akin to the kind of technology licensing agreements that one often sees in other industries where a technology owner not best-positioned to commercialise the technology outsources commercialisation to an external party. In 2015, the overall licensing deal value in the industry exceeded USD 46.2 billion across the globe [8].

A number of reasons have been given for a pharmaceutical company to engage in out-licensing, including budget limitation, lack of familiarity with the local market, and maximisation of portfolio growth [8]. A local partner may be particularly valuable due to its close relations with the local medical authorities [9: 331]. Regarding the maximisation of portfolio growth, the argument is that a branded manufacturer may have a large portfolio and may not have the capability to promote all the products in its portfolio effectively [8]. Through out-licensing, the manufacturer can engage a business partner to promote certain products, which may in turn allow the licensor to focus on its core and most profitable products.

For example, in March 2021, GlaxoSmithKline (GSK) signed a 3-year out-licensing agreement with Boston Pharmaceuticals (hereinafter called Boston Pharma) regarding several pre-Phase II drugs, including one for cancer treatment and one for a central nervous system disorder. Under the agreement, Boston Pharma will pursue a number of drug candidates through proof-of-concept studies, and then GSK has the option to reacquire the drug candidates for further development and commercialisation worldwide under pre-agreed terms [10, 11]. If GSK chooses not to reacquire the drug candidates, Boston Pharma will be allowed to continue with product development and will pay royalty to GSK [10, 11]. This example shows that licensing need not happen only when a product has been fully developed. It is possible to resort to licensing to outsource part of the product development to a development partner.

Aside from out-licensing and in-licensing agreements, two other kinds of licensing agreements are also found in the pharmaceutical industry. These are co-promotion and co-marketing agreements [9: 333–335]. Under a co-promotion agreement, "two pharmaceutical firms (one, the holder of an exploitation license for a substance acquired from another laboratory, the other, usually the creator of the drug) launch on the market a single product, under the same brand, with the same price, and a single marketing strategy" [9: 333]. The product is produced by one firm, but promoted and sold by two or more companies under the agreement. The promotion partner hence contributes its salesforce to another pharmaceutical company's product.

The main reason for drug developers to enter into such an agreement is to leverage the existing sales network of another pharmaceutical company [9: 334]. A firm may have developed a highly promising drug, but may lack the sales network to promote the drug effectively. Building a new sales network from scratch can be extremely time-consuming and costly. The firm may not have a sufficient pipeline of products to justify such an investment. In this case, it may choose to partner with another firm that already owns an established sales network.

Under a co-marketing agreement, "two (or more) pharmaceutical laboratories launch the same medicine (the same formula, galenic form, the same dose, the same administrative file) in the market, but under two different commercial names" [9: 334]. Patients or even doctors are often unaware that products sold under such an agreement are the same product under different brand names [9: 334]. These agreements began to emerge in the early 1980s and were most often found in nascent markets and for products with high prices and high growth potential [9: 335].

There are reasons to believe that no challenge clauses are unlikely to be an issue in co-promotion and co-marketing agreements. The economic interests of the licensor and the licensee under both types of agreement are aligned as far as patent validity is concerned. The revenue share of the licensee under a co-promotion agreement will be higher when the drug remains patented, which allows the product to command a higher price. A licensee under a co-marketing agreement likewise would have scant incentives to invalidate the patent as doing so would effectively open the market to more competitors, hence lowering the profit for all the parties involved in the agreement. If licensees under these agreements have no economic incentives to bring validity challenges, no challenge clauses will be largely redundant. Meanwhile, no challenge clauses are more likely to be found in an out-licensing agreement. A licensee in such an agreement stands to gain significantly from patent invalidation, especially if it acquires unique know-how or expertise in the development process that will offer it a competitive advantage over future rivals after the patent has been declared invalid.

10.3.2 The Pharmaceutical Industry in Japan

Japan remains one of the more important markets for pharmaceutical companies worldwide, although its share of global revenue has exhibited a steady decline from 11.7% in 2012 to 7.2% in 2019.[35] This is perhaps somewhat surprising given that the country has one of the greyest populations in the world. This is to be contrasted

---

[35] Distribution of global pharmaceutical market revenue from 2010 to 2019, by region (2021) Statista, Hamburg. https://www.statista.com/statistics/275535/distribution-of-global-pharmaceutical-market-revenue/. Accessed 10 June 2021.

with North America, including both the US and Canada, which accounted for close to half of the global pharmaceutical revenue in 2019. Nonetheless, Japan is the second-largest market for pharmaceuticals worldwide after the US [12].

Although Japanese pharmaceutical companies are probably not as globally renowned as household names in automobile and consumer electronics such as Toyota and Sony, Japan has a vibrant pharmaceutical industry. The largest Japanese pharmaceutical companies include Takeda, Daiichi Sankyo, Chugai, Astellas, Otsuka, and Mitsubishi Tanabe [13]. Foreign pharmaceutical companies also have a strong presence in Japan, with Pfizer, MSD, GSK, and Novartis among the top 10 largest pharmaceutical companies in the country in 2019 based on sales figures [13].

Japan has substantial pharmaceutical manufacturing capacity to match the size of its domestic market. There were a total of 164 drug manufacturing plants with a production value of over JPY 1 billion (approximately USD 10 million) in the country in 2019.[36] Total production in 2019 exceeded JPY 9.5 trillion (approximately USD 87 billion). The country seems to be relatively self-reliant in terms of its drug needs; most of its drug consumption is met by domestic production. Total import in 2019 was JPY 2.8 trillion (approximately USD 26 billion). Furthermore, Japan seems to export only a small proportion of its domestic production. Total drug export in 2019 amounted to JPY 442.5 billion (approximately USD 4 billion), or less than 5% of domestic production. Similar to most other OECD countries, a very high percentage of drug consumption is accounted for by generics. As of September 2020, 78.2% of prescription drugs in Japan by volume consisted of generics.[37]

The Japanese pharmaceutical industry is very active in R&D. In 2019, Japanese pharmaceutical companies spent a total of around JPY 1.3 trillion (approximately USD 12 billion) on R&D in total.[38] The top two leading investors in R&D that year were Takeda, with a spending of JPY 492.4 billion (approximately USD 4.5 billion), and Otsuka, with an R&D spending of JPY 224.2 billion (approximately USD 2 billion). The significant R&D expenditure resulted in a considerable number of patents. About 13,500 patents were granted in the pharmaceutical industry in Japan in 2019.[39] About 4500 of these were used in in-house production, and about 9000 of them were either left idle or licensed to third parties.[40] The utilisation rate of the

---

[36] Number of medical drug manufacturing plants in Japan in 2019, by production value (2021) Statista, Hamburg. https://www.statista.com/statistics/1223235/japan-number-drug-manufacturing-plants-by-production-value/. Accessed 10 June 2021.

[37] Volume share of generics in the prescription drug market in Japan from 2005 to 2020 (2021) Statista, Hamburg. https://www.statista.com/statistics/799622/japan-generics-market-volume-share/. Accessed 10 June 2021.

[38] Research and development (R&D) expenditures in the pharmaceutical manufacturing industry in Japan from fiscal year 2015 to 2019 (2021) Statista, Hamburg. https://www.statista.com/statistics/1108205/japan-research-and-development-expenses-pharmaceutical-industry/. Accessed 10 June 2021.

[39] Number of patents owned in the pharmaceutical industry in Japan in 2019, by type (2021) Statista, Hamburg. https://www.statista.com/statistics/1118004/japan-number-patent-pharmaceutical-industry-by-type/. Accessed 10 June 2021.

[40] Ibid.

patents owned in the industry was thus around 33.6%.[41] A total of 481 new drugs were approved by the Pharmaceutical and Medical Devices Agency in Japan in the fiscal year of 2019, 155 of which were newly applied and approved.[42] New drugs refer to drugs that are clearly different from existing drugs in terms of active ingredients, administration, indication, or dosage.[43]

10.3.3 Licensing in the Pharmaceutical Industry in Japan

Before the late 1980s, wholesale distribution of drugs in Japan were controlled by domestic pharmaceutical companies [14: 4]. Foreign pharmaceutical companies thus needed to collaborate with their Japanese counterparts in order to access the Japanese market [15]. It was noted that "most American and European companies were content to remain second-tier players via licensing agreements in a country whose investment laws and economic prospects neither pleased nor welcomed them" [15]. In-licensing by foreign companies to Japanese pharmaceutical companies was hence common.

This scenario began to change when distribution channels were gradually opened to foreign companies. By 2014, an executive in a Japanese pharmaceutical company noted that it was becoming impossible for Japanese companies to obtain licenses from foreign drug makers [14: 4]. These drug makers could now market their drugs directly to the Japanese public and no longer needed Japanese pharmaceutical companies as intermediaries. Having said that, in-licensing remains relatively prevalent in the Japanese pharmaceutical sector.

Out-licensing is said to be relatively rare in Japan before the 1970s as the Japanese pharmaceutical industry did not produce many novel drugs. The industry was not known for its innovation at that time due to a conscious decision to opt for "a business strategy aimed at developing numerous products requiring modest levels of innovation" [15]. The first notable out-licensing agreement signed by a Japanese pharmaceutical company was that by Fujisawa to Lilly regarding cefazolin, "the first injectable cephem that became the leading cephem worldwide in the 1970s" [15]. This out-licensing deal was met with immediate success "as Japan delivered a flow of important antibacterial innovations that they proceeded to commercialise at home and to license throughout the world" [15].

Increased competition from foreign pharmaceutical companies in what hitherto had been a relatively protected market spurred Japanese pharmaceutical companies to

---

[41] Ibid.

[42] Number of new drugs approved by the Pharmaceuticals and Medical Devices Agency (PMDA) in Japan from fiscal year 2014 to 2019 (2021) Statista, Hamburg. https://www.statista.com/statistics/1118447/japan-pmda-approved-new-medicines/. Accessed 10 June 2021.

[43] Ibid.

invest in R&D. New research facilities were built at a rapid pace, and Japanese pharmaceutical companies were catching up with their European and American counterparts in terms of patents received and new drugs approved [15]. With increased innovation by Japanese pharmaceutical companies, out-licensing became an increasingly important part of the competitive landscape. However, with its emphasis on incremental innovation, the Japanese pharmaceutical sector still lags behind its European and American counterparts in terms of breakthrough R&D [12].

Licensing is an important part of the business for Japanese pharmaceutical companies. Companies such as Otsuka place significant emphasis on their licensing activities [16]. A notable in-licensing agreement was that from the Korean company Kolon Life Science to Mitsubishi Tanabe involving Invossa, "the world's first cell-mediated gene therapy for the treatment of a long-acting growth hormone for the treatment of degenerative osteoarthritis" [17]. Another in-licensing agreement was that between the Swedish pharmaceutical company Gambro AB and Shimizu Pharmaceutical in Japan to promote the former's dialysis products in the Japanese market [17]. A notable out-licensing agreement was that from Nitto Denko to Bristol-Myers Squibb regarding "a small interfering RNA (siRNA) molecule targeting heat shock protein 47 in Phase 1b development for the treatment of nonalcoholic steatohepatitis (NASH)" [17]. A further example was Taiho Pharmaceutical out-licensing agreement for Lonsurf/TAS-102 (trifluridine and tipiracil hydrochloride) with Servier for development and commercialisation of the drug in Europe [10, 11].

Nishimura et al. [18: 4] report that there were 347 out-licensing agreements and 604 in-licensing agreements involving 54 Japanese pharmaceutical companies between 1997 and 2007. Their figures lend support to the notion that, despite increased innovation since the 1980s, Japanese pharmaceutical companies remain more likely to be recipients of in-licenses from foreign pharmaceutical companies for the purpose of product marketing in the domestic market. Unfortunately, the data set collected by Nishimura et al. does not distinguish the counterpart in the licensing agreement based on nationality. It is thus impossible to conclude how many of the in-licensing agreements are entered into for the purpose of introducing a foreign drug into the domestic market. In a later paper by two of the three authors, there is a slightly different data set that sets out the identity of the licensing partner. Their data indicate that roughly half of the partners in in-licensing agreements are foreign [19: 1255]. This suggests that a substantial number of in-licensing agreements may have been entered into to introduce a new drug into the domestic market.

Nishimura et al.'s study provides some important insights into the main drivers for Japanese pharmaceutical companies to engage in licensing activities. Their findings are consistent with what one would expect. They divide the lifecycle of drug product development into four stages: (1) drug discovery, (2) early development, (3) late development, and (4) marketing [18: 4]. They find that companies with fewer drug candidates in the late development and marketing stages are more likely to accept in-licenses at various stages of drug development. Conversely, a company with a richer pipeline of drug candidates in various stages of development is more likely to engage in out-licensing [18: 4]. They also find that larger companies as measured by sales are more likely to license in external drug candidates and less likely to license out candidates in their own pipelines [18: 15, 18]. The authors postulate that these companies have a lower propensity to out-license due to the rent dissipation effect, which holds that an out-licensor may lose revenue from out-licensing due to increased competition from the out-licensee [18: 15].

In-licensing and out-licensing agreements may need to be distinguished from the perspective of no challenge clauses. In an out-licensing agreement, a Japanese pharmaceutical company will be the licensor licensing its technology to another company, often overseas, for the commercialisation of its products. Conversely, in an in-licensing agreement, the Japanese company will be the licensee receiving a licensed technology from another pharmaceutical company, again, often overseas. When a Japanese pharmaceutical company imposes a no challenge clause in an out-licensing agreement with an overseas counterpart, the harm caused by such a clause will most likely be felt by overseas consumers. But when a no challenge clause is incorporated in an in-licensing agreement between a foreign and a Japanese phar-maceutical company, the domestic company is most often going to be the licensee. Given that many in-licensing agreements still seem to be mainly driven by a desire to break into the Japanese market, the consumers affected by such agreements will be domestic and a no challenge clause in an in-licensing agreement will be much more relevant from the perspective of the JFTC and the AMA.

10.4   Some Theoretical Issues

After introducing the state of the law on no challenge clauses in Japan and exam-ining the landscape of licensing activities in the Japanese pharmaceutical sector, the remainder of this chapter focuses on three theoretical issues that have arisen in competition law analysis of no challenge clauses. These are (1) the role of market power, (2) the role of patent validity, and (3) the relevance of the number of patents being licensed. As it turns out, the likelihood of consumer harm of a no challenge clause may vary depending on the number of patents covered by it. The use of no challenge clauses in portfolio licensing, which is common in the ICT industry, would be less likely to cause consumer harm than when these clauses are applied to a single or a small number of patents.

Before we explore these theoretical issues and their implications for pharma-ceutical licensing in Japan, we must first address an important question: should no challenge clauses be regulated under the AMA at all? Recall that these clauses are currently not regulated under US antitrust law and are dealt with as a matter of enforceability under patent law. In contrast, they have been held to be illegal under EU competition law under some circumstances and continue to be deemed an excluded restriction under the 2014 TTBER.

Commentators who have written about the issue under US law have tended to agree that these clauses should be within the purview of US antitrust law. This author [5: 507] has argued that no challenge clauses should be subject to a Rule of Reason analysis. Gal and Miller [20: 1528] go one step further and assert that these clauses should be presumptively illegal. The signpost for deciding whether a business practice should be subject to competition law scrutiny should be whether the conduct is capable of consumer harm. Given that the paramount, and in the US the exclusive, objective of competition law is the protection of consumer welfare, it should be uncontroversial that competition law should play a role when consumer welfare is implicated. It would require an extraordinary justification to argue against competition law regulation of a business practice that evidently has the potential to harm consumer welfare. This author so far has seen no persuasive justification against competition law intervention. While the appropriate legal framework remains to be determined, there would seem to be no sound basis upon which to exempt no challenge clauses categorically from competition law scrutiny.

10.4.1 The Role of Market Power

The first issue to be determined in designing the appropriate legal rule for no challenge clauses is whether proof of market power should be required. Put somewhat differently, the question is whether a rule of reason type analysis or a presumptive illegality or perhaps even per se illegality approach should be applied. The former requires proof of market power while the latter two do not.

No challenge clauses cause consumer harm when consumers are forced to pay supra-competitive prices for a patented technology or product even though the underlying patent is invalid. A patent, however, does not necessarily translate into supra-competitive prices. A patented technology or product would only be able to command such prices if it faces no reasonably close substitutes [5: 477]. In other words, the technology or product must possess some market power. The pricing power of a technology or product would be constrained by substitutes even if it is patented as patent protection does not necessarily preclude substitutes. This harkens back to the ruling in the *Illinois Tool Works* case decided by the US Supreme Court that the possession of a patent does not create a presumption of market power, which needs to be proved independently with facts from the market.[44]

Even though the foregoing would seem to suggest that a rule of reason type analysis would apply, the fact that consumer harm of a no challenge clause is premised on market power has not completely disposed of the issue of the appropriate legal rule for these clauses. Gal and Miller [20: 1528] concede that market power is a prerequisite for consumer harm of a no challenge clause. That concession, however, has not stopped them from proposing a rule of presumptive illegality for these clauses [20: 1528]. They make two arguments for this. The first one is that there is a lack of pro-competitive justifications for these clauses [20: 1529]. The extent to which this is true crucially depends on the validity of the underlying patent. If the underlying patent is invalid, a no challenge clause prevents the removal of an invalid patent and may cause consumer harm when accompanied by market power. If the underlying

---

[44] Illinois Tool Works, Inc. v. Independent Ink, Inc., 547 U.S. 28, 31 (2006).

patent is valid, however, the only consequence of a no challenge clause is to minimise unnecessary and wasteful litigation expenses [5: 503]. This will be further elaborated in the next section on the role of patent validity in the legal analysis of no challenge clauses.

The second argument is that there is no satisfactory temporal reference point for measuring market power [20: 1528]. On the one hand, measuring market power ex ante when the licensing agreement is signed would not make sense because many licensing agreements are signed before the product is commercialised and is put to test in the market [20: 1528]. This means that "these agreements have the potential to create significant anticompetitive effects even though it is often not clear at the time they are signed whether this potential will indeed be [realised]" [20: 1528]. On the other hand, assessing market power ex post when the patent has acquired market power would be equally problematic. Ex post assessment "adds to the uncertainty of the parties—most importantly the licensee—as to whether the clause is legal and to the potential costs of bringing a patent challenge" [20: 1528–1529]. A further argument is that deferring the assessment of market power may create uncertainty for the licensor who may, in good faith, believe that her technology or product is unlikely to possess or acquire market power and hence the no challenge clause should not cause consumer harm.

Gal and Miller [20: 1529] have not offered any persuasive argument as to why this uncertainty should be resolved in favour of the licensee-challenger as opposed to the patentee. They merely note that an ex post assessment "might directly frustrate our goal of increasing challenges of unwarranted patents." This, however, presumes that a majority or at least a significant number of the underlying patents are invalid. While some studies have suggested that this may be the case [21: 205], whether these studies provide a sufficient basis for what effectively amounts to a presumption of market power remains unclear. The establishment of market power in a rule of reason case is never easy; many rule of reason cases stumble at this hurdle. This, however, does not lend support for the abolition of the market power requirement in rule of reason cases in general. Given the consensus that market power is required for a no challenge clause to cause consumer harm, it would be quite extraordinary to excuse the plaintiff from the burden to prove market power simply because of the uncertainty regarding and difficulty to furnish such proof. By that same logic, the recoupment requirement in a predatory pricing claim under the US case of *Brooke Group* would be a prime candidate for abolition.[45]

A full exposition of the treatment of market power in a no challenge clause claim is beyond the scope of this chapter. Suffice it to note that the same argument raised by Gal and Miller can equally arise in a resale price maintenance (RPM) case. Under *Leegin*, most US courts have come to treat proof of market power as a threshold issue in an RPM case.[46] The kind of uncertainty due to changes in market dynamics highlighted by Gal and Miller can similarly arise in an RPM case where the manufacturer may not have possessed market power when the RPM scheme was first introduced

---

[45] Brooke Group Ltd. v. Brown & Williamson Tobacco Corp., 509 U.S. 209 (1993).

[46] Toledo Mack Sales & Service, Inc. v. Mack Trucks, Inc., 530 F.3d 204 (3d Cir. 2008).

but may subsequently acquire such power. To the best of the author's knowledge, no one has argued that RPM should be treated as presumptively illegal because of this uncertainty, although this author has previously argued that there may be other valid reasons for treating RPM as presumptively illegal [22]. Changes in market conditions could happen in every competition law case, and the possibility of such changes alone cannot justify foregoing a market power requirement altogether. If a hitherto lawful no challenge clause becomes illegal due to changes in market conditions, it should be incumbent upon the licensor to reassess her licensing practices and rescind the no challenge clause as appropriate.

Elimination of a market power requirement can only be justified if there are special reasons why the defendant should be entitled to rely on her ex ante judgment of market conditions and should not be held accountable for subsequent emergence of market power. If it is believed that the licensor deserves special protection from liability based on her ex ante good faith determination of her market position, the most that this justifies is an affirmative defence. The licensor can be excused from liability if she can demonstrate that at the time of the licensing agreement, she has made a good faith assessment that her technology or product does not possess market power and that it is reasonable for her not to be aware of the changes in market circumstances that may have since given her such power.

The foregoing discussion of the role of market power in the legal analysis of no challenge clauses is consistent with the position adopted by the JFTC in the IPR Guidelines. Under these Guidelines, it is stipulated that these clauses would only violate the AMA if they result in lessening of free competition, which requires proof of a modicum of market power or some leading position.

10.4.2 The Role of Patent Validity

The second important issue for designing the legal rule for no challenge clauses is the role of patent validity in the analysis. As suggested previously, whether valid pro-competitive justifications are available for these clauses is contingent on the validity of the underlying patent. If the underlying patent is valid, a no challenge clause avoids otherwise wasteful litigation expenses. Patent validity is not only relevant to the question of pro-competitive justifications, but it also has a bearing on consumer harm. A no challenge clause would allow a patentee to collect undeserved supra-competitive profit if the patent is invalid [5: 476]. On the contrary, the profit would be fully justified and deserved if the patent is valid. It is part of the implicit bargain of the patent system that an innovator should enjoy exclusivity, which may result in supra-competitive profit, for an invention that is novel, non-obvious and useful in the US and capable of industrial application in the EU. Patent validity is hence the lynchpin of the legal analysis of no challenge clauses.

This does not mean that every commentator agrees that patent validity should be a relevant consideration in the legal analysis of no challenge clauses. Unsurprising in light of their advocacy of a presumptive illegality rule, Gal and Miller [20] believe that patent validity should be ignored. Their main justifications are that determination of patent validity would introduce unnecessary complications to the legal proceedings and pro-competitive justifications for these clauses are lacking. In the slightly different context of reverse payment settlements, the US Supreme Court[47] and some prominent commentators [23: 289] have similarly argued that patent validity should be disregarded in the analysis of reverse payment settlements. Gal and Miller [20: 1529] themselves rely on the analogy between no challenge clauses and reverse payment settlements to bolster their argument.

This analogy between no challenge clauses and reverse payment settlements is not entirely apt and does not support the complete disregard of patent validity in a no challenge clause case. The main reason is that there is a readily available proxy indicator of patent validity in a reverse payment case: the size of the reverse payment. The size of the reverse payment is a reflection of the patentee's subjective assessment of the strength of her patent. The stronger she believes her patent to be, the fewer reasons she has to offer a large payment to a potential infringer. The US Supreme Court acknowledged in the *Actavis* case that there is no reason for a patentee to make a large payment to the alleged infringer if she is convinced about the strength of her patent.[48] An unusually large payment by the patentee to the potential infringer suggests that the patentee is keen to see off a validity challenge, indicating a lack of confidence in the validity of the patent.

No such proxy indicator exists in a no challenge clause case. In a no challenge clause case, the licensee pays a royalty to the licensor, which is the direction of payment that one would expect in a patent licensing agreement, as opposed to the reverse direction, which gives rise to the term reverse payment. The fact that the licensee makes royalty payments to the licensor does not eliminate the possibility of an implicit value transfer from the licensor to the licensee. The licensor may have offered an implicit discount to the licensee to induce the latter to accept the no challenge clause. The ascertainment of the size of the discount, however, would require a counterfactual analysis and would be highly difficult to carry out in practice. This would be especially the case when a no challenge clause is incorporated in all licensing agreements and hence a comparative analysis would be futile. There is hence no convenient proxy for patent validity in a no challenge clause case and a consideration of patent validity would seem inevitable.

A detailed exposition of the appropriate treatment of patent validity in a no challenge clause case is again beyond the scope of this chapter. This author has addressed this issue elsewhere and the full analysis will not be repeated here. Three points are worth mentioning here. First, patent invalidity is a necessary but an insufficient condition for consumer harm and hence illegality [5: 493–494]. A no challenge clause would surely be legal if the patent is valid. But it is not necessarily illegal if the patent is invalid. A no challenge clause would cause minimal consumer harm in the absence of market power. Therefore, the best way to structure the analysis would be to offer an affirmative defence based on patent validity under which the

---

[47] Federal Trade Commission v. Actavis, 570 U.S. 136, 158 (2013).

[48] Actavis, 570 U.S. at 154–55.

defendant would be absolved from liability if she could demonstrate the validity of the underlying patent.

Second, the validity of the patent should be assessed from an ex ante, rather than an ex post, perspective [5: 494]. This is consistent with the views of most commentators in the context of reverse payment settlements [5: 494]. An ex post perspective runs the risk of allowing the courts to second-guess the patentee with the benefit of hindsight after the patentee has made a good faith determination at the time of the agreement affirming patent validity [5: 494].

Third, patent validity should be assessed from an objective perspective rather than a subjective one [5: 494]. This implies that a patent would be deemed valid if a reasonable patentee would have thought so with the information at her disposal during the licensing agreement [5: 494]. This rule is sensible because relying on a subjective perspective would provide the patentee incentives to manipulate the process and produce self-serving statements to enhance her litigation position.

The foregoing analysis is consistent with the position taken by the JFTC in the IPR Guidelines that no challenge clauses can only be illegal if the underlying patent is invalid. In the absence of proxy indicators of patent validity similar to the case of reverse payment settlements, the only way to determine this is to require a direct proof of patent validity. The IPR Guidelines, however, do not specify whether patent validity is to be treated as a requisite element in the plaintiff's case or as an affirmative defence. This will need to await future enforcement action by the JFTC or court cases.

10.4.3 The Relevance of the Number of Patents Being Licensed

The final issue to address in the legal treatment of no challenge clauses is the number of patents being covered by a no challenge clause in a licensing agreement. The competitive impact of a no challenge clause can vary depending on the size of the patent portfolio being licensed. If only one or a handful of patents is licensed, the invalidation of one patent can have a significant impact on the patentee's market position. If only one patent is at issue, its invalidation would put an end to the patentee's market power, if any existed in the first place.

But if in contrast, a licensing agreement covers a large portfolio of patents, the impact of the no challenge clause may be much more attenuated. The patentee's market power may no longer emanate from one or a handful of patents. A considerable number of patents may together contribute to the patentee's market position. In this case, the invalidation of some of the patents in the portfolio may not materially alter the patentee's market position [24]. Therefore, it may be justified to have, in place, a general rule that no challenge clauses are presumptively legal if they apply to a sufficiently large patent portfolio. Nevertheless, this presumption should not apply if a small number of the patents in the portfolio are responsible for the patentee's market power and the remainder of the portfolio can be invented around or licensed from elsewhere. In this case, the invalidation of that small number of patents may alter the patentee's market position and may make a material difference in the incidence of consumer harm. The no challenge clause should be subject to meaningful scrutiny under competition law.

This consideration is likely to be less relevant in the context of the pharmaceutical industry, where licensing often only covers a small number of patents. Pharmaceutical products are different from those in the ICT industry, which typically involves hundreds if not thousands of patents [25: 1590–1591]. Meanwhile, a drug is often covered by a small number of patents [25: 1590–1591]. Therefore, the invalidation of a patent in a pharmaceutical licensing agreement will be likely to have a material impact on the licensor's market position and may significantly alter the incidence of consumer harm. The presumption of legality for a no challenge clause in the context of portfolio licensing has relatively little application in the pharmaceutical industry.

10.5 Conclusion

Evidence suggests that no challenge clauses seem to be prevalent in Japan, at least in the ICT industry. Yet enforcement experience against these clauses by the JFTC is relatively limited. These findings suggest that both market power and patent validity are critical considerations in the legal analysis of no challenge clauses. Patent validity can be incorporated as an affirmative defence in the legal framework, and market power should be a required element in a plaintiff's case. As much as the AMA's position on these clauses can be gleaned from the JFTC's IPR Guidelines, under which no challenge clauses are only illegal if the underlying patent is invalid and there is lessening of free competition, it seems that the position is consistent with the foregoing theoretical analysis. Japan may in fact have the theoretically soundest approach to no challenge clauses among all the major jurisdictions.

References

1. Orstavik, I. B. (2005). Grantbacks and no challenge clauses in the new EC technology transfer regulation. *International Review of Intellectual Property and Competition Law, 36*(83–112), 87.
2. Miller, A. D., & Gal, M. S. (2015). Licensee patent challenges. *Yale Journal on Regulation, 32*(121–160), 127.
3. Mitsubishi Research Institute Inc. (2015). Report on the research study on the relationship between the intellectual property system and competition policy, p. 2. https://www.global ipdb.inpit.go.jp/jpowp/wp-content/uploads/2015/11/1957cfd59e302225fbce87e7190c29ce. pdf. Accessed June 10, 2021.
4. Nakamura, T. (1982). Metoclopramide seizogyosha rano tokkyo ken ranyo jiken [On metoclopramide manufacturers' patent abuse case]. *Kosei Torihiki, 381,* 27–31.
5. Cheng, T. K. H. (2016). Antitrust treatment of no challenge clauses. *New York University Journal of Intellectual Property and Entertainment Law, 5*(2), 437–512

6. Taylor, C. T. (1993). No-challenge termination clauses: Incorporating innovation policy and risk allocation into patent licensing law. *Indiana Law Journal, 69*(215–254), 235–241.
7. Reepmeyer, G. (2006). *Risk-sharing in the pharmaceutical industry*. Physica-Verlag.
8. Dolinsky, P. (2021). Four reasons why pharma companies are turning to out-licensing to grow their brands. https://www.dksh.com/global-en/insights/tl-hec-pharma-companies-turning-to-outlicensing. Accessed June 10, 2021.
9. Simonet, D. (2002). Licensing agreements in the pharmaceutical industry. *International Journal of Medical Marketing, 2*(4), 329–341, 331
10. Pharmaceutical Technology. (2021). Boston pharma signs out-licensing agreement with GSL. https://www.pharmaceutical-technology.com/news/boston-out-licensing-agreement-gsk/. Accessed June 10, 2021.
11. Pharmaceutical Technology. (2021). New molecular entity in-licensing skewing later in drug lifecycle. GlobalData report. https://www.pharmaceutical-technology.com/comment/nmes-in-licensing-skewing/. Accessed June 10, 2021.
12. Mahlich, J. (2007). The Japanese pharmaceutical industry in transition: Has higher research orientation resulted in higher market value? *Asian Business & Management, 6*, 75–94.
13. Pharma Boardroom. (2021). Top 10 pharma companies in Japan. https://pharmaboardroom.com/articles/top-10-pharma-companies-in-japan/. Accessed June 10, 2021.
14. Yamasaki, M. (2014). Some new aspects of drug licensing in Japan, p. 4. http://plg-group.com/wp-content/uploads/2014/03/New-Aspects-of-Drug-Licensing-in-Japan-Motohiro-Yamasaki.pdf. Accessed June 10, 2021.
15. Neimeth, R. (1991). Japan's pharmaceutical industry postwar evolution. In: A. C. Gelijns, & E. A. Halm (Eds.), *The changing economics of medical technology*. National Academies Press. https://www.ncbi.nlm.nih.gov/books/NBK234305/. Accessed June 10, 2021.
16. Otsuka Pharmaceutical Co Ltd. (2021). Partnering/licensing activities. https://www.otsuka.co.jp/en/partnering-and-licensing/inquiry-form/form. Accessed June 10, 2021.
17. Engen, S. (2017). Japan licensing deals: A look back at 2016, and what to expect in 2017. https://www.locustwalk.com/japan-licensing-deals-a-look-back-at-2016-and-what-to-expect-in-2017-2/. Accessed June 10, 2021.
18. Nishimura, J., Okada, Y., & Takatori, T. (2009). Drug pipelines and pharmaceutical licensing. OPIR Research Paper Series No. 45, pp. 1–33, 4. http://www.jpma.or.jp/opir/en/issue/en_rs_045/paper_45.pdf. Accessed June 10, 2021.
19. Nishimura, J., & Okada, Y. (2014). R&D portfolios and pharmaceutical licensing. *Research Policy, 43*(1250–1263), 1255.
20. Gal, M. S., & Miller, A. D. (2017). Patent challenge clauses: A new antitrust offense? *Iowa Law Review, 102*(1477–1532), 1528.
21. Allison, J. R., & Lemley, M. A. (1998). Empirical evidence on the validity of litigated patents. *AIPLA Quarterly Journal, 26*(185–275), 205.
22. Cheng, T. K. H. (2017). A consumer behavioral approach to resale price maintenance. *Virginia Law and Business Review, 12*(1), 1–92.
23. Elhauge, E., & Krueger, A. (2012). Solving the patent settlement puzzle. *Texas Law Review, 91*(283–330), 289.
24. Sidak, J. G. (2016). Evading portfolio royalties for standard-essential patents through validity challenges. *World Company, 39*(2), 191–211.
25. Burk, D. L., & Lemley, M. A. (2003). Policy levers in patent law. *Virginia Law Review, 89*(1575–1696), 1590–1591.

Chapter 11
Will Authorised Biologics Deter Biosimilars?—Utilising JFTC's Expertise in Drug Pricing

Takanori Abe

Abstract In the US, the impact of authorised biologics on biosimilars is post-regulated by the competition authorities, while in Europe, pharmaceutical regulatory authorities consider competition impacts in addition to post-regulation by the competition authorities. In Japan, it is pre-regulated by the Ministry of Health, Labour and Welfare (MHLW) and the Central Social Insurance Medical Council (CSIMC), which consider competition at the point of drug price listing. Should the MHLW and CSIMC consider competition in drug pricing, it would be necessary to formulate systems to utilise the expertise of a competition expert, namely the Japan Fair Trade Commission (JFTC). When calculating the drug price of authorised biologics, reducing the cost of drugs should be prioritised over protecting the incentives for the development of biosimilars. Patient choice and the quality of healthcare should be emphasised more, taking advantage of the characteristic that the MHLW and CSIMC, who are drug experts, consider competition.

Keywords Authorised biologics · Authorised generics · Biosimilar · Drug price · Competition

0.7 or 0.5: that is the question.

T. Abe (✉)
ABE & PARTNERS, Osaka, Japan
e-mail: abe@abe-law.com

Graduate School of Medicine, Osaka University, Osaka, Japan

© The Author(s) 2022
A. Negishi et al. (eds.), *Competition Law and Policy in the Japanese Pharmaceutical Sector*, Kobe University Monograph Series in Social Science Research,
https://doi.org/10.1007/978-981-16-7814-1_11

11.1   Issue: Report of the Japan Biosimilar Association

On 16 May 2017, the Japan Biosimilar Association submitted a report titled 'The Impact of Authorised Biologics (provisional name) on the Development and Promotion of Biosimilars (Report)' to the Director of the Economic Affairs Division, Health Policy Bureau, MHLW.[1]

It reports as follows: 'Authorised biologics significantly impact the R&D and penetration of biosimilars and may ultimately hinder further development of the whole industry of biological medicinal products'. It continues that 'If authorised biologics, considered identical to originator medicinal products, are authorised while biosimilars have not yet progressed their wide understanding and penetration, such authorisation will have a serious impact on the penetration of biosimilars, which may lead to a loss of growth opportunities not only for biosimilars but also for the entire biologics industry, which may lead to stagnation of innovation. As a result, these impacts will negatively affect the public because of dependence on foreign countries for the stable supply of biological medicinal products, persistently high prices of medicines, and lack of progress as a whole in improving patient access to treatments with biological medicinal products'.

A biological medicinal product is a drug whose active ingredient is derived from proteins such as growth hormone, insulin, and antibodies.[2] In the field of biological medicinal products, generic biological medicinal products are called biosimilars, in contrast with originator biological medicinal products. While generic biological medicinal products are not identical to the originator biological medicinal product, they have been confirmed with clinical trials, etc. to have equivalent/homogeneous quality, safety, and effectiveness.[3]

On the other hand, while authorised generics (AGs) are not clearly defined, the term generally refers to generics that share not only active ingredients, but also APIs, additives, and manufacturing methods, etc. with the originator medicinal products. These are called 'authorised biologics' in biological medicinal products.[4] The name 'authorised generics' means they are marketed by the subsidiaries of originator companies or by generic industry companies under the authorisation of the originator companies.[5] AGs are characterised by the fact that, for physicians and patients, they have more similarities to originator medicinal products than generics,

---

[1] *Bio kozokuhin no kaihatsu sokushin ni taisuru bio AG (kashou) ga ataeru eikyou ni tsuite [The Impact of Authorised Biologics (provisional name) on the Development and Promotion of Biosimilars (Report)],* The Japan Biosimilar Association (16 May 2017).

[2] *Bio iyakuhin to biosimilar (bio kozokuhin) ni kansuru Q&A [Q & A on biological medicinal products and biosimilars],* The Japan Pharmaceutical Manufacturers Association, *available at* http://www.jpma.or.jp/medicine/bio/pdf/bio_03.pdf, last visited 7 February 2021.

[3] *Yaku-1 Jiki yakkaseido kaiaku ni mukete (4) [Yaku-1 The next Reform of the Drug Price System No.4]* The Drug Price Special Committee, CSIMC, MHLW at 41 (23 October 2019), *available at* https://www.mhlw.go.jp/content/12404000/000559485.pdf.

[4] *Id.* at 46.

[5] *Id.*

and AG companies may be able to sell AGs earlier than generics.[6] To secure market share, even if a generic competitor enters the market after the patent rights to the originator medicinal product expires, originator companies can take early advantage in the generic drug market by launching AGs before the patent right expires.

As they will be sold before the patent right expires, AGs will be launched if they are judged to be generally advantageous, even when they may cause the cannibalisation of originator medicinal products. Under the current Japanese drug price regulation system, generics are defined by the fact that their already listed products (originator medicinal products) sharing the APIs have finished the re-examination period, and they are marketed by different companies from their originator medicinal products. Since the definition of generics does not consider contractual relationships with the originator companies and differences in APIs, additives, and manufacturing methods, etc., AGs are treated as equivalent to generics in the drug pricing system.[7]

Is the concern of the Japan Biosimilar Association reasonable? How should we consider the impact of authorised biologics on biosimilars from the perspective of competition policy and health policy? The same issues have already been discussed in the US and Europe on AGs of small molecule products and authorised biologics, and some of their competition authorities or pharmaceutical regulatory authorities have expressed their views. This article first surveys the US and European situations, and then the Japanese situation to identify implications for Japan.

In addition to the difference in the names used to describe authorised biologics between countries, each country also has no consistent naming convention, causing confusion. Both the Central Social Insurance Medical Council (CSIMC)[8] and European Commission[9] stated the necessity of having a consistent name. In this article, 'authorised biologics' is used in principle for the US and Europe as well as Japan, and if different names are given in citations, it will be noted as such.

---

[6] *Id.*

[7] *Id.*

[8] At the Drug Price Special Committee of the CSIMC on 27 March 2019, the Chairman Hiroshi Nakamura stated the following: 'Today, I am very concerned that biosimilars are so-called follow-on biologics, and biosames are so-called generic biological medicinal products. Since documents include both follow-on biologics and generic biological medicinal products with a different "generic" position, it may cause confusion. I believe that each committee member had a very appropriate discussion about biosames and biosimilars today, but in future, to avoid confusion, we should discuss their name not only at this CSIMC but also at other places'. *Chuou shakai hoken iryo kyougikai yakka senmonbukai dai 151 kai gijiroku [No. 151 meeting minutes of The Drug Price Special Committee of the CSIMC]*, (27 March 2019), *available at* https://www.mhlw.go.jp/stf/shingi2/0000203254_00007.html, last visited 7 February 2021.

[9] *Duplicate marketing authorisations for biological medicinal products*, European Commission Health and Food Safety Directorate-General Pharmaceutical Committee (Nov. 7, 2019) *available at* https://ec.europa.eu/health/sites/health/files/files/committee/pharm780_duplicates_en.pdf. Here, it is stated that terms such as 'autobiologicals', 'biosimilars', 'biogenerics', 'autobiosimilars', 'autogeneric', 'bioidentical', 'biosimilar generics', etc. are used, which causes confusion.

11.2   The US[10]

Under the Hatch–Waxman Amendments[11] in the US, the first generic filing for paragraph IV of the Abbreviated New Drug Application (the 'first-filer') was granted
180-day exclusivity after launching its product. During this period, because of the
absence of competition with other generic companies, both the generic drug price and
the first-filer's revenues were significantly higher than they would have been when
there were additional generic competitors. In contrast, competition from AGs during
the 180-day exclusivity period has the potential to reduce both generic drug prices
and generic firm revenues. The courts have ruled that the 180-day exclusivity does
not preclude an originator company (brand-name company) from entering with its
own generic.[12] Therefore, originator companies frequently launch AGs to compete
with first-filers.

Thus, AGs have been the subject of controversy. Originator companies that offer
AGs contend that they are pro-competitive, namely that they make valuable products
available to consumers at lower prices than those of originator medicinal products
and provide competition that leads to lower generic prices. In contrast, some in
the generic drug industry contend that AGs harm competition by drawing revenues
away from first-filers during the 180-day exclusivity period and discourage generic
firms from challenging the patents of originator companies, thereby undermining
competition in the long run and the goals of the Hatch–Waxman Amendments.

Under these circumstances, Congress requested studies on the competitive effects
of AGs. Senators Leahy, Grassley, and Rockefeller commented that if the generic
industry were to be less incentivised to produce generic drugs to compete with originator drugs, possibly, fewer generic drugs would come to the market and the prices for
certain drugs would remain high for consumers. In addition, Representative Waxman,
a legislative sponsor of the Hatch–Waxman Amendments, stated that in response
to the tactics used by the pharmaceutical industry to delay generic competition,
Congress closed loopholes in the Hatch–Waxman Amendments in 2003. However,
he did not believe it was a coincidence that originator companies began to exploit
the practice of AGs after the closing of those loopholes.

In 2006, at the request of members of Congress, the Federal Trade Commission
(FTC) began its own study to examine the short- and long-term competitive effects
of AGs. In 2009, the FTC issued an Interim Report[13] that focused on the short-term

---

[10] Wong and Norey [12]; *Authorized Generic Drugs: Short-Term Effects and Long-
Term Impact*, FEDERAL TRADE COMMISSION (Aug. 2011) ('FTC 2011'), *available
at* https://www.ftc.gov/sites/default/files/documents/reports/authorized-generic-drugs-short-term-
effects-and-long-term-impact-report-federal-trade-commission/authorized-generic-drugs-short-
term-effects-and-long-term-impact-report-federal-trade-commission.pdf.

[11] Drug Price Competition and Patent Term Restoration Act of 1984, Pub. L. No. 98–417, 98 Stat.
1585 (1984).

[12] Teva Pharm. Indus. Ltd. v. Crawford, 410 F.3d 51, 54 (D.C. Cir. 2005).

[13] *Authorized Generic: An Interim Report*, FEDERAL TRADE COMMISSION (June 2009) ('FTC
2009') *available at* https://www.ftc.gov/sites/default/files/documents/reports/authorized-generics-
interim-report-federal-trade-commission/p062105authorizedgenericsreport.pdf.

effects of AGs and presented an analysis suggesting that consumers benefit and the healthcare system saves money when an AG enters the market because of the greater discounting that accompanies the added competition provided by the AG. In 2011, the FTC issued its Final Report,[14] concluding that the consumer benefitted from the introduction of AGs in the market, including paying lower prices from additional competition, and that patent challenges by generics have actually increased in the relevant period. The FTC Final Report is evaluated to have concluded that AGs are pro-competitive.[15]

While this debate may have worked on the assumption that AGs would be small molecule drugs, with the passing of the Biologics Price Competition and Innovation Act (BPCIA) in 2009,[16] and a recent increase in biosimilar activity in the US, the same debate has started to enter the fledgling biosimilar space, leading commentators to ask how authorised biologics[17] might affect biosimilars. The FTC has not yet expressed its opinion on authorised biologics. The differences between small molecule products and biological medicinal products mean that the debate about AGs in small molecule products cannot be directly applied to authorised biologics. That is, small molecule generic products are created to be therapeutically equivalent to their originator counterparts. As such, originator small molecule products may be substituted at the pharmacy counter for their generic counterparts without the need to involve the prescriber.

On the other hand, because of their nature and method of manufacture, truly identical copies of biologic products by others are considered impossible. Biosimilars are highly similar to and have no clinically meaningful differences from an existing reference product (i.e. originator drug) approved by the Food and Drug Administration (FDA). However, biosimilars cannot be substituted at the pharmacy counter for originator drugs without the prescriber's involvement. Furthermore, prescribing physicians may also be reluctant to switch patients who are stable on the reference product to a new therapy. Because the market penetration for biosimilars has not been as quick as for small molecule generics, there may be little market incentive for originator companies to join the biosimilar market in the form of an authorised biologic. If a biosimilar is expected to produce the same clinical result as the reference product in any given patient, it will be approved as interchangeable by the FDA. Since this interchangeable designation brings with it the ability to substitute the biologic for an interchangeable product at the pharmacy counter without the prescriber's involvement, authorised biologics will likely be realised after the FDA approves interchangeables.[18]

---

[14] FEDERAL TRADE COMMISSION, *supra* note 10.

[15] Feldman and Frondorf [5: 523], Dechert [1].

[16] Biologics Price Competition and Innovation Act of 2009, Pub. L. 111–148, 124 Stat. 119, 804 (2010).

[17] The name 'authorised biologics' or 'branded biosimilars' is used.

[18] McGowan [7] predicts that interchangeables will not be launched until 2023.

11.3 Europe[19]

On 7 November 2019, the Pharmaceutical Committee of the Directorate-General for Health and Food Safety (DG SANTE) at the European Commission presented the following regarding duplicate marketing authorisations for biological medicinal products.[20]

Article 82(1) of the Regulation of Community procedures for the authorisation and supervision of medicinal products for human and veterinary use and establishing a European Medicines Agency (Regulation (EC) 726/2004)[21] limits cases where the applicant or who obtained approval for one medicinal product to obtain multiple approvals, that is, cases of duplicate marketing authorisations for the same medicinal product. The first subparagraph of Article 82(1) provides that only one marketing authorisation may be granted to one applicant for a specific medicinal product. The 2nd subparagraph of Article 82(1) provides that the Commission shall authorise the same applicant to submit more than one application to the Agency for that medicinal product when there are objective verifiable reasons relating to public health regarding the availability of medicinal products to healthcare professionals and/or patients, or for co-marketing reasons. The Commission assesses whether the conditions of Article 82(1) are met on a case-by-case basis to determine whether to agree to the submission of a further application for the same medicinal product. According to Annex I.1 of the 2011 Commission[22] note on the Handling of Duplicate Marketing Authorisation Applications,[23] the first introduction of a generic product by the holder of the reference medicinal product (the originator medicinal product) can also improve the availability of a medicinal product. This is because the first entry of a generic into the market impacts availability, as it usually increases accessibility. While the 2011 Commission note did not include specific considerations regarding biological products and/or biosimilars, the granting of duplicate marketing authorisations as generics in the case of biological medicinal products has raised concerns from the generic industry about the likely impact on the biosimilar market. They considered that this would affect choice and competition, undermine the EU concept of biosimilars, and ultimately may limit the range of options available to patients.

The Commission launched a targeted consultation directed at stakeholders to seek their views on the issue of granting duplicate marketing authorisations for a first generic of biological medicinal products; specifically, on the impact that such authorisations would have on the availability of biosimilars to healthcare professionals and patients. One possible consideration was that such authorisations could have anticompetitive effects and undermine other treatment options available to patients.

---

[19] *supra* note 9.

[20] The European Commission has not adopted the document.

[21] OJ L 136, 30.4.2004, p. 30.

[22] Commission Directorate-General for Health and Consumers (DG SANCO, now DG SANTE).

[23] *Handling of Duplicate Marketing Authorisation Applications*, European Commission Health and Consumers Directorate-General (October 2011) *available at* https://ec.europa.eu/health/sites/hea lth/files/files/latest_news/2011_09_duplicates_note_upd_01.pdf.

A view in favour of stricter scrutiny for authorised biologics was submitted by Member State Competent Authorities, the generics industry, a patients organisation and a healthcare professionals organisation. That is, contrary to the position with small molecule products, only originator companies can produce authorised biologics[24] for manufacturing and technological reasons. This difference is the reason authorised biologics and their biosimilar counterparts may have a de facto uneven position in the national market. As a result, differences between Member State health systems can influence market access for certain competing products, which in time may result in a negative effect on the availability of medicinal products to patients and healthcare professionals. Contrary to the position of authorised biologics, biosimilars have to invest time and money in clinical studies, which also impacts their market entry. The vast majority of EU Member States do not allow pharmacy substitution for biosimilars, whereas substitution is in principle automatically allowed for authorised biologics, resulting in a privileged position of authorised biologics compared to biosimilars from the viewpoint of pharmacy substitution. Allowing authorised biologics can reportedly affect physicians' decision-making in treatment monitoring because of misconceptions regarding the inferior therapeutic properties of biosimilars compared to authorised biologics. While authorised biologics will almost certainly be marketed at a much lower price than their reference products, biosimilars are also subject to a price decrease. The resulting situation would allow originator companies to undercut the price of biosimilars while allowing the reference originator medicinal product to maintain a high price. In tendering procedures, authorised biologics can be used as a tool to influence pricing dynamics to drastically reduce the market value for biosimilars, or the originator company would essentially be competing against itself with two of its own medicinal products. Even though the introduction of authorised biologics in the market can initially have a positive effect on availability, in the long term, they may have a negative effect on the availability of biosimilars. A stakeholder expressed the view that duplicate authorisation should lose its validity once it is proven that biosimilar alternatives exist at a sufficient quantity to adequately meet demand and that the Commission should go even further, questioning whether authorised biologics should be allowed.

A view against stricter scrutiny of authorised biologics was submitted by originator companies. That is, the first introduction of authorised biologics will increase availability for patients and healthcare professionals. Furthermore, authorised biologics can be granted with a full label without carving out any indications, which may increase availability and accessibility for a larger section of the patient population. Authorised biologics should not be treated differently from the AGs of small molecule products and should be subject to the same authorisation criteria. The Commission proposes the following change in Annex I: 'Requests for duplicate marketing authorisations need to be properly substantiated and based on sound evidence'. However, the standard applied under this wording is quite high, and the wording is unclear. Since the current logic has been established for years and was

---

[24] The wording of 'autobiologicals' is used here.

issued at a time when biological medicinal products were well known and available on the market, any change to such practice needs to be properly justified.

The feedback received from Member State Competent Authorities showed that they had no experience regarding the actual effect of duplicate authorisations for authorised biologics. In addition, although in principle, the first introduction of an authorised generic (small molecules or biologics) improves availability and reduces prices, the originator companies do not have an interest in keeping prices permanently low. Thus, an authorised biologic could be used as a vehicle to deter competing biosimilars from entering or staying on the market. Therefore, the introduction of an authorised biologic to the market can have negative effects on long-term availability.

The European Commission concluded that most arguments are made on a theoretical basis, as there is still not enough experience to draw practical conclusions on the issue. The Commission is also considering amending Annex I.1 of the 2011 Commission note along the following lines, collecting the opinions of Member States. That is, duplicate marketing authorisation is an exceptional process, and for duplicates (small molecules or biologics) requested for public health reasons, the applicant should provide specific evidence to allow the Commission to verify a positive effect on availability. The first entry of a generic into the market is not automatically considered to increase the availability.

On 5 March, 2021, the European Commission published an updated version of the 2011 Commission note on the handling of duplicate marketing authorisation applications for medicinal products.[25] The updated note states experience shows that there is no automatic link between the introduction of a duplicate marketing authorisation by the holder of the original medicinal product (be it a chemical or a biological medicinal product) and increased availability. Taking into account that duplicate marketing authorisation can only be granted exceptionally, the applicant should provide the Commission with specific evidence that demonstrates that duplicate marketing authorisation is likely to increase availability, which should be assessed on a case-by-case basis.

11.4   Japan

Regarding the AGs of small molecule products, the following remarks and proposals were given at the meeting of the Japan Society of Generic Medicines in November 2014. 'Introducing AGs as safe because they are the same as the originator medicinal product will give rise to the implication that generics to date are not safe'. The only advantage of AGs is that they can be sold several months earlier than other generics.

---

[25] *Handling of duplicate marketing authorisation applications of pharmaceutical products under Article 82(1) of Regulation (EC) No 726/2004,* European Commission (5 March 2021) *available at* https://eur-lex.europa.eu/legal-content/EN/TXT/PDF/?uri=CELEX:52021XC0305(01)& from=EN. last visited 10 May, 2021.

It is better to lower drug price of the originator medicinal products than to allow AGs.[26]

Regarding authorised biologics, on 16 May 2017, the Japan Biosimilar Association submitted a report to the Director of Economic Affairs Division, Health Policy Bureau, MHLW, stating that authorised biologics may threaten the development and penetration of biological medicinal products. It was reported that this submission responded to the situation of Kyowa Hakko Kirin. The company considered commercialising the authorised biologics of Nesp, aiming to minimise the damage caused by the expiration of its patent in 2019 protecting its mainstay therapeutic agent for renal failure Nesp (generic name: Darbepoetin Alfa). It established a new company, Kyowa Kirin Frontier, to manage Nesp's authorised biologics business[27] of Nesp on 18 January 2017.[28,29]

After the authorised biologic of Nesp was approved, the Drug Price Special Committee of the CSIMC on 27 March 2019[30] discussed whether to calculate the drug price of an authorised biologic to be 0.5 times the price of the originator medicinal product, as is the norm with generic products, or 0.7 times the price, as with biosimilars. The tentative agreement was 0.7. The committee members expressed the following opinions: 'Considering the aim to move away from the model where originator companies rely on their long-listed products, I am very concerned that the originator companies try to remain in the market through their subsidiaries'.

Furthermore, 'Providing drugs with firmer efficacy and safety at low prices would be the most desirable for patients, and it is an important issue from the perspective of saving medical expenses. Thus, for AGs positioned similar to a biosame,[31] we should urgently deepen discussions on the drug price system to reduce the prices targeting the next revision, maintaining an appropriate competitive environment between companies, not preventing the development of biosimilars, authorised biologics, etc.'.

It was also stated that 'The authorised biologics are exactly the same product except for its packaging and are manufactured by a wholly-owned subsidiary. I would like to ask again: Why are the effectiveness and efficacy different even though they are the same products? ... I feel uncomfortable that the wholly owned subsidiary

---

[26] The Nikkan Yakugyo (17 November 2014).

[27] *[Kyowa Hakko Kirin] Nesp AG ga shounin shutoku—bio iyakuhin de wa hatsu [Nesp AG first authorised as a Biological Medicinal Product]*, Yakujinippo (21 August 2018), *available at* https://www.yakuji.co.jp/entry66762.html, last visited 7 February 2021.

[28] *Biosimilar kyougikai ga kenkai—Bio AG sannyuu wa bio iyakuhin sangyou zentai no hatten wo sogai [Bio AG launch hinders growth of the Biological Medicinal Products Industry* , MIX Online (17 May 2017), *available at* https://www.mixonline.jp/tabid55.html?artid=57513, last visited 7 February 2021.

[29] *Bio AG, sangyo wo obiyakasu—BS kyougikai ga kenkai [Japan Biosimilar Association concerns Bio AG threatened Biological Medicinal Products Industry]*, Yakujinippo (23 May 2017), *available at* https://www.yakuji.co.jp/entry58194.html, last visited 7 February 2021.

[30] *supra* note 8.

[31] This means authorised biologics.

may be the same company. I know that there is a rule, but I feel extremely uncomfortable that the same company launches drugs in this way to affect biosimilars, while understanding it as a company strategy'.

Furthermore, 'Authorised biologics will probably not be launched unless biosimilars are developed and apply for authorisation. I understand that originator companies can launch authorised biologics within the existing rule responding to the development of biosimilars, under the mechanism that their development funds, etc., can be recovered through evaluation of their new drugs. However, I feel that such a strategy is not sophisticated competition. In that sense, I agree with the Drug Supervisor about how to decide the drug price of authorised biologics in order to be in time for the drug price listing this June. However, this issue cannot be fully solved only with a price of 0.7. In cases where authorised biologics are launched, we should also consider how to deal with the drug price of substantially the same originator medicinal products'.

Finally, 'As for 0.7, you are right, and there is a problem whether it is appropriate to multiply by 7 (*sic*) like with biosimilars, although authorised biologics are authorised without clinical trials and with no development cost. However, more than 0.7 would cause various harmful effects, and less than 0.7 would also raise problems'.

In response, Kenichi Tamiya, the Drug Supervisor of the Medical Economics Division, Health Insurance Bureau, MHLW, stated, 'We are concerned that if pricing authorised biologics stagnates biosimilar development, this may cause a very negative impact from the perspective of reducing drug costs and promoting the R&D of biological medicinal products, including biosimilars. Sufficient attention is required to maintain an appropriate competitive environment'. He reiterated the need to 'maintain an appropriate competitive environment' and expressed concern that 'pricing authorised biologics could hinder biosimilar development'.[32]

The discussions continued at the Drug Price Special Committee of the CSIMC on 23 October 2019.[33] Tamiya, the Drug Supervisor, presented three ideas for a calculation rule for authorised biologics: (1) to multiply the drug price of the originator medicinal product by 0.5, as with a new generic; (2) to multiply the drug price of the originator medicinal product by 0.7, as with biosimilars; and (3) to have the same drug price as a succession item.

Committee members expressed the following opinions regarding these ideas: The originator company suggesting sales of authorised biologics to restrain the development and sales of biosimilars may not violate a rule, but it does bring a significant problem from the viewpoint of maintaining an appropriate competitive environment.

It was also stated that, 'The most important thing is to set prices encouraging the development of biosimilars and to create an appropriate competitive environment. From this perspective, the drug price should be set. For example, biosimilars

---

[32] *Nesp no biosame toujou de touseki sijou wa saranaru kyousou he biosame wa 0.7 gake ni [Nesp Biosame to bring further competition in Dialysis Market—Biosame pricing at 70%]* MIX Online (28 March 2019), *available at* https://www.mixonline.jp/tabid55.html?artid=67246, last visited 7 February 2021.

[33] *Chuou shakai hoken iryo kyougikai yakka senmonbukai dai 158 kai gijiroku [No. 158 meeting minutes of The Drug Price Special Committee of the CSIMC]*, (23 October 2019), *available at* https://www.mhlw.go.jp/stf/shingi2/0000203254_00016.html, last visited 7 February 2021.

may be 0.7 times the drug price of originator medicinal products because of higher manufacturing costs, including R&D, than generics. In addition, we should maintain the motivation to develop biosimilars, which requires clinical trials and an appropriate competitive environment. Therefore, one option is to raise the drug price of authorised biologics, which do not require clinical trials, to a little higher than 0.7, which is different from the biosimilars' 0.7. Then, regarding the drug price of originator medicinal products when their authorised biologics apply for authorisation, the relevant originator medicinal product should be priced at the same level as the authorised biologic at that time. However, considering sales competitiveness, it may be unavoidable to have a certain price difference'.

Finally, 'It is very difficult to rate the biosame[34] to promote the development and launch of biosimilars, but a higher drug price than that of biosimilars would cause various problems, and the lower price would also cause problems. Therefore, for the time being, adopting the same price is painful but inevitable'.

On 22 November 2019, the Drug Price Special Committee of the CSIMC[35] agreed that the drug price of authorised biologics would be 0.7 times that of their originator medicinal products, like biosimilars.

The history of the authorised biologic of Nesp is as follows: On 5 August 2019, Kyowa Kirin Frontier launched an authorised biologic of Nesp, the first authorised biologic in Japan. However, contrary to the prediction that the authorised biologic of Nesp would overwhelm the market, the demand for Nesp's biosimilars (Nesp BS) expanded. The supply of all three biosimilar companies, Kissei Pharmaceutical Co., Ltd., Mylan EPD, and Sanwa Kagaku Kenkyusho Co., Ltd., could not keep up with the strong demand. A nephrologist remarked, 'Based on my feeling at the site, the BS, having a lower delivery price than the authorised biologic, appears to be penetrated due partly to reduction in the unit price of dialysis'.

Reportedly, with a reduction in the bundled payment of medical expenses in dialysis, the adoption of BS is accelerating, which seems related to the delivery price difference between BS and authorised biologics.[36]

The JFTC has not issued any opinions on the AGs of small molecule products and biological medicinal products.

---

[34] This means authorised biologics.

[35] *Chuou shakai hoken iryo kyougikai yakka senmonbukai dai 160 kai gijiroku [No. 160 meeting minutes of The Drug Price Special Committee of the CSIMC]*, (22 November 2019), *available at* https://www.mhlw.go.jp/stf/shingi2/0000203254_00018.html, last visited 7 February 2021.

[36] The Nikkan Yakugyo (26 November 2020).

11.5 Implications for Japan

11.5.1 Differences Between the US, Europe, and Japan

As outlined above, the US, Europe, and Japan differ in terms of authorised biologics. Although the US issued a competition authority's view on the AGs of small molecule products, no view on authorised biologics has been issued and examples of authorised biologics are few. Europe issued views on the AGs of small molecule products and authorised biologics by the pharmaceutical regulatory authorities, which consider competition when examining duplicate marketing authorisation applications. However, there are few examples of authorised biologics. Japan already has an example of authorised biologics, in which the CSIMC discussed and approved the drug price. However, in Japan, the JFTC has not expressed its view on the AGs of small molecule products or authorised biologics.

These differences may reflect the differences between the US, Europe, and Japan in terms of the timing and authorities of considering competition with respect to AGs, that is, the presence or absence of post-regulation by competition authorities and consideration of competition by pharmaceutical regulatory authorities.

Post-regulation by competition authorities is implementable in the US and Europe,[37] while in Japan, such post-regulation is less likely. This is mainly derived from the different ways of drug pricing. That is, in the US[38] and many European countries, drug prices are in principle determined by drug manufacturers, which enables the competition authorities to apply post-regulation regarding the impact of authorised biologics on biosimilars. In Japan, drug pricing[39] is conducted by the MHLW and CSIMC[40] under the national health insurance system, with the application of the government's drug price standards (official prices at the retail stage). It is unlikely that the JFTC will point out that the drug price decided by the MHLW and CSIMC violates the Antimonopoly Act.[41] Although it may detect cartels of delivery prices, it is difficult to assume that the JFTC implements post-regulation.

---

[37] Alexander Roussanov (Partner of Arnold & Porter, former senior legal adviser in the Legal Department of the European Medicines Agency (EMA)) provided insight into the possible post-regulation by the European Commission's Directorate-General for Competition (DG COMP) after launch following a duplicate marketing authorisation by the European Commission.

[38] Kefauver [6: 16, 26] states, 'The pharmaceutical industry is particularly susceptible to monopoly control due to its unique market structure'. In addition, 'The usual laws of supply and demand do not apply here. Customers with a prescription can only purchase branded medicines prescribed by physicians'. He further criticises the high monopoly prices of pharmaceutical companies.

[39] Yakka seisaku kenkyukai [13: 138, 146] explains in detail the drug price system and its practice.

[40] Sato [11], based on the experience of actual engagement in revision discussions at the CSIMC, explains this in detail.

[41] Shiteki dokusen no kinshi oyobi kosei torihiki no kakuho ni kansuru horitsu [Antimonopoly Act] Act No. 54 of 14 April 1947, as last amended by Act No. 45 of 26 June 2019.

Regarding the consideration of competition by the pharmaceutical regulatory authorities, neither the US FDA[42,43] nor Japan's MHLW[44] have approval authority from a competition standpoint. However, in Europe, the European Commission[45] considers competition for duplicate marketing authorisation applications.[46]In Japan, the MHLW and CSIMC consider competition at drug price listing[47]after approval

---

[42] Since the FDA does not have the authority to consider competition in the approval process, the act of excluding competitors using regulations, known as 'Regulatory Gaming', is considered to be manifested (Competition Policy Research Center of the JFTC *'iyakuhin shijo ni okeru kyousou to kenkyu kaihatsu incentive—generic iyakuhin no sannyuu ga shijou ni ataeta eikyou no kenshou wo tsuujite—[Competition in the Pharmaceutical Market and R & D Incentives: Through Verification of the Impact of the Entry of Generic Drugs on the Market]'* 22 (2015), Dogan and Lemley [3: 708].

[43] The BIOSIMILARS ACTION PLAN of the FDA states—although not about the approval process itself—that the agency will focus on promoting innovation and competition in biological medicinal products and biosimilars. The FDA's key actions for achievement include developing and implementing new tools for FDA approval to improve the efficiency of the review process and to provide more information on the FDA's evaluation. (*BIOSIMILARS ACTION PLAN Balancing Innovation and Competition,* U.S. Food & Drug Administration (July 2018), *available at* https://www.fda.gov/media/114574/download).

[44] In reviewing the approval of pharmaceutical products, the Minister of Health, Labour, and Welfare considers matters related to quality, efficacy, and safety, and whether the methods to control manufacturing or the quality of the item at the manufacturing facility complies with the standards (Article 14(2) of Iyakuhin, iryokikito no hinshitsu, yukosei oyobi anzensei no kakuhoto ni kansuru horitsu [Pharmaceutical and Medical Device Act] Act No. 145 of 10 August 1960, as last amended by Act No. 63 of 4 December 2019.).

[45] The European Medicines Agency (EMA) adopted opinions based on scientific criteria for the evaluation of medicines, and the European Commission makes an administrative decision based on these opinions (Kenichi Hayashi *Canary Wharf dayori—Oushuu iyakuhinnchou (EMA) nite-dai 1 kai 2010nen 1 gatsu [News from Canary Wharf—at the European Medicines Agency (EMA)—(1) January 2010]* 27 January 2010), *available at* https://www.pmda.go.jp/int-activities/outline/0027.html, last visited 7 February 2021.

[46] According to Annex I.1 of the 2011 Commission note on the Handling of Duplicate Marketing Authorisation Applications, the first introduction of a generic product by the holder of the reference medicinal product (the originator medicinal product) can also improve the availability of a medicinal product. Furthermore, the Pharmaceutical Committee of the Directorate-General for Health and Food Safety (DG SANTE) and the European Commission on 7 November 2019 presented that the Commission launched a targeted consultation directed to stakeholders to seek their views on the impact of duplicate authorisations on the availability of biosimilars to healthcare professionals and patients. One possible consideration was that duplicate authorisations could have anticompetitive effects and undermine other treatment options available to patients. Dodds-Smith and Roussanov [2: 143] state that Article 82(1), which provides for duplicate authorisations, is seemingly based on the Commission's belief that if more than one authorisation was granted for the same product, it would allow companies to 'partition' the single market, which sometimes occurred in the national authorisation system. They added that it was competition law concerns, rather than concerns relating to quality, safety, and efficacy (the assessment criteria governing the grant of marketing authorisation) that drove this policy. Alexander Roussanov (Partner of Arnold & Porter, former senior legal adviser in the Legal Department of the European Medicines Agency (EMA)) provided the insight that the European Commission considers competition at duplicate marketing authorisation.

[47] Unlisted drugs in the drug price standard are not reimbursed by insurance; therefore, drug manufacturers want the drug price listing, which enables regulations to work in a virtual environment at this stage as well.

but before launch. This is clearly reflected in the repeated emphasis on 'maintaining an appropriate competitive environment' by Drug Supervisor Tamiya at the CSIMC.

11.5.2 Utilising the JFTC's Expertise in Drug Pricing

11.5.2.1 Pre-simulation

Fundamentally, in drug pricing, the MHLW and CSIMC consider efficacy, safety, etc.,[48] and it is questionable whether they can consider competition.[49] If they do, the current practice needs to be improved.

That is, as long as the MHLW and CSIMC have less expertise in competition than the JFTC, it is advisable to formulate the systems to utilise the expertise[50] of the JFTC, a competition expert, including its economic analysis. In fact, the JFTC enforces not only post-regulation conduct by detecting Antimonopoly Act violations, but also pre-evaluates regulations, targeting the establishment or alteration/abolition of regulations.[51] Applying the JFTC's expertise to the current regulatory practices and operations and utilising it in drug pricing by the MHLW and CSIMC will make it easier to achieve 'maintaining an appropriate competitive environment'. In assessing a drug price for authorised biologics and preventing biosimilar companies from giving up biosimilar development because they cannot recover their invested capital owing to the launch of the authorised biologics,[52] they could run simulations using a model to derive the relationship between the drug price, wholesale price, delivery

---

[48] Notification No. 0207-1, issued by Health Insurance Bureau, *Yakka santei no kijun ni tsuite* [Criteria for drug pricing] (7 February 2020).

[49] On the other hand, if the MHLW and CSIMC never consider competition, it will not be considered in drug pricing. Because it is unlikely that the JFTC will post-regulate the drug pricing by the MHLW and CSIMC, drug pricing will take place without considering competition and problems may occur.

[50] See *Kyousou seisaku de tsukau Keizai bunseki handbook* [Economic Analysis Handbook Used in Competition Policy: CPRC Handbook Series No. 1], Competition Policy Research Centre of the JFTC (2012).

[51] Kisei no seisaku hyouka ni okeru kyousou joukyou heno eikyou no haaku bunseki ni kansuru kangaekata ni tsuite [Considerations on Understanding and Analyzing the Impact on Competitive Conditions in Regulatory Policy Evaluation], The General Secretariat, JFTC (31 July 2017).

[52] To evaluate 'maintaining an appropriate competitive environment', it is necessary to consider not only the situations of biosimilar companies but also those of the originator companies. That is, at how much the drug price of authorised biologics is set will the originator companies abandon the selling of authorised biologics, and maintain a balance between them. At the Drug Price Special Committee of the CSIMC on 25 September 2019, regarding AGs in general, the Drug Supervisor Tamiya stated the following, indicating the necessity of also considering the circumstances of the AG: 'When authorised generics were launched, it was pointed out that the price of long-listed products should be lowered to the price of AGs. If a rule is set that the drug price of long-listed products is lowered to that of AGs, I have a concern whether the AGs will be licensed by the originator companies to launch, which needs consideration. In that case, licensing authorised generics and granting manufacturing and marketing approval of generic products may not occur, so we need to discuss this'. *Chuou shakai hoken iryo kyougikai yakka senmonbukai dai 156 kai gijiroku [No. 156 meeting minutes of*

price, and market share of authorised biologics and biosimilars, and predict how the profits of biosimilar manufacturers will change depending on the drug price setting. The cost of biosimilar manufacturers is predicted based on development costs, including clinical trials and manufacturing costs. Based on these results, the break-even point for biosimilar manufacturers can be determined. Through the above simulation, it will be possible to some extent to find a turning point at which drug price biosimilar companies are unlikely to recover their invested capital.[53] Drug Supervisor Tamiya's proposal and committee members' remarks at the CSIMC reached the 0.7 times drug price for authorised biologics and biosimilars after deliberating various factors.[54] This leaves the rest to a 'competition under price-cap regulation'[55,56] and

---

The Drug Price Special Committee of the CSIMC], (25 September 2019), *available at* https://www. mhlw.go.jp/stf/shingi2/0000203254_00014.html, last visited 7 February 2021.

[53] See Nagate [9: 13, 16–17]. It builds a simple market model for originator medicinal products and biosimilars, and analyses the source of profits of the biosimilar business. Nagate points out that if originator medicinal products have brand value, and the price of the originator medicinal products is equal to that of biosimilars, the market share of originator medicinal products may be 100%, because the originator medicinal products become dominant against biosimilars. On the other hand, even though the price of biosimilars is lower than that of originator medicinal products, the price of the originator medicinal products may remain high because there is no competition for price devaluation between the originator medicinal products and biosimilars, leaving a producer surplus for biosimilar manufacturers. This model will also be helpful in predicting the prices, market share, and producer surplus of authorised biologics that can inherit the brand value of the originator medicinal products and biosimilars. In Dubois and Lasio [4: 3685], the impact of drug price regulation on demand, margins, and costs of the originator medicinal products and generic products is estimated via an economic analysis using a model that explores the Nash equilibrium of Bertrand competition in France, where drug prices are regulated as in Japan. This estimation was made in the case where the drug price was regulated under the actual French system and in the case where the drug price was determined by the free market unlike the actual system. The cases were then compared. The estimates and comparisons clarified that the drug price of originator medicinal products is easily reduced by price constraints, which stimulates demand, and with a smaller wedge between originator medicinal products and generics, demand shifts from generics to the originator medicinal products, and drug costs will be reduced by an average of 2%, etc. In France, where as mentioned, drug prices are regulated as in Japan, a method for estimating demand, margins, and costs with a Bertrand competition model is used, which is helpful in predicting the demand, revenue, and cost of authorised biologics and biosimilars in Japan.

[54] Both payer and physician committee members at the Drug Price Special Committee of the CSIMC on 27 March 2019 questioned the following problem: 'Although authorised biologics were approved without clinical trials and development costs, is it allowed to multiply it by 7 (sic) like for biosimilars?' Here, the addition of 0.2 cannot be explained theoretically.

[55] Competition Policy Research Center, of the JFTC, *supra note 42*, at 69.

[56] In fact, since then, competition has emerged between the authorised biologic of Nesp and Nesp BS because of differences in delivery prices.

can be evaluated as a 'painful but inevitable decision'.[57] However, the JFTC's expertise including economic analysis would allow more objective rather than intuitive evaluations and decisions.

The JFTC's expertise can be used by applying the current system,[58] but establishing new systems is also worth considering, such as an opinion request system and opinion statement system (Article 79 of the Antimonopoly Act, Article 180(2) of the Patent Act[59]) to provide an opportunity for the JFTC to express opinions on drug pricing. Similarly, systems of judicial research officials (Article 57 of the Court Act[60]) and technical advisers (Article 92(2) of the Code of Civil Procedure[61]) could be instituted to enable them to hear expertise on competition from JFTC officials, academics and practitioners with deep knowledge of the Antimonopoly Act and obtain the expertise involved in the drug pricing discussion. Moreover, the findings of the US and European competition authorities may lead to an optimal solution, although the systems are largely different from the Japanese one.

11.5.2.2   Post-verification

In addition, any drug price decided through a pre-simulation should be post-verified. While the current legislation arranges post-verification by annual drug price surveys,[62] in this case, it is essential to verify the outcome of the sales of authorised biologics and biosimilars after setting the drug price of authorised biologics as 0.7 times the originator price. In the Nesp case, contrary to the prediction that authorised biologics of Nesp would overwhelm the market, Nesp BS expanded its demand, which could not be covered by the supply. This partially results from the success of the Japan Biosimilar Association's lobbying activities,[63] but undoubtedly relies

---

[57] First, drug prices should be derived deductively and should be calculated by policy judgment. The question of whether the drug price of authorised biologics should be multiplied by 0.7, 0.5, or 1 is based on the inductive idea of whether it should be the same as the drug price of biosimilars— i.e. 0.7—or be less or more expensive than that. Based on this idea, 0.7 times will be a standard, obsessed with that number.

[58] This is the said pre-evaluation system for regulations. The Coordination Division of the Economic Affairs Bureau of the JFTC coordinates with each ministry and agency to prevent the bills drafted and measures taken by each ministry and agency from limiting or hindering fair and free competition.

[59] Tokkyoho [Patent Act] Act No. 121 of 13 April 1959, as last amended by Act No. 3 of 17 May 2019.

[60] Saibanshoho [Court Act] Act No. 59 of 16 April 1947, as last amended by Act No. 44 of 26 June 2019.

[61] Minji Soshoho [Code of Civil Procedure] Act No. 109 of 26 June 1996, as last amended by Act No. 22 of 24 April 2020.

[62] For the reality of the drug price survey, see Yakka seisaku kenkyukai [13] *supra* note 39:138, 146.

[63] At the Drug Price Special Committee of the CSIMC on 27 March, 23 October, and 22 November 2019, the expert advisors on originator companies did not make particular remarks regarding authorised biologics. However, at the Drug Price Special Committee of the CSIMC on 25 September 2019, regarding AGs in general, the expert advisors on originator companies made the following

largely on the fact that the delivery price of Nesp BS was less expensive than that of Nesp AG, with the reduction of bundled dialysis medical expenses. Based on this, close attention should be paid to the sales of authorised biologics and biosimilars under fee-for-service medical expenses if the delivery price of authorised biologics is reduced to the same level as biosimilars. What should be done if in these cases authorised biologics are adopted more than biosimilars,[64] even though both drug prices are 0.7 times the originator price? It should be evaluated whether 'an appropriate competitive environment' is maintained under which biosimilars just lose the competition and should not receive further relief, or if 'an appropriate competitive environment' is lost, based on which the drug price of authorised biologics should be changed.[65]

In addition, in conducting post-verification of whether 'maintaining an appropriate competitive environment' has been achieved, operational and institutional design should be built to utilise the expertise of the JFTC, which is a competition expert. The evaluation of 'maintaining an appropriate competitive environment' in the market of biological medicinal products is close to the evaluation in post-regulation routinely conducted by the JFTC; that is, an evaluation of the substantial restriction of competition or inhibition of fair competition in a certain trading field to determine whether or not it corresponds to a private monopolisation, an unreasonable restraint of trade, or unfair trade practices. Based on the above, the JFTC's expertise can be used more directly.

---

remarks: 'There were various discussions about AGs, but I think AGs promoted the replacement with generics in some aspects. Since AGs are not clearly defined in the drug price system, I desire careful discussion about changing the system from the perspective of AGs, including whether it is really appropriate'. *Chuou shakai hoken iryo kyougikai yakka senmonbukai dai 156 kai gijiroku [No. 156 meeting minutes of The Drug Price Special Committee of the CSIMC]*, (25 September 2019), *available at* https://www.mhlw.go.jp/stf/shingi2/0000203254_00014.html, last visited 7 February 2021.

[64] It is unclear which drug spreads more widely under the fee-for-service system when both authorised biologics and biosimilars are priced at the same 0.7 times the drug price. The result may depend not only on differences in patient burden under the High-Cost Medical Expense Benefit System and economic incentives for medical institutions, but also on the preferences of patients and physicians in the qualitative differences between authorised biologics and biosimilars.

[65] While difficult to imagine in reality, theoretically, if the difference between the bundled payment and fee-for-service is pointed out as the main factor regarding whether authorised biologics are used more than biosimilars, it will be necessary to consider whether to allow flexible drug price calculation by intentionally making the drug prices of authorised biologics inconsistent between the bundled payment and the fee-for-service, even though the drug price is determined in units of biosimilars, etc., not after further subdivision ('The criteria for drug price calculation' (Health Insurance Bureau, *supra* note 48).

11.5.3   Emphasis on Patient Choice and Quality of Healthcare in Drug Pricing

When considering competition in the drug pricing of authorised biologics, not only incentives to develop biosimilars but also patient access, quality of healthcare, therapeutic decisions by physicians, and patient choice, etc. must be considered.

The discussions at the CSIMC seemed to overemphasise the incentives to develop biosimilars, i.e., the protection of biosimilar companies. Fundamentally, the protection of incentives to develop biosimilars ultimately aims to reduce drug costs. When authorised biologics are priced at 0.5 times the originator price, such pricing might lower the total drug cost compared to setting it at 0.7 times, which has been apparently never examined.[66] This attitude would unavoidably provoke criticism that the national policy of promoting biosimilars has been overemphasised ahead of the ultimate goal of reducing drug costs.

From the viewpoint of patient choice and quality of healthcare, patients desire to obtain good quality medicines at a low price,[67] and for that purpose, authorised biologics priced 0.5 times the originator price seems more beneficial for patients.[68] However, the physician committee members gave no opinions to support this viewpoint. Taking advantage of the characteristic that the MHLW and CSIMC, the drug experts, consider competition and perform assessments in Japan, it may be necessary to examine the impact of authorised biologics with further emphasis on the factors of patient choice and healthcare quality.

Acknowledgements I thank Akira Negishi (emeritus professor, Kobe University), Kensuke Kubo (associate professor, Keio University Faculty of Business and Commerce), and Alexander Roussanov (Partner of Arnold & Porter, former senior legal adviser in the Legal Department of the European Medicines Agency (EMA)) for their helpful comments; Kosuke Uetake (associate professor, Yale School of Marketing) for providing helpful articles; and the Ministry of Health, Labour and Welfare and the Japan Fair Trade Commission for answering questions.

---

[66] The committee members' remarks highlighted strong doubt regarding the scheme of authorised biologics, which might have hindered discussions on promoting authorised biologics.

[67] As the payer committee member stated at the Drug Price Special Committee of the CSIMC on 27 March 2019, 'Providing drugs with firmer efficacy and safety at a low price would be the most desirable for patients'. Nagasaka [8: 109] also provides a general remark on the Japanese drug price system, stating, 'From a financial viewpoint, drug compression would be welcomed to ease patients' burden. However, from the viewpoint of patient access to the latest best medicines, low cost is not necessarily good'.

[68] The patient burden will be lower with the 0.5 times drug price of authorised biologics than the 0.7 times to which the High-Cost Medical Expense Benefit System is not applied. For example, insulin preparations, both insulin glargine (Lantus), an originator medicinal product, and insulin glargine BS, are not covered by High-Cost Medical Expense Benefit System. According to Nakamura [10: 41], 'The High-Cost Medical Expense Benefit System applies to biologic medicinal products, which are expensive, and exempts patient burden from a certain amount or more. Therefore, even if originator medicinal products are switched to the biosimilars, the patient burden may not change'. In that case, the patient burden may not change for authorised biologics or biosimilars.

References

1. Dechert, L. L. P. (2011). The FTC finds that authorized generic drugs yield procompetitive benefits. Dechert On Points 65. https://s3.amazonaws.com/documents.lexology.com/742 d89d3-2ac8-48f0-972c-cd88ebe2f526.pdf
2. Dodds-Smith, I., & Roussanov, A. (2020). Duplicate marketing authorisations in the EU: Evolution of the regulatory framework and practical implications. *European Pharmaceutical Law Review, 4*(3), 142–152.
3. Dogan, S. L., & Lemley, M. A. (2009). Antitrust law and regulatory gaming. *Texas Law Review, 87*, 685.
4. Dubois, P., & Lasio, L. (2018). Identifying industry margins with price constraints: Structural estimation on pharmaceuticals. *American Economic Review, 108*(12), 3685–3724.
5. Feldman, R., & Frondorf, E. (2016). Drug wars: A new generation of generic pharmaceutical delay. *Harvard Journal on Legislation, 53*, 500–561.
6. Kefauver, C. E. (1965). *In a few hands: Monopoly power in America*. Pantheon Books. Japanese edition: Kefauver, C. E. (1966). *Shosuusha no te ni—dokusen tono tatakai no kiroku (trans: Ohara, K.)*. Takeuchi Shoten.
7. McGowan, S. (2021). The US biosimilar market: Predictions for 2021. https://pharmaphorum.com/views-and-analysis/biosimilar-market-predictions-2021/
8. Nagasaka, K. (2010). *Nihon no iryou seido sono byouri to shohousen [Japanese medical system: Its pathology and prescription]*. Toyo Keizai.
9. Nagate, T. (2018). Jigyou yosoku biosimilar business no micro keizaigakutekina kousatsu—Biosimilars: The new long listed products?—[Business forecast: Microeconomic consideration of biosimilar business–biosimilars: The new long listed products?]. *Kokusai Iyakuhin Joho, 1098*, 13–18.
10. Nakamura, H. (2018). Yakkaseido no kangaekata, tokucho to yakka wo torimaku kadai [Concepts and characteristics of the drug price system and problems around drug price]. In K. Oguro & T. Sugahara (Eds.), *Yakka no keizaigaku [Economics of drug price]* (pp. 27–47). Nikkei Publishing.
11. Sato, T. (2018). *THE chuuikyou, sono hensen wo fumae kenkouhoken seido no 'ima' wo saguru [THE CSIMC, Exploring the 'Now' of the health insurance system based on the transition]*. Yakuji Nippo.
12. Wong, H. K. & Norey, E. L. (2019). Will authorized biologics disrupt the market for biosimilars? Biosimilar Development. https://www.biosimilardevelopment.com/doc/will-authorized-biologics-disrupt-the-market-for-biosimilars-0001
13. Yakka seisaku kenkyukai (2020). *Kaihoken to iyakuhin sangyo no mirai ni mukete –yakka seido 70 nen wo furikaeru [Toward the future of national health insurance and the pharmaceutical industry: Looking back on the 70 years of the drug price system]*. Shakai hoken kenkyujo.

Part III
An Economic Analysis of the Pharmaceutical Industry and Trade Practices in Japan

Chapter 12
The Pharmaceutical Industry in Japan: A History of Its Development

Kenta Nakamura

Abstract This chapter provides insight into the evolution and contemporary characteristics of the Japanese pharmaceutical industry. The first half presents an overview of the history, which, like that of other industries, is one that is catching up with Western countries. After World War II, foreign products were introduced in Japan; thereafter, the country's firms endeavoured to independently develop products, gradually improving drug discovery technology and resulting in the production of many innovative new drugs starting in the mid-1980s. During this period, the government established and implemented various laws and regulations, including medical insurance, patents and drug pricing systems. Pharmaceutical companies had to change their policies to adapt to these systemic changes. In the second half of the chapter, I describe the contributions of science to innovation in drug discovery and the relationship between patent protection and competition in the pharmaceutical industry, based on case studies of the development of 14 drugs created by Japanese pharmaceutical companies.

Keywords Pharmaceutical industry · Japan · History · Innovative drugs · Science · Patents

12.1 Introduction

This chapter presents basic materials of the characteristics of the Japanese pharmaceutical industry, but does not delve into ongoing research and development (R&D) and market competition. The focus is on the development of the Japanese pharmaceutical industry from the post-war period to the year 2000. The challenges facing the Japanese pharmaceutical industry today include the sustainable creation of innovative new drugs and management of global competition, which are both relevant and highly universal challenges. Understanding the historical circumstances of

K. Nakamura (✉)
Graduate School of Economics, Kobe University, Kobe, Japan
e-mail: knakamura@econ.kobe-u.ac.jp

the Japanese pharmaceutical industry will offer an informative clarification of its innovation process.

This chapter consists of two parts. In the first part, the history of the post-war development of the pharmaceutical industry is divided into four stages: (i) post-World War II to the 1950s, (ii) the 1960s, (iii) the 1970s to the mid-1980s and (iv) the mid-1980s to 2000. It touches upon the effects of the implementation of, as well as changes to, laws and regulations, including systems for national health insurance, patents and drug pricing, on the behaviour of Japanese pharmaceutical companies. The second half presents case study summaries on the development of 14 drugs created by Japanese pharmaceutical companies, the subsequent contributions of science to innovation in drug discovery, and the relationship between patent protection and competition in the pharmaceutical industry.

12.2   The History of the Pharmaceutical Industry in Japan: An Overview

Prior to the Meiji Restoration (1868), Japanese medicine was largely based on Chinese medicine, using natural sources including roots and tree bark as Japanese or Chinese medicinal herbs.[1] Following the Meiji Restoration, the government's modernisation policy shifted mainstream medicine from traditional Japanese medicine to Western medicine, which was strongly influenced by the emergence of the chemical industry. However, because Japan did not have the capacity to manufacture Western medicines at the time, it relied on imports from Europe (primarily Germany) and the United States for most of its supply of Western medicines.

This changed drastically with the outbreak of World War I. Imports from Germany were significantly reduced, while the domestic production of pharmaceuticals in Japan became an urgent matter. Two factors incentivised domestic pharmaceutical companies to manufacture medicines. First, the start of the war led to a sudden increase in the price of pharmaceuticals. Second, the Wartime Law on Industrial Property of 1917 essentially invalidated patents held by applicants from countries at war with Japan. This law enabled Japanese companies to manufacture drugs of German origin without fear of being sued for patent infringement. In addition, the pharmaceutical industry began to develop its capacity for synthetic chemistry during this period, with major pharmaceutical companies opening research laboratories and launching independent R&D initiatives.

---

[1] This section is based on Odagiri and Goto [13], Ch. 11), Kuwashima and Odagiri [10], Anegawa [2], and A Contemporary History of the Japanese Pharmaceutical Industry (1980–2010) Task Force [1].

12.2.1 The Era of Foreign Technology Introduction: Post-World War II Through the 1950s

During World War II, Japan fell far behind the rest of the world in terms of drug discovery technology, as it lost access to previously available advanced scientific and technological knowledge from overseas. To make up for the lost time, Japan decided to introduce technologies from Western companies following the war. The first of these was penicillin. Penicillin, an antibiotic discovered by Alexander Fleming in 1928, was first produced in Japan during the war in 1944. However, it was only after the introduction of strains and culturing methods from the United States following the war that Japan was able to produce large quantities of high-quality penicillin. At that time, infectious diseases were a major challenge in Japan due to malnutrition and unsanitary living conditions, and penicillin proved to be an effective way to combat these infections. In addition to pharmaceutical companies, many companies from other industries, such as the food, beer, sake brewing, miso/soy sauce, dairy and chemical industries, started producing penicillin. Accordingly, the penicillin manufacturing industry grew into an export industry soon after production began. Consequently, many companies eventually abandoned the industry due to overproduction and falling prices.

Technologies for the production of major antibiotics other than penicillin, such as streptomycin (introduced by Merck in 1951), were licensed by Japanese companies throughout the 1950s. Similarly, advanced technologies were introduced in the field of pesticides and agrochemicals, such as dichlorodiphenyltrichloroethane (DDT).

12.2.2 The Era of Rapid Growth: The 1960s

The Japanese economy underwent rapid growth after World War II, and the pharmaceutical industry was no exception. The total production value of pharmaceutical products exceeded 100 billion JPY in 1956, continued to proliferate, and surpassed 1 trillion JPY in 1970 (Annual Report on Pharmaceutical Industry Production Statistics, Ministry of Health and Welfare).

In 1961, Japan initiated universal healthcare coverage, significantly reducing the financial burden of medical care for its citizens. This led to an increase in the number of medical examinations and in demand for pharmaceuticals, resulting in a subsequent increase in prescription drug production. During this time, the proportion of prescription drugs in the pharmaceutical industry increased.[2] However, this trend was not due to a decline in demand for over-the-counter (OTC) drugs [7]. The demand for OTC drugs also increased during this time due to the increase in the popularity of mass media—mainly television—and the resulting advertising war, which promoted

---

[2] According to the Annual Report of Pharmaceutical Industry Production Statistics, the shares of OTC and prescription drugs in 1960 were 46% and 54%, respectively; however, 10 years later, they were 25 and 75%, respectively.

vitamin B1 and other health supplements. Thus, the development of the pharmaceutical industry was driven by two factors: the mass use of medicines spurred by universal healthcare coverage and the mass consumption of OTC drugs by the public. The 1960s was a time of remarkable growth in the Japanese pharmaceutical industry. However, it was also a time when the side effects of pharmaceuticals, including the infamous teratogen thalidomide, posed a serious public health threat.

12.2.3   The Era of Independent Development of New Drugs: The 1970s to the Mid-1980s

In the 1970s, Japanese pharmaceutical companies began to develop new drugs independently in earnest. This shift in focus to drug discovery was brought about by several institutional factors, in addition to the expansion of the domestic pharmaceutical market and the growth of Japanese pharmaceutical companies with the introduction of the national health insurance system.

First, Japan liberalised the foreign direct investment limits in the pharmaceutical industry in 1975. This institutional change amplified the competitive pressures faced by Japanese companies, as larger Western pharmaceutical companies with higher R&D budgets were able to freely enter the Japanese market.[3] Second, the substance patent system (1976) was introduced via revisions to the patent law. These revisions categorised pharmaceutical patents into substance, process and use patents.[4] A *substance patent* is granted to an applicant for the invention of a new compound, and all uses of the compound (even off-label uses not anticipated by the inventor) are included in the scope of the patent. This type of patent is extremely powerful. The introduction of a strong patent system enhanced the private incentives for pharmaceutical companies to conduct R&D, offering promising prospects for revenue gains from innovations.[5] Third, in 1978, the National Health Insurance Drug Price Standard was changed from one that favoured generics (a unified limited list system) to one that favoured new drugs (a brand-specific listing system). This enabled brand-name products to maintain high prices.

These institutional changes emboldened companies to independently develop new drugs; however, many of the new drugs developed during this period were similar in

---

[3] For details on economies of scale and economies of scope in pharmaceutical companies, see Henderson and Cockburn [8] and Okada and Kawara [14].

[4] A *process patent* gives the applicant rights to a process for the manufacture of a chemical substance, such as a component of a drug, whereas a *use patent* is granted for a new use or effect of a specific substance. Prior to the introduction of the substance patent system, the aim was to protect the profits of pharmaceutical inventions by obtaining a patent on the manufacturing method; however, despite this, the same substance could be manufactured using alternative methods.

[5] Kosaka [9] demonstrated that the introduction of the substance patent system increased R&D expenditure and the number of substance patents filed by Japanese pharmaceutical companies and concludes that the strengthening of the patent system promoted innovation in the pharmaceutical industry.

structure and composition to existing drugs and so were called 'new and improved' drugs ('me-too' or 'follow-on' drugs). Despite the increase in the number of new drugs launched by Japanese companies, overseas expansion did not progress, and the ratio of overseas sales remained low. Yet in Japan, the development of these new drugs played a crucial role in improving drug discovery technology.

12.2.4 The Era of Innovative Drug Development: From the Mid-1980s Onward

In the mid-1980s, following the introduction of foreign products and independent product development, drug discovery technologies accumulated by pharmaceutical companies came into full use, and Japanese companies began to produce innovative new drugs that saw popular use worldwide. In addition to the accumulation of drug discovery technologies, three factors contributed to Japanese companies' development of world-class new drugs during this period.

First, social concerns created pressure to suppress the domestic pharmaceutical market. In the 1980s, national healthcare costs continued to rise because of the chronic ageing of the population. Drug prices were reduced as a means to curb soaring medical costs. This resulted in insufficient prospects for expansion in the Japanese market, causing domestic pharmaceutical companies to have no choice but to accelerate overseas expansion and strengthen global competitiveness.

Second, foreign companies, mainly those from the United States, targeted the Japanese market, intensifying competition. Despite the complete liberalisation of capital in 1975, the complex distribution structure of the Japanese pharmaceutical market presented a bottleneck that made it difficult for foreign companies to enter the market. The expansion of foreign companies in the Japanese market generally requires equity participation from or acquisition by a Japanese company. In the 1990s, however, foreign companies established their own distribution systems. As a result, joint ventures and sales alliances between foreign and domestic companies began to dissolve.

Finally, a number of systems that offer incentives for the development of innovative new drugs have been introduced. The introduction of the patent term extension system in 1988 motivated companies to develop innovative new drugs by ensuring the duration of patent rights lasted long enough for companies to recover R&D costs. In addition, new price calculation systems, additional allowance for breakthrough drugs (1992) and additional allowance for efficacy (1996) were introduced.

12.3   Lessons from the Development of Innovative New Drugs in Japan

This section presents case study summaries revealing the scientific origins of 14 innovative drugs developed by Japanese pharmaceutical companies. These case studies were conducted by the Research Institute of Science and Technology for the Society of the Japan Science and Technology Agency (JST/RISTEX) R&D programme, 'Science Origins of Innovations and its Economic Effects'. This programme aimed to develop a systematic understanding of the contribution of science to the process of innovation by directly collecting information from contributors to drug discovery innovations.[6]

The case studies cover the following innovative drugs developed in Japan (generic name of molecules followed by product names, the discovery company and therapeutic domain):

- **compactin**
  - discontinued in Phase II
  - Sankyo (now Daiichi Sankyo)
  - high cholesterol

- **pravastatin**
  - Mevalotin, Pravachol
  - Sankyo (now Daiichi Sankyo)
  - high cholesterol

- **rosuvastatin**
  - Crestor
  - Shionogi
  - high cholesterol

- **leuprorelin**
  - Leuplin, Lupron, Viadur
  - Takeda Pharmaceutical
  - prostate cancer

- **ofloxacin**
  - Tarivid, Floxin
  - Daiichi Pharmaceutical (now Daiichi Sankyo)
  - broad-spectrum antibiotic

- **levofloxacin**
  - Cravit, Levaquin

---

[6] The principal investigator was Sadao Nagaoka, Tokyo Keizai University. I participated in this research programme.

- Daiichi Pharmaceutical (now Daiichi Sankyo)
- broad-spectrum antibiotic

- **tamsulosin**

  - Harnal, Flomax
  - Yamanouchi Pharmaceutical (now Astellas Pharma)
  - prostatic hyperplasia

- **pranlukast**

  - Onon
  - Ono Pharmaceutical
  - bronchial asthma

- **tacrolimus**

  - Prograf
  - Fujisawa Pharmaceuticals (now Astellas Pharma)
  - organ rejection prophylaxis

- **pioglitazone**

  - Actos, Glustin
  - Takeda Pharmaceutical
  - diabetes

- **donepezil**

  - Aricept
  - Eisai
  - Alzheimer's

- **candesartan**

  - Blopress, Atacand, Amitas
  - Takeda Pharmaceutical
  - high blood pressure, congestive heart failure

- **tocilizumab**

  - Actemra
  - Collaboration between Chugai Pharmaceutical, the UK Medical Research Council, and Osaka University
  - rheumatoid arthritis

- **nivolumab**

  - Opdivo
  - Ono Pharmaceutical in cooperation with Medarex USA and Kyoto University
  - cancer

These drugs studies were selected in cooperation with the Office of Pharmaceutical Indus-try Research (OPIR) of the Japan Pharmaceutical Manufacturers Association (JPMA). Discovered relatively recently, tocilizumab (1992) and nivolumab (2005) are antibody drugs (biopharmaceuticals), whereas the others are small-molecule compounds. The diseases discussed in the case studies are common, and many people are affected by them across the globe. Exploratory research on the drugs mentioned above began between the early 1970s and the early 2000s. It took an average of 16 years from the start of the research (basic R&D) to the first approval or market launch for these drugs. Many have novel mechanisms of action and are marketed in numerous countries. The sales of each drug significantly contributed to the performance of the related pharmaceutical company, accounting for an average of about 20% of company sales at their peak.

Each case study analysed the contribution of science to an innovative drug project, from conception to implementation, as well as the mechanisms used. They are based on interviews with key researchers responsible for the discovery of drugs, as well as an analysis of relevant literature describing the drug discovery process, patent data, scientific papers and drug sales. This section provides a summary of the cases and outlines the significance of the contributions of scientific innovation in drug discovery, as well as the relationship between patent protection and competition in the pharmaceutical industry.[7]

12.3.1 Drug Discovery and Science

The case studies analysed demonstrate the importance of leveraging the scientific progress in drug discovery. Scientific progress creates opportunities for drug discovery through the identification of new drug targets, the development of new research tools and the proposal of new uses for existing inventions. To make the most of scientific progress in drug discovery, the capacity for continuous scientific engagement—company researchers must be able to understand and critically evaluate the latest scientific advances and then apply them to drug discovery—is vital.

The pharmaceutical industry is a science-based industry. A strong basis in science (or 'science linkage') is critical for drug discovery technology.[8] However, the perception of science and industry as directly linked is not entirely correct. It is more accurate to state that the pharmaceutical industry is more closely linked to science than other industries. In practice, universities and national research institutes virtually never provide seeds for drug discovery in a form that can be easily formulated into a drug. Instead, drug discovery often begins with an incomplete understanding of the relevant science. Surprising as it may seem, the function of the drug target and the

---

[7] For more details on individual cases, see Nagaoka et al. [15].

[8] The concept of science linkage is a widely used quantitative method to measure the relationship between science and technology based on the frequency of citations to scientific papers within a patent.

mechanism of action of the molecules acting on the target may not become apparent until the drug is actually used.

For example, in the case of tacrolimus (Prograf), an immunosuppressant, the mechanism of action was revealed at a very late stage of drug development, just before it was administered to a transplant patient for the first time. While the mechanism of action was studied by Fujisawa Pharmaceutical (the company that developed the drug) Stuart Schreiber and his colleagues at Harvard University made a significant contribution to the understanding of its mechanism. Schreiber discovered the FK506 binding protein (FKBP) in 1988 and subsequently found that tacrolimus by itself had no effect as a pharmaceutical agent and only exhibited immunosuppressive activity when it binds to FKBP to form a complex.[9]

12.3.2 Researcher-Initiated Drug Discovery

The case studies demonstrate that many of the discovery projects that resulted in innovative drugs were initiated by individuals rather than organisations. The drivers of the freedom afforded to researchers include Japanese pharmaceutical companies being small in scale, newly established exploratory laboratories founded at geographically distant locations from headquarters, young researchers being assigned to these laboratories, and the possibility for voluntary research outside prescribed working hours.

In general, when research projects are selected based on organisational consensus, projects that involve a high degree of uncertainty tend to be ignored. However, the case studies selected involve research projects with high uncertainty, but with revolutionary implications that would make a significant contribution to the company's profits if successful. This may be a result of researchers taking initiative in their choice of topic, deviating from the existing routine and becoming Schumpeterian entrepreneurs in an attempt to advance innovation. Such projects are risky, so it is essential to ensure there are opportunities for recovery in case of failure. The system of long-term employment (in which individuals are employed by the same company until retirement), adopted by many Japanese companies, encourages researchers to take on the challenge of highly uncertain projects as it allows for their long-term evaluation.

12.3.3 Developing Researcher and Human Network Capabilities

Japanese companies that have developed innovative new drugs are able to take advantage of scientific advances primarily because they actively invest in the development

---

[9] FK506 is the development code name for tacrolimus.

of researchers' capabilities with a view to long-term returns. For example, a company may send researchers to study at universities and research institutions in Japan or overseas and encourage them to obtain doctoral degrees after joining the company. The long-term employment system cultivates a long-term perspective on human resource investment.

Face-to-face networking, such as placing the company's researchers in university laboratories, is a necessary investment that results in the development of innovative drugs. This suggests cutting-edge scientific knowledge and drug discovery technologies are likely a form of tacit knowledge. This is consistent with the work of Zucker [18, 19], who emphasised the critical role of geographic proximity in biotechnology-related industry–academia collaboration on the basis that the sharing of tacit knowledge only takes place on a local scale.

12.3.4 Global Clinical Development and Sales Capabilities

Of the 14 projects in the case studies, only three involve Japanese pharmaceutical companies conducting independent clinical trials in Europe and the United States.[10] A primary reason for poor international brand awareness of major Japanese pharmaceutical companies, despite the fact that they have produced a number of innovative drugs since the mid-1980s, is that the clinical development and marketing of new drugs is conducted overseas by licensing them to major foreign pharmaceutical companies.

Licensing to major overseas pharmaceutical companies allows Japanese companies to leverage the complementary assets of other companies, such as their development experience and sales networks. For example, AstraZeneca, a company licensed in the compound, succeeded in developing rosuvastatin (Crestor), a treatment for dyslipidemia, when Shionogi, the discoverer of the compound, had given up on its development. In contrast, transaction costs remain an obstacle when forming alliances. In the case of innovative projects with high uncertainty, the costs involved in searching for and negotiating with clinical development partners tend to be high and time consuming. The longer the process takes, the shorter the remaining period of patent protection for the new drug, making it more difficult to market it overseas.

Pranlukast (Onon), a bronchial asthma drug developed by Ono Pharmaceutical, is the only drug in the case studies that was put on the market, but not sold in the United States and Europe.[11] It is the world's first cysteinyl leukotriene receptor antagonist drug and became available in Japan in 1995. Ono Pharmaceutical planned to expand its business globally, but at the time, the company did not have the capability to develop and market the drug overseas.[12] In 1993, Ono Pharmaceutical licensed out

---

[10] Yamanouchi's tamsulosin, Takeda's pioglitazone, and Fujisawa's tacrolimus.

[11] The drug has been marketed in Asia and South America.

[12] Although the timing was slightly off, Ono Pharmaceutical's consolidated overseas sales accounted for only 1% of total sales in the 1999 fiscal year.

pranlukast to SmithKline Beecham (SKB) in the United Kingdom, with the goal of expanding sales channels using SKB's strong sales network. According to media reports at the time, the licence agreement gave SKB exclusive rights to develop, manufacture and sell drugs outside Japan, Taiwan and Korea. SKB began Phase II clinical trials in Europe, but the licence agreement was terminated in 1999. Pranlukast was never launched by SKB, despite the company trademarking 'Ultair' for the product. Although SKB was one of the world's leading pharmaceutical companies, respiratory diseases such as bronchial asthma were not among their specialties, which might explain why overseas development did not proceed as expected. Thereafter, Ono Pharmaceutical continued to seek a licensee in the United States and Europe. However, due to the limited amount of time left on the patent and the appearance of competing products, it has not been licensed in Western countries.

The case studies reveal that it is critical for Japanese companies to enhance their clinical development capabilities in overseas markets when attempting to expand highly uncertain discovery projects and address rare diseases. This does not mean it is always best for Japanese companies to attempt to expand overseas independently; however, even when forming alliances with foreign pharmaceutical companies, it is important for Japanese companies to expand overseas themselves, and to increase their bargaining power in alliance agreements.

Japanese pharmaceutical companies became active in overseas clinical development around the year 2000. In 1996, Japan, Europe and the United States agreed on an international standard for conducting clinical trials (GCP-E6). In 1997, clinical data from overseas became available for use in the approval process for drugs in Japan. In addition, the inability to resolve problems with clinical trials in Japan (e.g., high clinical development costs and refusal of foreign regulatory authorities to use Japanese data because of complications regarding the credibility of data collected at Japanese medical institutions) also led Japanese companies to shift their clinical development bases overseas. After 1997, many leading Japanese pharmaceutical companies began to develop new drugs in Japan and the United States simultaneously, or in Japan, Europe and the United States. Asian countries with lower costs, especially China, are now become crucial clinical development bases for these countries' pharmaceutical companies [17].

12.3.5 Patent Protection

To provide incentives for companies to invest in R&D in an environment of high uncertainty, there must be the potential to secure significant returns from the creation of innovative drugs. Patent protection as a significant factor in securing profits for pharmaceutical companies has been asserted in various studies on the mechanisms of appropriability [4, 11]. This is supported by the drastically reduced profits of the pharmaceutical company that held the patent after the appearance of generic drugs following patent expiration.

Considering the time between the discovery of a new drug candidate, drug approval and market availability, the terms of patent protection are relatively limited. The case studies show it takes approximately 11 years from the time the basic patent for the active ingredient is filed to the time the drug is first approved for use worldwide. This indicates that, by the time a drug is launched, the remaining patent protection period is less than ten years, making the additional protection period afforded by the patent term extension system exceedingly important. As the extension of the patent term delays the entry of generic drugs into the market, evaluating the impact of the system on social welfare is also essential. Conversely, considering the therapeutic area as the unit of analysis, an empirical study found the number of patent applications, a proxy variable for R&D investment, increases as the patent term is extended [16]. Cockburn et al. [3] also indicate that drugs launch earlier in countries with higher levels of patent protection. Recognising the fact that new drugs are paving the way for generic drugs is important.

12.3.6 Three Types of Competition in the Pharmaceutical Industry

Competition in the pharmaceutical industry is often said to have two stages: the competition to discover new drugs based on new mechanisms of action, and the competition amongst drugs with the same active ingredients after the patent of a new drug expires (i.e., new drugs versus generics). However, based on a comparative analysis of new innovative drugs, Nagaoka [15] maintains it is more appropriate to think of competition as occurring in three stages. First, because exploratory research in the search for novel mechanisms of action is often unique and highly uncertain, there is very little competition during the early stages of discovery. Once a compound is successfully discovered, resolving the uncertainty, competition in R&D for early launch and best-in-class drugs becomes exceptionally intense. The first drug to be launched is deemed the first-in-class, and if several drugs are subsequently launched with the exact mechanism of action but different active ingredients, they are called 'me-too' or 'follow-on' drugs. The second stage of competition is market competition amongst drugs with the same mechanism of action. Finally, the third stage of competition is marked by the entry of generic drugs into the market.[13]

The first person or entity to invent a drug with a novel mechanism of action in a drug discovery study can obtain patent rights (usually a substance patent) for the invention. Yet there is always the possibility that another compound that makes use of the same mechanism of action will be synthesised or that a natural substance will be discovered. Therefore, patent protection does not necessarily guarantee the elimination of potential competitors. If a company enters discovery research late and is better able to synthesise a compound or conduct clinical trials, the pioneer

---

[13] In addition, at times drugs with different mechanisms of action compete with each other in the treatment of the same disease.

company that first discovers the drug with a novel mechanism of action may lag behind its competitors in bringing it to the market. Many Japanese companies in the case studies presented in this chapter missed the global first market launch for this reason.

In answering the question of whether the second or third type of competition is a more serious problem for pharmaceutical companies. Lichtenberg and Philipson [12] argue the impact of the third type of competition (competition with generic drug manufacturers) is overemphasised, whereas the second type of competition is underestimated. They estimate that the decrease in the discounted value of the innovator's return due to the second type of competition is equal to or greater than the impact of the third type of competition.

12.3.7   'Me-Too' or 'Follow-On' Drugs

There are conflicting views on the development of 'me-too' or 'follow-on' drugs. The pessimistic view is that not all resource allocations are socially optimal due to overlapping investments in virtually identical R&D projects to maximise the private benefits of pharmaceutical companies. The optimistic mindset is that generic drugs are socially beneficial because they often provide useful, affordable alternatives or treatments with enhanced efficacy and safety for specific patients as well as bring about price competition. For example, tacrolimus (Prograf) is a commercially available drug with the exact mechanism of action of the drug cyclosporine. However, tacrolimus is a more effective immunosuppressant and has fewer adverse effects. Therefore, the introduction of tacrolimus into the medical field has significantly improved the success rate of transplants. In addition, rosuvastatin (Crestor) was launched whilst many other powerful statins with the same mechanism of action, as well as generics, were on the market. Nonetheless, royalty income from the licensee, AstraZeneca, to Shionogi peaked at 65.7 billion JPY in 2013. This indicates Crestor's contribution to patient health is significant.

When knowledge of a new mechanism of action is disclosed through the publication of a patent application, and clinical trials confirm the likelihood of a new drug's commercial success, knowledge spillover from the disclosure of the invention through the patent system may lead to competition in the development of new drugs based on the same mechanism. Scientific progress might also reveal promising drug targets, and similar exploratory research will begin around the world, resulting in competition for the development of drugs with the same mechanism of action. If the former explanation is more accurate, the disclosure of the patented invention will have a negative effect on the applicant's profits, as it will encourage the entry of follow-on drugs into the same market in the future while creating a socially desirable knowledge spillover. In other words, it can be interpreted that the protection of the invention is understated with respect to the disclosure of the invention. However, DiMasi and Paquette [6] and DiMasi and Faden [5] are sceptical of the view that follow-on drugs are products of imitation, and suggest considering first-in-class and follow-on drugs as being determined by competition based on analyses of development history and patent application timelines is reasonable.

The results presented here are limited and further research is needed prior to the assertion of any general conclusions. However, a basic understanding of the process by which follow-on drugs arise is necessary to determine the appropriate patent protection.

12.4   Conclusion

This chapter provides insight into the characteristics of the Japanese pharmaceutical industry. The first half of the chapter provides an overview of the history of its expansion, which, like that of other industries, is a history of catching up with Western countries. After World War II, foreign products were introduced into Japan. Thereafter, the country's firms worked on independently developing their own products, gradually improving their drug discovery technology, which resulted in the production of many innovative new drugs beginning in the mid-1980s. During this period, the government introduced various laws and regulations, including systems for national medical insurance, patents and drug pricing. Pharmaceutical companies altered their approaches and strategies to keep up with these systemic changes. The second half of the chapter summarises case studies on the development of 14 innovative drugs made by Japanese pharmaceutical companies, the subsequent contributions of science to innovation in drug discovery, and the relationship between patent protection and competition in the pharmaceutical industry.

The topics discussed in this chapter are well-known characteristics of the pharmaceutical industry. For example, it seems the importance of patents in the pharmaceutical industry is self-evident. However, as mentioned in Sect. 3.7, other aspects of the patent system require clarification, including how the patent system should be designed to encourage the creation of innovative new drugs, whether patent protection for pioneer inventors is underdeveloped, whether the development of follow-on drugs enhances social welfare, and how the patent system should be complemented or replaced by a new drug pricing system as an overarching incentive mechanism. The chapter helps in better understanding the innovation process in the pharmaceutical industry in general and the Japanese pharmaceutical industry in particular.

References

1. A Contemporary History of the Japanese Pharmaceutical Industry (1980–2010) Task Force. (2014). A Contemporary History of the Japanese Pharmaceutical Industry (1980–2010). *Jpn J Hist Pharmacy, 49*, 18–38.
2. Anegawa, T. (2002). Japanese pharmaceutical industry: Success and failure. *J Health Care Med Commun, 12*(2), 49–78.

3. Cockburn, I. M., Lanjouw, J. O., & Schankerman, M. (2016). Patents and the global diffusion of new drugs. *The American Economic Review, 106*, 136–164.
4. Cohen, W. M., Goto, A., Nagata, A., et al. (2002). R&D spillovers, patents and the incentives to innovate in Japan and the United States. *Research Policy, 31*, 1349–1367.
5. DiMasi, J. A., & Faden, L. B. (2011). Competitiveness in follow-on drug R&D: A race or imitation? *Nature Reviews Drug Discovery, 10*, 23–27.
6. DiMasi, J. A., & Paquette, C. (2004). The economics of follow-on drug research and development: Trends in entry rates and the timing of development. *PharmacoEconomics, 22*, 1–14.
7. Hasegawa, H. (1986). In *Pharmaceuticals: Industry's social history*. Nihon Keizai Hyoronsha.
8. Henderson, R., & Cockburn, I. (1996). Scale, scope, and spillovers: The determinants of research productivity in drug discovery. *The Rand Journal of Economics, 27*, 32–59.
9. Kosaka, K. (2012). The impact of revisions of the patent system on innovation in the pharmaceutical industry. *IIP Bull, 21*, 1–5.
10. Kuwashima, K., & Odagiri, H. (2003). The pharmaceutical industry in Goto. In Akira & H. Odagiri (Eds.), *Science-based industries* (pp. 325–403). NTT Publishing.
11. Levin, R. C., Klevorick, A. K., & Nelson, R. R., et al. (1987). Appropriating the returns from industrial research and development. *Brookings papers on economic activity, 3*, 783–820.
12. Lichtenberg, F., & Philipson, T. J. (2002). The dual effects of intellectual property regulations: Within- and between-patent competition in the U.S. pharmaceuticals industry. *Journal of Law and Economics, 45*, 643–672.
13. Odagiri, H., & Goto, A. (1996). *Technology and industrial development in Japan: Building capabilities by learning, innovation and public policy*. Oxford University Press.
14. Okada, Y., & Kawara, A. (2004). Research productivity in the Japanese pharmaceutical industry: Economies of scale, economies of scope and spillovers. OPIR Research Paper Series No.15.
15. Nagaoka, S. (2019). *Drug discovery in Japan: Investigating the sources of innovation*. Springer.
16. Sano, S. (2012). The effect on investment in research and development of new drugs due to extension of the duration of the patent right. *JIPAJ, 9*, 69–88.
17. Yongue, J. S. (2014). The internationalization of the Japanese pharmaceutical industry (1980–2010). *Jpn J Hist Pharmacy, 49*, 77–83.
18. Zucker, L. G., Darby, M. R., & Armstrong, J. (1998). Geographically localized knowledge: Spillovers or markets. *Economic Inquiry, 36*, 65–86.
19. Zucker, L. G., Darby, M. R., & Brewer, M. B. (1998). Intellectual human capital and the birth of U.S. biotechnology enterprises. *The American Economic Review, 88*, 290–306.

Chapter 13
Trade Practices in the Japanese Pharmaceutical Market: A Simulation Analysis of Improvement Policies

Konosuke Noto

Abstract Various trade practices exist in the Japanese pharmaceutical distribution market, such as rebates and allowances between pharmaceutical companies and wholesalers, lump-sum bulk purchases, and unsettled provisional delivery between wholesalers and medical institutions. The Ministry of Health, Labour and Welfare has sought to reduce opaque trade practices to increase the reliability of the National Health Insurance (NHI) Drug Pricing System listing the distribution prices. In this chapter, I estimate the long-term impact of policies aiming to improve trade practices involving distribution prices, NHI prices and the profit structure of distribution players through modelling and a simulation analysis of distribution transactions with trade practices. The results suggest the impact of policies on the distribution market and NHI prices can be considerably reduced by simultaneously improving the upstream and downstream trade practices equitably. This may improve the negative primary sales margins of wholesalers, which is a policy objective, without significantly affecting the profits of other distribution players.

Keywords NHI drug pricing system · Trade practice · Distribution transaction · Pharmaceutical markets · Model simulation

13.1 Introduction

The various trade practices of the Japanese pharmaceutical distribution market include rebates and allowances between pharmaceutical companies and wholesalers (upstream trade practices), and lump-sum bulk purchases and unsettled provisional delivery between wholesalers and medical institutions (downstream trade practices). The Ministry of Health, Labour and Welfare (MHLW) has sought to reduce opaque trade practices to increase the reliability of the National Health Insurance (NHI) Drug Pricing System that reflecting the distribution prices on NHI prices.

This chapter is an updated version of Noto and Innami [11, 12].

K. Noto (✉)
Keio Research Institute at SFC and Dentsu Inc, Fujisawa, Kanagawa, Japan
e-mail: kouno3@sfc.keio.ac.jp

© The Author(s), under exclusive license to Springer Nature Singapore Pte Ltd. 2022   219
A. Negishi et al. (eds.), *Competition Law and Policy in the Japanese Pharmaceutical Sector*, Kobe University Monograph Series in Social Science Research,
https://doi.org/10.1007/978-981-16-7814-1_13

The stability of these trade practices in the distribution market indicates trade practices might have an impact on distribution prices. Thus, any improvement in these trade practices is likely to affect the NHI pricing and profit structure of the distribution players through changes in the distribution prices. In this chapter, I estimate the long-term impact of policies that aim to improve trade practices on distribution prices, NHI prices and the profit structure of distribution players through modelling and a simulation analysis of pharmaceutical distribution transactions with trade practices.

This chapter is organised as follows: Sect. 13.2 explains trade practices in the Japanese pharmaceutical market. Section 13.3 discusses the relationship between distribution prices and trade practices. In addition, I model the pharmaceutical distribution market with trade practices for the policy simulation. Section 13.4 simulates the long-term impact of improvement policies under several scenarios. Section 13.5 concludes.

13.2 Pharmaceutical Distribution Market and Trade Practices

13.2.1 The NHI Drug Pricing System

Ethical drugs produced by pharmaceutical companies are distributed via wholesalers to medical institutions, which dispense them to patients. In other words, the distribution market of ethical drugs involves two transaction relationships: one between pharmaceutical companies and wholesalers (upstream relationship) and the other between wholesalers and medical institutions (downstream relationship). Transaction prices in the upstream relationship are called invoice prices whilst those in the downstream relationship are called wholesale prices. Medical institutions charge patients for their share of the cost using the NHI price list and bills the insurance company for the remaining share.

The NHI price is determined by the brand name based on the NHI Drug Pricing System and is revised every two years[1] in April under the NHI price revision rule (weighted average market price adjustment method) based on the following formula:

$$\text{Revised NHI price}$$
$$= \text{weighted average marketprice}$$
$$\times (1 + \text{sales tax rate}) + \text{adjustment range}$$

where the market price is the average wholesale price minus the sales tax. The wholesale prices are ascertained through a market price survey conducted in the

---

[1] Japan has been revising NHI prices every two years since 1988. However, it was decided in 2020 to revise the NHI prices annually for drugs meeting certain conditions, starting in 2021. See MHLW [9], pp.1–3 for details.

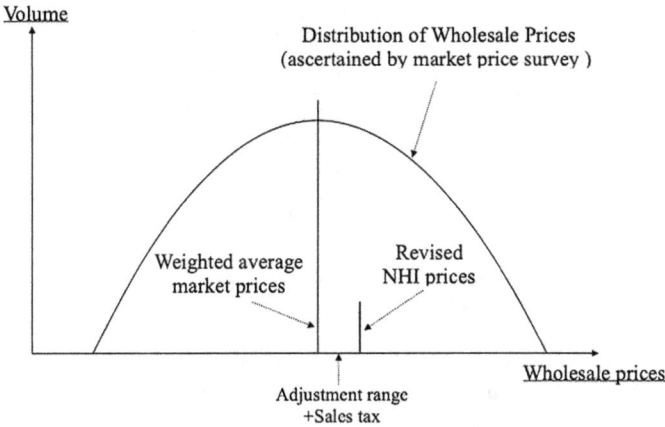

Fig. 13.1 NHI price revision rule

September prior to the revision. The NHI price is revised by adding a sales tax and an adjustment range to the market price. In other words, the NHI Drug Pricing System reflects market prices. Therefore, it is necessary for the market price survey to be accurate to maintain the system's credibility (Fig. 13.1).

13.2.2   Trade Practices in the Pharmaceutical Market

The NHI Drug Pricing System requires an accurate survey of distribution market prices. However, trade practices in the distribution market are detrimental to such accuracy.

The payment of rebates and allowances by pharmaceutical companies to wholesalers are post-transaction compensation payments. Typically, such payments are intended to compensate wholesalers for their discounts or promotional incentives in other industries. However, such payments in the Japanese pharmaceutical market vary and fill ambiguous roles, and account for a large share of wholesalers' profits. The wholesalers' profit margin, which has remained at a negative level in recent years, is routinely compensated through rebates and allocations [6]. The MHLW has criticised this process and requested pharmaceutical companies to simplify and reduce their rebates and allowances because ambiguous and large compensation payments make price formation opaquer.

Meanwhile, lump-sum bulk purchases between wholesalers and medical institutions involve multiple brands of drugs, combined and delivered in bulk to medical institutions at a single price or discounted rate. When multiple brands of drugs are traded at bulk prices, individual values, such as the supply and demand relationship and inventory management and delivery costs, are not reflected in wholesale prices. The MHLW requires wholesalers and medical institutions to engage in single price

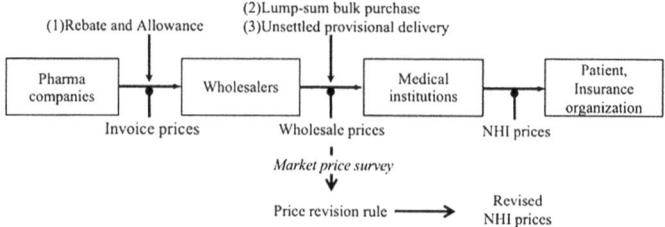

Fig. 13.2 NHI price revision process and trade practices

transactions per item based on the brand-specific NHI price list [6]. However, lump-sum bulk purchases accounted for about 40% of all transactions conducted by major medical institutions (hospitals with more than 200 beds and chain pharmacies) in 2013 [7].

In addition, unsettled provisional delivery exists between wholesalers and medical institutions. As drugs are a necessity for medical institutions, wholesalers generally deliver them without agreeing on a price. However, unsettled prices undermine the credibility of the market price survey. The MHLW defined an unsettled provisional delivery as one that remains unsettled for more than six months. The percentage of overall transactions settled is the price settlement rate. In September 2013, this rate was about 70%, although the rate was only about 50% for large medical institutions [7]. The MHLW requests that medical institutions and wholesalers reach early price settlements after delivery.

These three trade practices undermine the credibility of the NHI pricing system through opaque distribution prices. Figure 13.2 summarises the relationship between them.

13.2.3 Response to Trade Practices

The MHLW responded to the issue of trade practices by establishing two councils. The Council for the Modernisation of Drug Distribution was established in 1983. This council has been improving the trade practices by formulating and disseminating model contracts among the distribution players. Moreover, the council has released several reports, such as the 'Modernisation of the Distribution of Ethical Drugs and NHI Prices' in 1990 and the 'Promotion of Modernisation of the Distribution of Ethical Drugs' in 1995 to ensure free competition, transparency and a fair distribution market under the NHI drug pricing system.

In 2004, the MHLW established a private advisory board called the Council on Improvements in the Distribution of Ethical Drugs (CIDED) to take over from the previous council and discuss methods to improve trade practices. Meanwhile, the Central Social Insurance Medical Council then released its report that lump-sum bulk purchases and unsettled provisional delivery must improve reliability based on market price surveys from 2005. Additionally, the Japan Fair Trade Commission (JFTC) released the 'Investigation Report on the Actual Conditions of Distribution of Ethical Drugs' in 2006. This report investigated conditions of rebates and allowances based on questionnaire surveys and interviews with pharmaceutical companies, wholesalers and medical institutions. The JFTC noted these may present a challenge under the Antimonopoly Act, and therefore it will continue to monitor trade practices. In response to these reports, In 2007, the CIDED released the 'Urgent Proposal to Improve the Distribution of Ethical Drugs'. The report strongly urges distribution players to specify possible efforts for improvement of trade practices. However, Mimura [10] indicates no significant improvement has occurred even after the urgent Proposal. The CIDED then released the 'Promotion of Improvement in the Distribution of Ethical Drugs' in 2015 also, although it differs little from the 2007 proposal.

As mentioned above, the traditional MHLW response to trade practices has been limited to recognising issues involving the reliability of the NHI price system. However, no quantitative analysis of the role of trade practices in transactions, the relationship between trade practices and distribution prices, or how improvements of trade practices could affect NHI prices and the profits of distribution players has been performed.

Several studies in industrial organisation literature examine post-compensation such as rebates and allowances. These studies note post-compensation inhibits fair competition in the distribution market. Numerous empirical and theoretical studies involving post-compensation in the pharmaceutical market have been performed outside Japan [2, 5]. However the relationship between the distribution market and the drug pricing system differs greatly from country to country, it would be inappropriate to apply these studies' findings to the Japanese pharmaceutical system.

Research on trade practices in the Japanese pharmaceutical market is limited. Possible reasons for this include the fact that researchers rarely have access to data on pharmaceutical distribution in Japan, making it difficult to properly assess transactions. Most studies to date are limited to theoretical analyses of pharmaceutical distribution transactions and simplified verification of implications using corporate financial or questionnaire data [14–16].

The MHLW introduced a penalty system to combat unsettled provisional delivery in 2014. Under this system, if the price settlement rate is less than 50% at the end of September in the market survey year, medical institutions' medical fees and basic pharmacy fees will be significantly reduced. Yet even after the introduction of this system, there has been no discussion or quantitative analysis of the long-term impact on the pharmaceutical market.

13.3 Drug Price Revision Rules and Trade Practices

In this section, I discuss how the incentive structure is defined under the drug price revision rules of the NHI drug pricing system and the role of each trade practice in the distribution market, based on Ogura and Hagino [13].

13.3.1 Market Under Drug Price Revision Rules

Equation (13.1) is a simplified version of the NHI price revision rule.[2]

$$P_{t+1} = P_t^w + r_{t+1} P_t \qquad (13.1)$$

where t is the time index, P_{t+1} is the revised drug price in period $t + 1$, P_t^w is the wholesale price and r_{t+1} is the adjustment rate ($0 \leq r \leq 1$) in period t. This rate is multiplied by P_t to establish the adjustment range, which is added to P_t^w, becoming the revised drug price for period $t + 1$. The current drug price P_t is then subtracted from both sides of the equation.

$$P_{t+1} - P_t = \left(P_t^w - P_t \right) + r_{t+1} P_t \qquad (13.2)$$

This is converted to Eq. (13.3).

$$RP_{t+1} = -\pi_t^m + r_{t+1} P_t, \qquad (13.3)$$

where RP_{t+1} is the difference between the revised price P_{t+1} and the previous price P_t and π_t^m is the NHI price margin for medical institutions ($P_t - P_t^w$). Equation (13.3) provides the pricing structure of NHI drug prices. In other words, when medical institutions obtain a discount in the previous year, the extent of the discount rate exceeding the adjustment range will be reflected as a NHI price reduction in the next price revision. On the other hand, if the discounted rate is within the adjustment range, the NHI price will not be reduced.

Thereafter, Eq. (13.3) is revised to Eq. (13.4).

$$\frac{RP_{t+1}}{P_t} = -\frac{\pi_t^m}{P_t} + \frac{r_{t+1} P_t}{P_t} \qquad (13.4)$$

To simplify the notation, Eq. (13.4) is further revised to Eq. (13.5).

---

[2] For the sake of simplicity, Eq. (13.1) does not distinguish between the wholesale and weighted average market prices.

$$R_{t+1} = -\beta_t^m + r_{t+1} \tag{13.5}$$

where R_{t+1} is the NHI price revision rate and β_t^m is the NHI price margin rate for medical institutions. As Eq. (13.5) demonstrates, the revision rate is the NHI price margin rate minus the adjustment rate. The adjustment rate functions as a buffer for the revision. When the adjustment rate is high, sellers (pharmaceutical companies and wholesalers) can more easily offer discounts to medical institutions. Thus, the adjustment range performs the role of 'guaranteed NHI price margin' for medical institutions.

When the current price revision rule was introduced in 1992, the adjustment rate was set at 15%. The NHI price margin rate then was 23.1%, and medical institutions could receive a total margin of almost two trillion yen. Furthermore, the drug cost ratio was considerably higher than most advanced European countries [13]. In view of these financial burden, the government gradually reduced the adjustment rate from 15 to 2% by 2000. Following this reduction, the NHI price margin rate declined to 6.3% in 2003. It has remained at an estimated 8%–9% in recent years.[3]

13.3.2 Rebate, Allowance and Adjustment Rate

The factors influencing the setting of invoice prices for pharmaceutical companies include manufacturing costs, competing products, product life cycle, product portfolio and the medical representative sales force. However, the most critical factor is the NHI price. For pharmaceutical companies with minimal marginal production costs, it is profitable to maintain a higher NHI price as this results in higher profit overall, with no sales price fluctuation risk for two years. Hence, under the NHI price revision rule, pharmaceutical companies have an incentive to maintain a high distribution price level by setting the invoice price at a higher level.

As mentioned in Sect. 13.3.1, as long as the adjustment rate is established at a high level, a decrease in distribution price might not result in a major price revision. Therefore, it is easy for pharmaceutical companies to implement marketing strategies to increase their market share by discounting their invoice price. However, if the adjustment rate is reduced, the companies may be reluctant to sell at discounted prices, because lowering invoice prices could directly lower NHI prices. Thus, pharmaceutical companies may strategically set higher invoice prices by committing to pay post-transaction compensation (rebates and allowances) to wholesalers before the transaction. Table 13.1 shows the industry-average annual trends in the distribution market during 1992–2014.

As the adjustment rate declines, the rebate, allowance and invoice prices increase simultaneously. While the adjustment rate has remained fixed at 2% since 2000, the invoice price has been stable at 93–94%. Additionally, the increase in invoice price is

---

[3] See Fig. 13.3 for the relationship between adjustment rate and NHI price margin rate.

Table 13.1 Industry-average annual trends in the distribution market, 1992–2014 (NHI price during each period = 100)

Year	Adjustment rate (%)	Invoice price	Wholesale price	Wholesaler's primary margin	Rebate and allowance	Wholesaler's gross margin
1992	15	77.20	82.61	5.41	6.90	12.31
1993	15	77.20	82.32	5.12	7.04	12.16
1994	13	79.80	83.66	3.86	7.58	11.44
1995	13	79.60	83.49	3.89	7.25	11.14
1996	11	81.30	85.77	4.47	6.54	11.01
1997	10	84.50	87.84	3.34	6.95	10.29
1998	5	89.50	92.66	3.16	7.31	10.47
1999	5	89.30	91.70	2.40	7.18	9.58
2000	2	93.00	95.01	2.01	6.99	9.00
2001	2	93.50	94.00	0.50	8.17	8.67
2002	2	94.20	94.20	0.00	8.60	8.60
2003	2	94.10	92.90	−1.20	9.50	8.30
2004	2	94.30	92.83	−1.47	9.43	7.96
2005	2	94.10	91.73	−2.37	10.28	7.91
2006	2	94.86	94.01	−0.91	9.16	8.25
2007	2	94.67	92.19	−2.69	10.76	8.07
2008	2	93.94	92.06	−1.88	9.15	7.27
2009	2	94.04	91.14	−2.90	8.82	5.92
2010	2	94.08	91.50	−2.58	8.60	6.02
2011	2	94.08	90.20	−3.88	9.20	5.32
2012	2	94.00	91.60	−2.40	8.60	6.20
2013	2	94.00	90.90	−3.10	8.80	5.70
2014	2	94.10	91.40	−2.70	8.80	6.10
Average		89.97	90.25	0.26	8.33	8.60

Source The Council on Improvements in the Distribution of Ethical Drugs

accompanied by the wholesale price increase, although not at the same rate. Thus, the wholesalers' primary margins have continued to fall since 1992 and have remained at a negative level since 2003. This negative margin is compensated for by rebates and allowances. The wholesalers' gross margin (primary sales margin plus rebates and allowances) is always positive.

Flexible rebates and allowances allow pharmaceutical companies to meet the participation constraints of wholesalers (0 ≤ wholesalers' gross margin) while maintaining their invoice prices at a higher level. As such, rebates and allowances serve as an NHI price maintenance strategy to raise the invoice prices in the drug distribution market under the NHI drug pricing system.

13.3.3 NHI Price Margin and Adjustment Rate

Under the current NHI drug pricing system, the NHI price is set for two years, while the wholesale price (the procurement price for medical institutions) is market price. Since medical institutions do not purchase drugs at wholesale prices above the NHI price, there is always a NHI price margin in the transaction of ethical drugs. This official margin profit (generated by simply buying and selling) is an important revenue source for medical institutions, which are labour-intensive and generally have low profits.[4] Figure 13.3 illustrates the adjustment rate and the average NHI

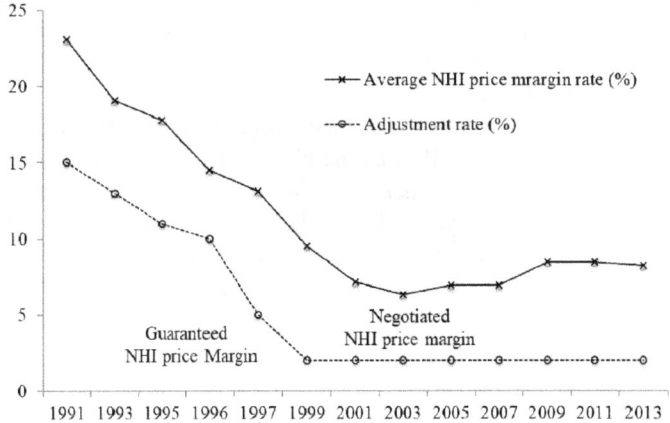

Fig. 13.3 Adjustment rate and average NHI price margin, 1991–2013. *Source* The Council on Improvements in the Distribution of Ethical Drugs

price margin rate in 1991–2013.

Although the NHI price margin rate has diminished with the reduction in the adjustment rate as guaranteed NHI price margin, the NHI margin rate for medical institutions consistently exceeds the adjustment rate. Therefore, the NHI price margin can be deconstructed into a *guaranteed NHI price margin*, representing the adjustment range, and a *negotiated NHI price margin*, obtained through price negotiations. Therefore, the NHI price margin level is determined by the adjustment rate and the bargaining power of medical institutions. In the following, I discuss the relationship between price negotiations and trade practices of medical institutions in downstream transactions.

---

[4] This is also true for pharmacies, where dispensing fees account for the majority of income.

13.3.4 Lump-Sum Bulk Purchase as Price Negotiation

In lump-sum bulk purchases, multiple products are traded at a single price or discount rate, making the cost of negotiation lower than that of individual price transactions. This allows wholesalers to offer discounts and medical institutions to obtain the NHI price margin more easily. The JFTC [4] points out the wholesalers' marketing specialists have less knowledge regarding pharmaceuticals than the marketing representatives of pharmaceutical companies. Therefore, the sole sales strategy for wholesalers to increase their market share is to sell the 'price' (NHI price margin) and not the 'value' (drug properties related to the diagnosis, treatment, and preventive effects of diseases) [3]. As a specific means to achieve this, marketing specialists combine different products to reduce negotiation costs. In other words, lump-sum bulk purchasing is a trade practice based on medical institutions' pursuit of NHI price margins and wholesalers' sales strategies.

Table 13.2 reveals the average NHI price margin by transaction type. The 2007 NHI price survey shows the NHI price margin rate in single price transactions for 94 branded drugs. The NHI price margin rate in single price transactions is less than the overall transactions average, including lump-sum bulk purchases. This trend remains consistent when examining different types of drugs. Although such consistency cannot be easily extended to alternate drugs, it illustrates that medical institutions often receive significant NHI price margins when making lump-sum bulk purchases.

Table 13.2 Average NHI price margin by transaction type

Transaction type	Average NHI price margin (%)
Single price transactions per item (94 brand name)	3.3
Overall transactions	6.9
Drug class (Number of brands)	**Average NHI price margin (%)**
Radiopharmaceuticals (44)	3.2
Agents for peritoneal dialysis (13)	3.4
Agents for artificial kidney dialysis (4)	6.3
X-ray contrast agents (4)	5.5
Proteins, amino acid and preparations (3)	3.1
Antibiotics (3)	3.8

Source Central Council of Social Insurance Medical Services

13.3.5   Unsettled Provisional Delivery as Price Negotiation

When NHI prices are established through the biennial NHI price revisions, price negotiations between wholesalers and medical institutions commence. During this process, medical institutions employ a negotiation method called 'retroactive discounting'. In the negotiation, drugs are delivered at a provisional price, and then the price is re-negotiated based on transaction prices of other medical institutions as a reference. The re-negotiated price is applied to the already delivered drugs. Figure 13.4 reports the monthly trend of the price settlement rate by medical institution type and size.

The price settlement rate is minimal at the time of the NHI price revisions (April 2008, 2010, 2012, 2014); however, it increases by the end of the fiscal year (the following March). A comparison of the price agreement rates of hospitals with more than 200 beds and chain pharmacies with those of clinics and small pharmacies shows the settlement rates for large medical institutions are relatively low and occur gradually. Additionally, large medical institutions re-negotiate the wholesale price every April, even if the NHI price has not been revised. This is a transactional behaviour that is not observed in smaller medical institutions. This indicates that the larger the size of the medical institution, the more likely it is to conduct price negotiations through unsettled provisional delivery. A possible rationale for this is that large medical institutions can negotiate more favourable prices through retroactive discounts based on large transaction volume (compared to smaller institutions). For medical institutions, long-term price negotiations result in a loss in terms of opportunity cost. Therefore, it is reasonable to assume that the discount rate in unsettled provisional delivery is exceed the cost.

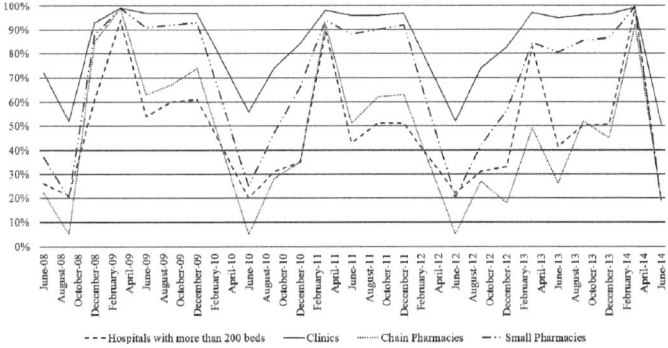

Fig. 13.4 Price settlement rate by medical institution type. *Source* The Council on Improvements in the Distribution of Ethical Drugs

13.3.6   Transaction Model with Trade Practices

The NHI drug pricing system provides economic incentives for each distribution player to engage in above three trade practices. Additionally, each trade practice may affect the distribution prices and NHI prices through the NHI price revision rules. At the conclusion of this section, I model a pharmaceutical distribution transaction in which the transaction price is influenced by each trade practice.

First, the model assumes the invoice price P_t^C in period t is as indicated in Eq. (13.6). The NHI price P_t multiplied by β_t^C. This parameter is the pricing strategy of the pharmaceutical company.

$$P_t^c = \beta_t^c P_t \tag{13.6}$$

The pharmaceutical company remits rebates and allowances V_t to the wholesaler post the transaction. Here, V_t is a fixed percentage of the NHI price: $V_t = v_t P_t$ $(0 < v_t < 1)$. As mentioned in Sect. 3.2, the payment of rebates and allowances V_t is a pharmaceutical company NHI price maintenance strategy. The pricing strategy β_t^c for the invoice price is an increasing function, $\beta_t^c = \theta_t^c v_t$, where θ_t^c is a parameter representing the strength of the relationship between the invoice price and the amount of the rebates and allowances. When R&D and production costs are not considered, the pharmaceutical companies' profit is the invoice price minus rebates and allowances. The pharmaceutical companies' profit π_t^c is found using Eq. (13.7).

$$\pi_t^c = \beta_t^c P_t - V_t \tag{13.7}$$

The wholesaler purchase drugs at the invoice price P_t^C, and sell to the medical institution at the wholesale price P_t^w. The wholesale price is the invoice price P_t^c plus the wholesalers' primary margin π_t^w. From the medical institutions' perspective, the wholesale price is the NHI price P_t minus the NHI price margin (the medical institutions' profit) π_t^m, as shown in Eq. (13.8).

$$P_t^w = P_t^c + \pi_t^w = P_t - \pi_t^m \tag{13.8}$$

The wholesaler's primary margin π_t^w is obtained by subtracting the invoice price P_t^C from the wholesale price P_t^w or by multiplying the wholesalers' primary margin β_t^w by the NHI price P_t, as shown in Eq. (13.9). The wholesalers' primary sales margin can be negative and therefore, β_t^w can be a negative value.

$$\pi_t^w = P_t^w - P_t^c = \beta_t^w P_t, \tag{13.9}$$

where $\beta_t^w = \theta_t^w P_t^c$. Parameter θ_t^w is the elasticity $\left(\Delta P_t^w / P_t^w\right)/\left(\Delta P_t^c / P_t^c\right)$ of the wholesale price with respect to the invoice price and represents the wholesalers' bargaining power that determines the wholesalers' primary margin. When $\theta_t^w > 1$, the wholesaler holds strong bargaining power over medical institutions, such that the wholesaler can produce a profit by further increasing the wholesale price (selling price) in response to an increase in the invoice price (purchase price) established by the pharmaceutical company. When $\theta_t^w = 1$, the wholesaler passes on the increase in invoice price as the wholesale price and the change in the invoice price does not change the wholesalers' profits; therefore, the wholesaler plays a neutral role in the distribution transaction. When $\theta_t^w < 1$, the medical institution holds strong bargaining power over the wholesaler, preventing them from increasing their prices sufficiently in response to an increase in invoice prices.

Additionally, the wholesaler receives rebates and allowances from pharmaceutical companies after their sales to medical institutions. The primary margin π_t^w plus V_t is the wholesalers' gross margin Π_t^w.

$$\Pi_t^w = \pi_t^w + V_t \tag{13.10}$$

The NHI price margin π_t^w of medical institutions is the NHI price margin rate β_t^m multiplied by the NHI price P_t, or the NHI price minus the wholesale price.

$$\pi_t^m = \beta_t^m P_t = P_t - P_t^w \tag{13.11}$$

As noted in Sect.3.3, the NHI price margin rate β_t^m can be deconstructed into the guaranteed NHI price margin rate $(r_{t+1} P_t)/P_t$ and the negotiated NHI price margin rate $(\pi_t^m - r_{t+1} P_t)/P_t$, which is obtained through price negotiations. The model assumes the NHI price margin rate can be decomposed into the adjustment range as the guaranteed NHI price margin and the negotiated NHI price margin rate σ_t. If the guaranteed NHI price margin rate is θ_t and the negotiated NHI price margin rate is σ_t, then the NHI price margin rate β_t^m is found using Eq. (13.12).

$$\beta_t^m = \theta_t + \sigma_t, \tag{13.12}$$

where $\sigma_t = \rho_t C_t$, the negotiated NHI price margin rate σ_t depends on the level of lump-sum bulk purchases and unsettled provisional delivery C_t in t period, and ρ_t is the parameter.

Finally, to summarise the model described thus far, the NHI price P_t can be deconstructed into the invoice price $\beta_t^c P_t$, the wholesalers' primary sales margin $\beta_t^w P_t$ and the NHI price margin of the medical institution $\beta_t^m P_t$.

$$P_t = \beta_t^c P_t + \beta_t^w P_t + \beta_t^m P_t \tag{13.13}$$

Here, $\beta_t^C + \beta_t^w + \beta_t^m = 1$, where each β_t represents the price bargaining power that determines the distribution prices. And, each trade practice creates an impact on its respective β_t.

13.4 Policy Simulation

In this section, I conduct a policy simulation to improve trade practices. First, a hypothetical drug price approximated from an aggregate data is applied to the model to estimate the impact of trade practices on the NHI price and the profits of each distribution player during each period. I then estimate the long-term effects on the NHI price and profit structure of each distribution player by reducing the level of trade practices in the model under the parameters set from the empirical analysis [12].

13.4.1 Hypothetical Drug

The NHI price P_t for the hypothetical drug at the time of launch is set at 100. The NHI price revision rate and the distribution price are approximated based on the average revision rate for all 372 drugs listed in the NHI drug pricing system between 1990 and 1991 and sold until 2015. These drug prices were revised 13 times between 1992 and 2015.[5] Using these data, the model simulates the long-term average market trends under the current NHI pricing system.

Table 13.3 displays the estimation results produced by applying the hypothetical drug to the drug distribution transaction model. Although the primary margins are negative over all periods except for the year of launch and the period prior to the fifth revision, the wholesalers' gross margins are positive over all periods. In addition, negotiated NHI price margins are generated over all periods. Thus, this hypothetical drug is able to represent the characteristics of drug distribution transactions using trade practices.

13.4.2 Simulation Setup

As stated in Sect. 2.3, the penalty system for unsettled provisional delivery was introduced in 2014. Policies limiting lump-sum bulk purchases, which undermine the credibility of NHI price surveys, are expected to continue. Moreover, as rebates and allowances have increased in recent years despite the government's longstanding request to pharmaceutical companies to reduce them, a penalty for the use of these practices may soon be imposed. Therefore, the simulation assumes both upstream and downstream trade practices are an improvement from the current baseline level.

The model assumes rebates and allowances perform a role in pharmaceutical companies' NHI price maintenance strategies. In other words, β_t^c represents the companies' pricing strategy for the invoice price, which is assumed to be an increasing function of rebates and allowances ($\beta_t^c = \theta_t^c v_t$). The simulation differentiates

---

[5] See Noto [12], pp. 61–62 for detailed calculation methods for the hypothetical drug.

Table 13.3 Estimation results of applying hypothetical drug

Revision Number	Elapsed Years	NP (P)	NPRR (PR) (%)	IV (P^c)	WP (P^w)	PCP (π^c)	WPM (π^w)	R (C^R)	A (C^A)	WGM (Π^w)	NPM (π^m)	NNPM (σ)
Launch	0	100.0		77.20	78.69	70.30	1.49	5.52	1.38	8.39	21.31	6.31
1	2	93.69	−6.3	72.33	71.68	65.73	−0.65	5.28	1.32	5.95	22.01	9.83
2	4	83.86	−10.5	66.75	63.55	60.67	−3.20	4.86	1.22	2.88	20.31	11.08
3	6	72.78	−13.2	61.50	58.26	56.44	−3.24	4.05	1.01	1.82	14.52	7.24
4	7	66.67	−8.4	59.67	56.97	54.80	−2.70	3.90	0.97	2.17	9.70	6.37
5	8	60.30	−9.6	53.85	54.85	49.52	1.00	3.46	0.87	5.33	5.45	4.24
6	10	56.06	−7.0	52.41	48.80	47.83	−3.61	3.66	0.92	0.97	7.25	6.13
7	12	49.92	−10.9	46.98	46.09	42.24	−0.89	3.79	0.95	3.86	3.83	2.83
8	14	47.09	−5.7	44.31	43.39	39.47	−0.93	3.87	0.97	3.92	3.70	2.76
9	16	44.33	−5.9	41.96	41.52	37.19	−0.45	3.82	0.95	4.32	2.81	1.92
10	18	42.40	−4.3	39.88	39.32	36.14	−0.55	2.99	0.75	3.19	3.08	2.23
11	20	40.17	−5.3	37.79	37.43	34.10	−0.36	2.96	0.74	3.33	2.74	1.94
12	22	38.23	−4.8	35.94	35.41	32.58	−0.53	2.69	0.67	2.83	2.83	2.06
13	24	37.18	−2.7	–	–	–	–	–	–	–	–	–

Note NP: NHI Price, NPRR: NHI Price Revison Rate, IV: Invoice Price, WP: Wholesale Price, PCP: Pharma Company Profit, WPM: Wholesalers' Primary Margin, R: Rebate, A: Allowance, WGW: Wholesalers' Gross Margin, NPM: NHI Price Margin, NNPM: Negotiated NHI Price Margin

between rebates and allowances. The empirical analysis[6] demonstrates rebates have a clear impact on the invoice price, whereas allowances have no such affect. The parameter representing the relationship between rebates and invoice price is assumed to be 1 throughout the period $\left(\theta_{1,...,13}^{c,r} = 1\right)$, whereas allowances are assumed to be 0—incurring no effect $\left(\theta_{1,...,13}^{c,a} = 0\right)$.

Elasticity of wholesale price to invoice price θ_t^w represents the bargaining power of wholesalers. The simulation assumes change of the parameter after the launch of generic drugs, as shown in [12]. From the 1st to the 6th revision (10th year on the market), the value is 1 $\left(\theta_{1,...,6}^w = 1\right)$ and from the 7th (12th year in the market) to the 13th (up to the 24th year in the market) revision, the value is 0.5 $\left(\theta_{7,...,13}^w = 0.5\right)$. This setting is intended to approximate the average life cycle of the original drugs that the generic products are launched between the sixth (10th year on the market) and seventh (12th year on the market) revisions.

The trade practices in downstream transactions (lump-sum bulk purchases and unsettled provisional delivery) enhance medical institutions' bargaining power in negotiating the NHI price margin σ_t. Therefore, the simulation assumes the negotiated NHI price margin rate σ_t will decrease: the relationship between the negotiated NHI price margin rate σ_t and the improvement level of trade practices in downstream trade practice C_t is assumed to be $\sigma_t = \rho_t C_t$. The parameter ρ_t assumes the value of 1 throughout the period $\left(\rho_{1,...,13} = 1\right)$ based on [11]. When downstream trade practice C_t improves by 1%, the negotiated NHI price margin rate σ_t diminishes by 1%.

Based on the above parameters, the following three cases are simulated: Case (1), improving only upstream trade practices (rebates and allowances); Case (2), improving only downstream trade practices (lump-sum bulk purchases and unsettled provisional delivery); Case (3), improving trade practices in upstream and downstream transactions simultaneously. In each case, 25, 50, 75 and 100% improvement rates are set.

13.4.3 Simulation Results

Table 13.4 summarises the simulation results (cumulative results of 13 revisions and percentage change from the baseline).

In Case (1), the invoice price affected by rebates declines, as does the wholesale price. This results in a more significant NHI price revision and a more rapid decline in NHI prices. This decline reduces the pharmaceutical companies' profits. In addition, the wholesalers' primary margin will improve slightly as the invoice price declines; however, their gross margin will deteriorate significantly compared to the baseline, owing to the reduction in post-compensation rebates and allowances. In the case of a 100% improvement rate, the wholesalers' primary margin and gross margin

---

[6] Noto [12], pp. 25–58 estimates impact of rebates and allocations on distribution prices θ_t^c and elasticity of wholesale prices to invoice prices θ_t^w using the panel data analysis of five branded drug transactions provided by a major Japanese pharmaceutical wholesaler.

Table 13.4 Summary of simulation results[7]

		NP (P)	Rate of change (%)	PCP (π^c)	Rate of change (%)	WPM (π^w)	Rate of change (%)	WGM (Π^w)	Rate of change (%)	NPM (π^m)	Rate of change (%)
Baseline (%)		832.69	–	627.00	–	−14.61	–	48.96	–	119.55	–
Case (1)	25	771.91	−7.3	584.48	−6.8	−11.28	22.8	32.81	−33.0	123.39	3.2
	50	717.02	−13.9	545.73	−13.0	−8.60	41.1	18.63	−62.0	126.50	5.8
	75	667.42	−19.8	510.42	−18.6	−6.48	55.7	6.16	−87.4	128.97	7.9
	100	622.57	−25.2	478.23	−23.7	−4.80	67.1	−4.80	−109.8	130.91	9.5
Case (2)	25	945.89	13.6	711.64	13.5	1.29	108.8	73.77	50.7	111.89	−6.4
	50	1079.13	29.6	810.55	29.3	20.93	243.2	103.87	112.2	101.61	−15.0
	75	1235.91	48.4	927.91	48.0	45.14	408.9	140.35	186.7	88.04	−26.4
	100	1420.32	70.6	1060.86	69.2	74.94	612.9	184.50	276.9	70.37	−41.1
Case (3)	25	846.25	1.6	639.20	1.9	1.53	110.5	50.11	2.4	120.92	1.2
	50	859.95	3.3	651.52	3.9	18.26	225.0	51.25	4.7	122.33	2.3
	75	873.79	4.9	663.99	5.9	35.59	343.5	52.39	7.0	123.78	3.5
	100	887.76	6.6	676.59	7.9	53.53	466.3	53.53	9.3	125.26	4.8

Note NP: NHI Price, PCP: Pharma Company Profit, WPM: Wholesalers' Primary Margin, WGW: Wholesalers' Gross Margin, NPM: NHI Price Margin

---

[7] See Noto [12], pp. 65–75 for detailed simulation results.

will be at the same, negative level. Meanwhile, the NHI price margin for medical institutions will increase. A reduction (improvement) in rebates and allowances will greatly accelerate a decrease in drug prices and affect the distribution players' profit structure.

In Case (2), the wholesale price increases from the reduction in medical institutions' NHI price margin as a result of improved downstream trade practices, maintaining higher NHI prices. The policies meant to improve trade practices in downstream transactions reduce consumer benefits as well as public insurance financial benefits due to lowering NHI prices from the price negotiation efforts of medical institutions. Thus, a trade-off occurs between reducing downstream trade practices and decreasing NHI prices. This result contradicts the purpose of the current NHI drug pricing system, which is to reflect the market price. Thus, it is necessary to discuss how to evaluate lump-sum bulk purchases and unsettled provisional delivery as a price negotiation technique by medical institutions.

In addition, the profits of pharmaceutical companies and the wholesalers' primary and gross margins increase significantly while NHI prices remain high in Case (2). On the other hand, the NHI price margin for medical institutions will be reduced. However, drugs that have been on the market for many years (as in this simulation), the impact of decrease in NHI price margin can be mitigated in the long term by maintaining the NHI price. Thus, the rate of change is minimal compared to the profits of the wholesalers.

Finally, in Case (3), where both upstream and downstream trade practices are improved, the rate of change from the baseline is extremely minimal, except for a major increase in the wholesalers' primary sales margin. The impact of policies on distribution and NHI prices can be considerably reduced by simultaneously improving upstream and downstream trade practices. This should also fulfil the policy objective of improving the wholesalers' negative primary sales margins without significantly affecting the profits of other distribution players.

13.5   Conclusion

If the current NHI pricing system continues, it will be necessary to improve trade practices. This chapter estimates the long-term impact of policies to improve trade practices on distribution prices, NHI prices and the profit structure of distribution players through modelling and simulation analysis of distribution transactions that rely on trade practices. The analysis illustrates the long-term effects as well as the side effects of policies to improve trade practices.

The results show upstream and downstream trade practices may be considered a single complementary system in the pharmaceutical distribution market under the NHI drug pricing system. Rebates (upstream trade practice) may raise the distribution price, whereas lump-sum bulk purchases and unsettled provisional deliveries (downstream trade practices) may lower the distribution price. If pharmaceutical companies do not maintain the distribution price through rebates, their profits may be greatly impaired in the long term. Alternatively, if medical institutions do not implement lump-sum bulk purchases and unsettlement provisional deliveries, they will be unable to obtain the NHI price margin profit and the NHI price will remain high. When such upstream and downstream trade practices are implemented as rational strategies in distribution transactions under the NHI drug pricing system, the system will have the institutional complementarity and robustness to change in the external environment [1]. To improve this situation, it is necessary to improve upstream and downstream trade practices in a balanced manner, as described in Simulation Case (3). In addition, policy evaluation and system reforms should be required to consider an incentive structure for each distribution player defined by the NHI drug pricing system to prevent unexpected trading behavioural changes.

The Central Social Insurance Medical Council approved the NHI drug pricing system reform in December 2017; this included annual price revisions and the long-term listed drug price reviews. These upcoming reforms are expected to affect trade practices and distribution prices through changes in the distribution structure. The impact of these interactions can be examined by applying the analytical framework in this chapter. However, in the analysis, the model assumes the trading behaviour of each player remains unchanged and a simple relationship exists between downstream trade practices and wholesale prices. By empirically examining these points, this analysis should be useful when creating policies to improve trade practices.

References

1. Aoki, M. (2001). Toward a comparative institutional analysis.Cambridge, MIT Press.
2. Graf, J. (2014). The effects of rebate contracts on the health care system. *The European Journal of Health Economics, 15*(5), 477–487.
3. Hodaka, E. (2012). Sinyaku sousyutu Kasan to ryuutuu toumei ka ato ga nai orosi keiei [The price maintenance premium and distribution transparency: Wholesaler management with no postponement]. Pharmaceutical Distribution Frontier Years Book '12-'13. Elsevier Japan.
4. The Japan Fair Trade Commission. (2006). Iryou you iyakuhin no ryuutuu zittai ni kan suru tyousa houkokusyo [Investigation report on the actual conditions of distribution of ethical drugs]. https://www.jftc.go.jp/houdou/pressrelease/cyosa/cyosa-ryutsu/h18/060 92702_files/06092702-hontai.pdf Accessed 10 January 2020
5. Kakani, P., Chernew, M., & Chandra, A. (2020). Rebates in the pharmaceutical industry: Evidence from medicines sold in retail pharmacies in the U.S. NBER (National Bureau of Economic Research) Working Paper No.26846.
6. Ministry of Health, Labour and Welfare (MHLW). (2007). Iryou you iyakuhin no ryuutuu kaizen ni tui te(kinkyuu teigen) [Urgent proposal to improve the distribution of ethical drugs]. https://www.mhlw.go.jp/shingi/2007/10/dl/s1010-8a.pdf Accessed 10 January 2020
7. Ministry of Health, Labour and Welfare (MHLW). (2014). Heisei 26 nendo kamiki (4~9gatu) no ryuutuu zittai [Distribution situation in the first half of 2014]. https://www.mhlw.go.jp/file/ 05-Shingikai-10801000-Iseikyoku-Soumuka/0000067957.pdf Accessed 10 January 2020
8. Ministry of Health, Labour and Welfare (MHLW). (2015). Iryou you iyakuhin no ryuutuu kaizen no sokusin ni tsuite (proposal) [Promotion of improvement in the distribution of ethical drugs]. https://www.mhlw.go.jp/file/05-Shingikai-10801000-Iseikyoku-Soumuka/000 0096099.pdf Accessed 10 January 2020

9. Ministry of Health, Labour and Welfare (MHLW) .(2020). 2021 (Reiwa 3) nendo yakka kaitei no kossi [Outline of FY2021 NHI price revisions]. https://www.mhlw.go.jp/content/12404000/000706832.pdf

10. Mimura, Y. (2011). Public pricing policy and trade practices in pharmaceutical distribution: A research group report on pharmaceutical distribution. *Journal of Health Care, Medicine and Community, 21*(2), 137–162.

11. Noto, K., & Innami, I. (2017). What happens to pharmaceutical prices when trade practices are improved: A simulation study. *Public Choice Studies, 68*, 5–26.

12. Noto, K., & Innami, I. (2018). Bargaining power and trade practices in the distribution of ethical drugs: Empirical analysis using micro panel data and policy simulation for improving trade practices. Institute for Health Economics and Policy research report 2018.

13. Ogura, S., & Hagino, T. (2003). Why do the Japanese spend so much on drugs?. In S. Ogura, T. Tachibanaki & D. A. Wise (Eds.), Labor markets and firm benefit policies in Japan and the United States (National Bureau of Economic Research Conference Report) (pp. 229–265). University of Chicago Press.

14. Sakurai, H., Tanno, T., Masuhara, H., Hayashi, Y., & Yamada, A. (2019). Wholesale price and marketing channel type of prescription drugs. *JSMD (Japan Society of Marketing & Distribution) Review, 3*(1), 11–18.

15. Sakurai, H., Tanno, T., Masuhara, H., Hayashi, Y., Onda, M., & Yamada, A. (2016). Distribution analysis for prescription medicines: Empirical study on wholesaler functions and information provision. *Journal of Marketing and Distribution, 19*(1), 15–24.

16. Tanno, T., & Hayashi, Y. (2014). Bargaining power and NHI drug price standard in ethical pharmaceutical distribution. *Studies in Applied Economics, 8*, 115–127.

Index

© The Editor(s) (if applicable) and The Author(s), under exclusive license to Springer Nature Singapore Pte Ltd. 2022
A. Negishi et al. (eds.), *Competition Law and Policy in the Japanese Pharmaceutical Sector*, Kobe University Monograph Series in Social Science Research, https://doi.org/10.1007/978-981-16-7814-1